ALSO BY SUSAN STRIKER

The Anti-Coloring Book, with Edward Kimmel

The Second Anti-Coloring Book, with Edward Kimmel

The Third Anti-Coloring Book

The Fourth Anti-Coloring Book

The Fifth Anti-Coloring Book

The Sixth Anti-Coloring Book

The Anti-Coloring Book of Exploring Space on Earth

The Inventor's Anti-Coloring Book

The Super Powers Anti-Coloring Book

The Mystery Anti-Coloring Book

The Newspaper Anti-Coloring Book

The Circus Anti-Coloring Book, with Jason Striker

The Anti-Coloring Book of Celebrations

The Anti-Coloring Book of Masterpieces

The Anti-Coloring Book of Red Letter Days

Nature's Wonders

Artists at Work

Please Touch

Young at Art

Young

at Art

Teaching Toddlers Self-Expression, Problem-Solving Skills, and an Appreciation for Art

Susan Striker

An Owl Book
Henry Holt and Company New York

Henry Holt and Company, LLC
Publishers since 1866
115 West 18th Street
New York, New York 10011

Henry Holt® is a registered trademark of Henry Holt and Company, LLC.
Young at Art® is a registered trademark of Susan Striker.

Halftone drawings by Frank Post from photographs by Susan
Striker. Black-and-white drawings by Judy Francis. Music copyist
Emma Rodriguez Oberheuser.

Library of Congress Cataloging-in-Publication Data

Striker, Susan.
    Young at art / Susan Striker.—1st ed.
        p. cm.
    "An Owl book."
    Includes bibliographical references and index.
    ISBN 0-8050-6697-7 (pbk.)
    1. Art—Study and teaching (Early childhood)   I. Title.

LB1139.5.A78 S77   2001
372.5'044—dc21   2001024777

Henry Holt books are available for special promotions and
premiums. For details contact: Director, Special Markets.

First Edition 2001

Designed by Oksana Kushnir

Printed in the United States of America
3 4 5 6 7 8 9 10

With love and admiration, to the many Jason Scot Frederic Strikers; the baby, the child, the boy, and the man. Always the imaginative problem solver, creative artist, flexible and independent thinker, loving and forgiving human being, and inspiration to his mom

Creativity stands at the center of all education.

—Bruno Bettelheim

CONTENTS

INTRODUCTION   1

CHAPTER 1 Drawing   24

CHAPTER 2 Painting   56

CHAPTER 3 Printing   87

CHAPTER 4 Paper   94

CHAPTER 5 Sculpture   109

CHAPTER 6 Exploring Color   120

CHAPTER 7 Exploring Shapes
and Art Concepts   138

CHAPTER 8 Birthday Parties
and Group Activities   150

CHAPTER 9 Books About Art
for Children   168

CHAPTER 10 Songs About Art   216

APPENDIX 1 Art Concepts   261

APPENDIX 2 Art Supplies   265

APPENDIX 3 Art Suppliers   268

BIBLIOGRAPHY   271

ACKNOWLEDGMENTS   275

INDEX   277

Young at Art

Introduction

When babies are developmentally ready to stand and walk, they can pull themselves up on the nearest piece of furniture and go. But when babies are developmentally ready to begin the scribbling experiments that will lead the way to reading and writing later on, they need a sensitive adult to have a crayon and paper ready for them. With the exception of baby's first steps, there is no more significant milestone in your child's development than the first mark he or she makes on paper. These squiggles herald the start of a lifetime of writing and drawing.

These two milestones both happen near baby's first birthday. Nurturing parents want to do much more than just hand a child a crayon; your enthusiasm helps encourage future exploration. In *Young at Art* I will show you many ways to facilitate your child's early artwork to make it especially meaningful and productive.

I believe that children engage in critical thinking and learn how to become problem solvers when they are allowed to work, within very clear parameters but with complete freedom, with basic art materials. In this book, I will suggest projects that work toward that end. I will offer hints that prevent the kind of messiness many of us fear when young children work with art materials. I will also demonstrate that the early sequence of scribbling all children engage in is not meaningless. On the contrary, scribbling leads very clearly and directly toward developing the ability to read and write. Early childhood educator and author Rhoda Kellogg studied thousands of children's drawings and made a diagram that shows how closely related the marks all children make are to every known written alphabet. Her analysis of children's scribbles is to me like the Rosetta stone, which translated mysterious Egyptian hieroglyphics into a known Roman language, allowing us to understand them. The scribble chart that appears on page 27 will reveal to you the important connection between scribbling and writing. I hope to help you see the value and impact of early childhood art. It is not a "frill," not merely "charming," but the very foundation upon which all later reading, writing, and drawing are built.

The information in this book will make you want to encourage your child to experiment with early art as much as possible. Art activity is so crucial to your child's development that you can't wait for an art "expert" to teach your child. I will share with you many secrets I have developed over the years as both a parent and an art teacher. You don't need to be an artist yourself to supervise sound, sequential, well-planned art activities for your child. After all, you don't need to be a doctor to take responsibility for your child's health.

I also have very strong feelings about how traditional art activities can be detrimental to our children's development and stifle their creativity. I will talk about the kinds of activities to avoid, and why. I will always offer you alternative activities to substitute for them.

This book explores drawing, painting, printing, paper, and sculpture. I have included music and fine children's literature to enrich every art experience, and games and movement are coordinated with each project to reinforce and expand learning. You will develop realistic expectations as you come to understand typical development in each of the media. Running throughout all of these chapters is a common thread, introducing basic art concepts to your child. At the end you will find a chart that ties it all together. You will be able to immerse your child in related activities in all areas that will ensure a full understanding of the many skills and concepts your child needs to proceed in school and in life.

I have often heard people who are not used to looking at art say, "My two-year-old paints better than that," when confronted with modern art. Picasso often expressed his desire to be more childlike in his work. Klee used childlike symbols in his work. Chagall did many fairy-tale-like works and the great modern portraits can be as expressive as a child's. There is a certain honesty and confidence that children bring with them to art that allows them to regularly make new discoveries and breakthroughs. Rather than forcing children to draw and paint like adults, we should be concentrating on producing adults who still have the capacity to draw and paint like children! Art doesn't have to be pretty to be great any more than literature has to be happy to be considered important. Many adult artists paint "pretty" pictures that are admired for a while and then forgotten. Real art is not merely decorative, and many things that we find pretty have nothing to do with art. Occasionally, a Michelangelo, van Gogh, or Picasso comes along to shock or outrage the public with new ideas, only later to be recognized as having changed the way the rest of us look at the world.

Art presents children with problems that can be solved in an infinite number of correct ways. The freedom, curiosity, and sense of adventure with which young children approach art is very difficult to relearn once it is squelched. Children who begin to view art as copy work rarely regain the true creative spirit that is required for the production of innovative great art and confident independent thinking.

I did not create the art lessons in this book. Children have been doing them for generations. Not one of them is cute or clever. So many art projects offered by well-meaning adults that children do are so terribly "clever" that the children who do them are overwhelmed by them. They approach the next art project with all of the inhibitions that go into making a child an underachiever.

Basic art materials can be used in an infinite number of ways. Children understand this and never tire of repeating activities. Although parents and teachers feel the need to always offer something new, really exciting things happen when children work with simple materials they are very familiar with and have confidence in working with.

You and I and our children started scribbling precisely the same way Rembrandt, Michelangelo, Picasso, and other great artists did. Later on they were influenced by society, but early on their art was spontaneous. The vehemence with which they continued their art careers, while many of the rest of us abandoned art, was, I feel, largely environmental. For example, Pablo Picasso's father was a painter and professor of art. Picasso grew up surrounded with art materials. His father dedicated himself to his son's education, encouraged him to paint very early, and bolstered his confidence in his talent through constant attention and lavish praise. Contrast his behavior with that of most other parents, whose major role in supervising art too often involves curbing and criticizing art activities. Parents, day care workers, and teachers must come to understand the importance of scribbling. Only when they consider it a worthwhile activity can they best create a climate conducive to learning. Although the true nature of creativity is somewhat elusive, it is certain that, as Peggy Davison Jenkins, author of *Art for the Fun of It*, has said (page 70),

Creativity is not so much an aptitude as an attitude.

The meaning and significance of each stage of scribbling still needs to be further studied. One thing is clear: children need to produce their own art, and they don't benefit at all from completing adult-made projects. When pushed to do something they are not ready to do, they suffer by stifling their own needs.

Portrait by Giovanni Francesco Caroto

This portrait of a young child by sixteenth-century artist Giovanni Francesco Caroto shows a child doing a schematic drawing exactly like drawings children do today. Neither geography, period in time, nor society's attitudes about the value of children's art can change the look of children's drawings.

We tend to compartmentalize different subjects and think of art as being quite separate from writing or mathematics. Children are learning mathematical and scientific facts as they work with art materials; removing or subtracting clay as they model, adding on when they create constructions, experimenting with balance as they build. A child who is exposed early to positive creative art activities, and who is allowed to develop freely and naturally (with adults offering encouragement instead of direction), will take to writing very easily when the time comes, and will continue using art as a means of self-expression. Scribbling progressively introduces children to both the symbol recognition and production required in later reading and writing. A child can have real trouble making the transition to writing if his or her scribbling development has been disrupted by such things as the imposition of an adult drawing "for" the child, adults who encourage the child in the scribbling stage to prematurely write or draw recognizable objects, introduction of coloring book activities with the accompanying encouragement to "stay within the lines," adult criticism, or siblings who make fun of scribbles. Too many parents and educators think of art as decoration and are unaware of the crucial link between scribbling and writing. It is difficult for them to believe that a second grader's problems with penmanship can sometimes be traced back to a disruption of scribbling development between ages one and four. More important, children who are discouraged from scribbling lose confidence in their ability to express themselves through art and eventually abandon it. Many day care centers and nursery schools persist in having one-to four-year-olds make things like pumpkins for Halloween and Santas for Christmas, thereby squelching normal development, perpetuating our mundane stereotypical expressions, and trivializing our feelings for meaningful holidays. They are also producing students who are insecure about the value of their own art. Often these children are destined for later reading and writing difficulties. In fact, children up to the age of six are motivated to produce art by the size, shape, texture, and possibilities of materials. Adults are more likely to be motivated by subject matter, and therein may lie the great failure to communicate that separates children and adults, and ultimately serves to separate children from art. The sad fact is that although art teachers must take

English, history, math, and science courses to become certified, it is possible in many areas to become a certified early childhood teacher without ever taking an art course. You may find that your child is being taught art by a teacher who knows absolutely nothing about it. If that happens, please speak up. After all, you would not tolerate a person who could not play a piano giving piano lessons to your child.

Learning cannot be thought of as a patchwork quilt. Children do not learn art from 9:00 to 9:30 and reading from 9:30 to 10:00. They are developing visual impressions when they read, and verbal and symbolic skills when they draw, paint, and sculpt. I am not suggesting that art is important only because it aids in teaching other subjects. It does, but the real value of art should not be limited to that aspect of it.

Roger M. Williams reminds us that "Plato perceived that the natural laws governing the universe—harmony and proportion, balance and rhythm— also govern music, dance, painting, poetry, and so on; he therefore urged making these art forms a foundation of educational method."

My own Anti-Coloring Books motivate children to draw pictures about many different subjects, including holidays. I wouldn't dream of offering them to any child under the age of six. Frequently, people tell me that even though they know the books are intended for older children, they give them to a three- or four-year-old because "the child is very smart." Just because a child is smart doesn't mean that he should be pushed to skip normal stages of development. Being more advanced on a developmental scale is not the same as being "better." As Jane Cooper Bland of the Museum of Modern Art said, "Allow children to be three before they are four and don't try to push a child into doing what older children do before he is ready to move ahead."

When economic conditions necessitate cutting back funding in many homes and schools, art materials are frequently the first things to be eliminated. Art is often thought of as a decorative frill, and art materials can be costly. Since art experiences aid in early symbol recognition and lay the groundwork for writing skills, this unfortunate solution can be a cause of reading difficulties. In reality, it would be possible to teach an art program rich in varied art experiences with only the most basic supplies. Allowing in-depth exploration of materials through offering these basics repeatedly maximizes learning. It is not the materials that should be constantly changing, it is the child!

Learning-disabled children of all ages benefit enormously from creative art experiences, but are the most likely to be given highly structured projects such as copy and color-in work by adults who undervalue their creative potential. These children can be wonderfully expressive and free if given enough time and space, appropriate materials, and encouragement. It is imperative here that supervising adults offer encouragement to children who are working at their mental or developmental age, if not at their chronological age. Clear directions need to be given, and, as with younger children, they need to be given one at a time.

The directions should have nothing to do with what the picture should ultimately look like. The object or picture being made must always be completely the child's. Praising accomplishments can help these children improve their often damaged ego and sense of self. Creativity does not depend on high intelligence, as is so often believed by people working with retarded children. People with high IQs are not necessarily also creative. People with low IQs can be creative or not, depending on the individual. Creativity has to do with an approach to thinking. It is a tragedy to take a child whose intellectual abilities are limited and rob him or her of creative potential as well.

Emotionally disturbed children and normal children going through difficult times (and who doesn't?) can use art to help themselves work out problems and to express their feelings. Positive early art experiences lay the foundation for this later use of art as a means of coping with life.

Creativity is an overused word. I have seen it applied to many activities, usually unrelated to art, that stifle rather than encourage creative thinking. Creative thinking involves a fresh approach and original ideas. Through various activities, children can be encouraged to solve their own problems and explore new materials and situations with confidence. It is important to begin fostering this kind of thinking very early. Children form their patterns of behavior in the early months, and parents' attitudes are strong motivating factors at this time. By age three, some children already refuse to "get dirty" while others adventurously paint with self-confidence and intellectual curiosity. Scribbling and free-drawing experiments are probably the most important art activities in which a child can engage. Art for kids is a sense of adventure. They never know what they will find and learn with each new experience. You need to set aside a special place in your home, as well as in your heart, for your child's art. Materials that are left in view will be all that's needed to tempt your child to draw almost every day. Manipulative work with responsive materials with which the child has direct physical contact, such as finger paint and clay, in addition to crayons and paint, are significant and contribute to the child's intellectual and creative development.

A well-organized, attractive workspace is necessary for effective use of art materials. You cannot be creative if you cannot find a paintbrush! The space itself, with materials *always* available, can be tempting enough to stimulate creative activity. When the child is under two, and you are concerned that he or she may draw on walls, you can leave the crayons in view, but out of reach. That way the child can ask for them, alerting you to supervise the activity. If the child can only paint outdoors, when the weather permits or when a parent has the time and inclination to drag out the easel, many learning opportunities are lost forever. It is essential that the child not have to worry about spills or messes while working.

Once you understand how important art activity is for a young child, you will want to encourage your own child to engage in it as often as possible. One way to do so is to set up an art studio at home. After all, you have special places in your home set aside for other important activities, such as eating, sleeping, and viewing TV. Having a special place in your home for making art is one way of demonstrating how highly you value the activity. It will also simplify your life considerably not to have to set up and clean up every time your child wants to paint. Keep all art supplies in the art studio, as well as an extra roll of paper towels. Close proximity to water is helpful. Whether it is a corner of a bedroom or a separate space, it should be a place that can get messy. A vinyl or linoleum floor or a plastic tablecloth over carpet are both ways of making spilled paint less of a problem. I helped my neighbor convert the awkward space under a staircase from a closet into an art studio. The hooks that had previously hung there held a few smocks, plastic buckets, and pails of paintbrushes. Two side-by-side wall-hung easels was one way she encouraged her child's friends to paint when they visited. On the opposite wall we installed a small desk. An old mirror was hung at the far end of the space, which gave the art studio the illusion of being much bigger than it really was. The mirror was also an ideal surface on which to paint with tempera. On the back of the door a large shoe organizer held paints, markers, and all sorts of other art supplies. When company came, the door could be closed and the house looked as neat as a pin.

Other friends of mine set up a painting space in the basement of their large suburban home. Many changes were made to their home to accommodate their growing family over the years, but the painting space has remained. When their four daughters got older, they always had handy the supplies they needed for the science and history projects that their high school teachers assigned. The room is quiet now, but two of the girls are already married and it's not going to be long before visiting grandchildren will make good use of the studio.

Laura, the reading teacher in the school where I teach, started out with an "art cart" that she made from a multidrawer closet organizer. She told me that she did it out of desperation, because she always seemed to be running around the house looking for art materials and she wanted to put everything in one place. She was able to wheel the cart all over her house, which was convenient. She labeled every drawer with a picture of what she kept in the drawer so that her daughter, Raine, could find things without asking for help. The art cart has since been eliminated and everything is kept on a table now, because Raine couldn't reach all of the drawers and still needed a place to work. Laura finally set up an "art table" for her daughter in the mudroom of her home. She recently had to turn her mudroom into a guest room and mentioned to me that she had moved the art table into her living room. I asked her what she would do if Raine spills paint. "Oh!" she said. "Raine is four years old now. She never spills anything anymore!" Laura covered the table with a transparent plastic shower curtain. She keeps four bins on it: one with markers, one with crayons, one with pencils, and a fourth for staplers, scissors, glue, a hole punch, and stamps. She also has seven spill-proof paint pots with paint and brushes always in them. Raine is free to work at her art table whenever she wants and rarely needs to ask her mother to get anything for her. The table is rectangular and big enough for two children to work at, so it is frequently used during play dates. There is also a wooden holder for paper that Raine rolls out and cuts to the size she wants. Perhaps because of her mother's interest in reading, Raine considers herself a book illustrator. She and her mother often sit together at the art table and write books together. Raine dictates the words for her mother to write while she does the drawings to illustrate the story.

The wealthy parents of one of my students had an elegant playhouse built in their large backyard. It had a freestanding double easel and one wall was painted with chalkboard paint. A more economical alternative might be to put together one of those ready-made toolsheds that you can buy at Home Depot and other houseware supply stores.

Art materials are not the only way to encourage critical-thinking skills and creativity. Toys can also be chosen to stimulate creativity as well. Toys that play by themselves, such as those that are battery-operated rather than child-driven, are to be avoided. Consider limiting the amount of time your child uses toys that have only one correct answer—such as puzzles. Act pleased when your child uses toys, tools, or art materials in ways that the manufacturer did not intend. Appropriate art projects alone won't make a child creative or inclined to make independent decisions. Creative people need self-confidence. The key ingredients contributing to independence and self-confidence are:

- Parents' attitudes about how and why limits are set
- Parents who communicate that they trust the child, and who inspire trust in themselves
- Parents who clearly communicate love, respect, and approval

Many creative activities happen outside the realm of drawing, painting, and sculpture offered by you. The most exciting thing in the world is to watch a child planning and implementing an artistic endeavor, from inception to completion. The child purposefully sets out to do some piece of work that may baffle an adult. It is difficult to distract a child from this kind of activity, but no sensitive adult would want to. Often these creative masterpieces have little to do with your carefully planned "art corner" and utilize none of the expensive art materials you've gone to such trouble to obtain. These original works of conceptual art should be saved for a time to let the child know how valuable the work was. My son, Jason, chose to decorate a window with pencil sketches he had made on self-stick paper, which he meticulously secured to very specific spaces. Jason also once strategically arranged twenty or so paper coffeepot filters on the kitchen floor with all the care and attention Michelangelo must have given to painting the ceiling of the Sistine Chapel!

The problems he encountered in these self-motivated creations were thought out and solved alone. Conceptual artists would do well to study some two- and three-year-olds going about this business. Arranging and controlling shapes in space are a very real part of these valuable experiences. Many projects that have enormous creative potential lose that potential because of poor adult presentation. Decorating Easter eggs is one project that comes to mind. Even very young children can scribble on an egg with a wax crayon and dip it in color. There is no sound reason to purchase overpriced kits that come with decals of adult drawings for the scribbler to stick on the egg.

Putting self-adhesive notes on window, an example of conceptual art

Sensitive parents sometimes need to sacrifice neatness and order at home and will know when to make suggestions to stimulate more adventurous uses of materials. It is time to introduce new materials when the child seems to feel totally at ease with the first. Basic art materials, those with which the child is familiar and comfortable, are generally more conducive to innovative thinking and creative behavior than a wide variety of ever-changing, expensive materials. Children need to experience all five of the major media of art: drawing, painting, collage, printmaking, and sculpture. The projects suggested in *Young at Art* are offered as guidelines for parents, and suggestions should not always be taken literally. You defeat the purpose of the book if you say, "No, that's not right," when the project calls for the child to "scribble with a red crayon," and he or she pastes something on it, or takes a blue crayon to the page. That child is working toward his or her own goals and should receive positive reinforcement from you. It is essential to view these art project ideas as starting points—not as ends in themselves. The scribbler who affixes something to a drawing, tears it, or moves off the page onto the table or floor surface may be exhibiting an early example of the creative thought process. Please, never give a child coloring books, dot-to-dot, magic paint with water, or similar anti-art toys. These items are counterproductive and children can become dependent on them very quickly. It is through these kinds of art activities that we inadvertently rob children of self-confidence and joy in producing their own work. For this same reason it is also never helpful to create art for or about holidays. Jack-o'-lanterns, turkeys, bells, Santas, trees, bunnies, bonnets, silhouettes of Abraham Lincoln or Martin Luther King Jr. have absolutely no place in the home or in any school program below grade two. They do not help a child understand the meaning of a holiday at all. If you need to wean yourself from holiday art gradually, then do so by setting out orange paint and black paper at Halloween time, red paint and green paper at Christmas, and purple paint and green paper at Easter time. Let the subject of the completed picture be completely the child's creation. (Be aware, however, that these color presentations may be out of sequence for a more effective way of learning about colors.) Holiday art is adult-pleasing. For preschoolers it is inappropriate. Their own development is frequently arrested at this point. Adults who entertain their children by drawing for them can have the same devastating effect. Art projects that look like people, animals, or holiday symbols had to have been done under suffocating supervision. In group situations such as play groups, day care centers, nursery schools, or camps, it is safe to say that no art experience has taken place if all of the children's work looks alike. Assembly-line art is worse than none at all. Intervention in the form of "correcting" or "helping" the child discourages creative thinking. Adults who spend their time and money securing elaborate materials can be as stifling as those who spend their time reproducing coloring book pages or cutting children's paintings into turkey shapes.

Parents, teachers, and older siblings, proud of their own drawing accomplishments, often inadvertently stifle learning and creativity because of their own preconceived notions. I had a real problem with one of my elementary school students, who started each project with an "I can't" and grew teary whenever I tried to persuade him to try a new project. I had no real success with him for his first three years of school, but always jumped in with public, lavish praise when he did try something and achieve some success. Even I was surprised when in third grade he created quite a masterpiece. I went overboard praising him and sent him to the principal so that she could congratulate him as well. After that, he started "hanging out" in the art room, visiting me at lunchtime, and often electing to come to the art room during his recess period. We had time to talk and it was during one of these visits that he brought in some drawings his older brother had done to show me. They were the drawings of a very talented young man. Fortunately for Nick, that older brother was now off at college, freeing Nick to get out from under his shadow. I suggested to Nick that he was probably intimidated by his brother's talent, but also pointed out that they shared the same genes. Nick really blossomed by fourth grade and became known as "artistic" among his peers. He was a perfect example of how stifling it can be to be exposed constantly to adult art before being given a chance to try things on your own.

Any attempt to depict a realistic object should originate with the child. This probably will happen sometime around the fourth birthday, though it can come later and still be in the normal range. If that first attempt at realism is the first thing that meets with obvious parental approval, your child's first three years of artistic endeavor are trivialized. This can also serve to discourage the regression back to scribbling that is still necessary for a long time to come. Children do some scribbling through age six or seven, and it is not helpful to demean the activity.

Various skills used in producing art, such as coloring, cutting, or pasting, are most effectively learned when they carry out the child's goals rather than some adult-conceived project. Spills and messes can happen when the child is excited by the activity and too engrossed in work to stop and think about neatness. Most often these disasters occur because the supervising adult did not plan the space or lay out the materials efficiently. Occasional messing also may signal unhappiness or frustration in other areas of the child's life, and this can open communication between you if you are not too quick to reprimand. Parents can learn so much about their children by studying their art and their methods of work. They learn most about their offspring, however, by observing the process of creativity. It is essential, therefore, that parents supervise meaningful art projects at home to further enhance parent-child communication. Leaving it to the child's teacher is simply not enough. Seeing scribbling as "just scribbling" or, worse, as "a mess" is most certainly interpreted by children as a form of rejection. Please be accepting of your children's ideas in art and don't try to force-feed preconceived art notions to them.

In their rush to prepare children for life, people tend to forget that the real basics are the growing and learning done through play and art experiences. Children are better prepared to read through independent scribbling activities than they are by coloring in pictures or underlining them in workbooks. Help children understand that they only have to please themselves during creative work. The process of working, never the finished product, should be important. Art that is viewed as destructive by parents, such as coloring on walls or painting on furniture, is usually done when supervising adults are busy elsewhere and therefore not responding to the child's cues. With a child under the age of three, it most likely happens because the child was stimulated by the sight of tempting materials, became engrossed in enjoyable, constructive motor activity, and has not yet come to understand the family's sense of right and wrong. Yelling or punishing does not help the child internalize the moral issue at hand and serves to lessen the child's enjoyment and spontaneity in subsequent art activities. The negative feelings of parental disapproval carry over to the next experience and will probably not have changed the child's perception of the meaning of a "neat home environment." Art activities become stressful, which prevents future learning. You serve both your own and your child's interest if you can sensitively and gently channel your child's artistic enthusiasm to large paper instead of a wall, or an old carton instead of your favorite table.

It is clearly necessary for parents to sometimes be willing to discard some of their own preconceived notions of cleanliness and good behavior. Babies can be encouraged to touch and explore the items with which they come in contact. When a child reaches for a dangerous object, don't scream, "No!" as instinct sometimes dictates. Instead, drop what you are doing, take the child on your lap, look at the object, and talk about it together. This is essential if you wish the child to grow up with the same curiosity and intense interest in life that all children are born with. Let your child make some decisions from the very beginning, like when to eat, sleep, or stop to examine something. Continue letting your child know that his or her opinion is not less important than yours. Stop with your child to examine and discuss rocks, leaves, tree bark, fabrics, tools (even sharp ones), and everything else that fascinates him or her. You cannot expect a child who hears "Don't touch" all day to approach art materials with wild abandon. To a baby, "Don't touch" translates as "Don't learn." I wrote another book entitled *Please Touch,* which expands on my philosophy in this area.

In addition to the simple art projects presented in this book, there are many other things you can do with your child to encourage creative and independent thinking. Let your infant explore the world as much as possible through his or her eyes, mouth, and hands. Take your child to see great art, to smell the grass, and to lie on his or her back and watch the changing images in the clouds. Viktor

Lowenfeld, one of the great innovators in the field of art education, said, in his book *Creativity, Education's Stepchild: A Sourcebook for Creative Thinking*:

> Creative persons, we find, are among other things unusually sensitive to what they see, hear, touch, etc. They respond rapidly to the "feel" and grain of a piece of wood, the texture and flexibility of clay, things often hidden.

The projects presented here are designed for children aged six months through six years. They are most beneficial when begun at the six-month level and continued on a regular (even daily) basis. They can and should be repeated literally hundreds of times, and should always meet with praise, appropriate comments, and encouragement. Although the materials do not change, the child will! Each new approach to old materials comes with a different perspective and a greater storehouse of knowledge. The look and feel of various art materials are enough in themselves to stimulate genuine creativity. Hang your child's work in a prominent place in your home and treat it as if it is the most important accomplishment in the world. It is! A magnet on the refrigerator does not convey the same sense of importance as does a picture in a frame over the living room sofa. You can also have your child's pictures turned into silver pins and pendants you can proudly wear or give as gifts (see Appendix 3, "Art Suppliers"). These early art projects are your child's first steps in problem solving and independent thinking. They free your child for later intellectual development, just as the first tentative steps in walking allow your child to run later.

Toddlers have an insatiable desire to manipulate different kinds of materials. Through this kind of experimentation, their perception and understanding of the world are increased. It is just this free, self-motivated kind of exploration that teaches children how to use their minds and think for themselves. Children learn far more about their own capabilities through this kind of play than they do from adult-imposed rules and warnings. Each child's interests and abilities vary somewhat, but here are some guidelines for when to offer these art activities:

- finger "painting" with food should be available from the time the child is six months old
- an unwrapped, large black crayon and large white paper as long as the

child's arm can be offered between *eight months* and *one year*, with more
varied drawing experiences being gradually introduced
- by *eighteen months* the child can paint with a one-inch brush and one
  color of paint and can work with some form of play dough or Crayola
  Model Magic
- the *twenty-month-old* child will adore tape and self-stick stickers, and will
  be able to handle glue at *two-and-a-half* to *three years*
- after some preliminary exploration of how scissors work, the child can
  usually make slits in paper at age *two* to *two-and-a-half*
- the *three-year-old* can paint with two colors and should be making the
  transition from play dough to clay

If materials have been presented singly, with additions made gradually as
recommended in this book, the three-and-a-half-year-old will be experienced
enough to handle multiple colors. Printing will evolve naturally from painting.
Remember that the older child who has missed out on these experiences at peak
readiness time still needs to experience them before doing more advanced work.

You will need the following art materials to do the projects in this book. In
the appendix you'll find a list of suppliers for items that may not be readily
available.

- Applesauce, whipped cream, pudding, or other food
- Unwrapped crayons
- Fat pencils
- Water-soluble felt-tip markers
- Red, yellow, and blue finger paint
- Crayola Model Magic and/or play dough
- Chalk and dark paper and/or chalkboard
- Drinking straws
- Scraps of sponge
- Red, yellow, blue, green, purple, orange, black, and white tempera paints
- Paintbrushes
- Glue (Elmer's, Sobo, or Crayola Art and Craft)
- Tape
- Hole punch
- Paint roller
- Pipe cleaners
- Colored chalk or Craypas

- Self-adhesive stickers from the stationery store
- Food coloring
- Scissors
- Cardboard
- 11" × 17" white paper
- Colored construction paper

A Roughneck Carry Caddy by Rubbermaid is useful for storing most of your art materials. Keep crayons, chalk, pencils, etc., in separate cups or boxes so that you have the option of taking one material out at a time or all the materials at one time. If it suits your furniture arrangement, try a lazy Susan.

I feel that with very young children 11" × 14" paper is the smallest-sized paper that can be effectively used. Paper should be at least as long as the child's arm. Each suggested project in this book is most effective when repeated ad infinitum, until the child is ready to move on to the next. New artists are extremely prolific. The child who is offered, for example, white paper and a black crayon for the first time can use up reams of paper without losing interest. Under these circumstances, it is tempting to buy the cheapest possible paper. However, inexpensive paper, such as newsprint, can become brittle in no time, and can crumble and disintegrate. Children's paintings, if they are to be valued by the child as well as parents and teachers, should be done on 70-pound or 80-pound paper if at all possible. These quality-weight papers take paint and paste well, and can be rolled or folded without mishaps. Newsprint, computer paper, and old paper bags, however, are certainly better than nothing. Giving no paper to the child means that the child will ultimately draw on the walls. I feel that if at all financially feasible, you should buy children decent-quality paper from the very beginning. Art and stationery stores sell high-priced pads, and this can discourage parents. You can order good-quality drawing paper by the ream through school suppliers at a fraction of the cost. Order one ream of white and one ream of black. Your child will be set for years of creative activities. From time to time, challenge your child by offering something different than he or she has become accustomed to. If the child usually uses 11" × 14" paper, a piece of round paper or a sheet of 8" × 10" paper will be a challenge.

You will also want to have colored paper. Construction paper that is 80-pound or 85-pound paper is a fairly good quality, but all construction paper fades with time. Fadeless art paper is also available. It comes with one color on the front and a contrasting color on the back. It is ideal for paper sculpture, and easier to cut and tear than construction paper. Bristol board or cardboard is the perfect background for collage. The following are the four most common mistakes one can make regarding paper:

1. Offering pieces too small for a young child
2. Offering paper that is cheap and won't absorb paint, or will curl when paste is applied
3. Offering children paper that is precut into shapes such as turkeys, butterflies, flowers, etc.
4. Giving children printed paper with distracting pictures on it, such as flowers or animals, that are found in wallpaper books

Elmer's, Sobo, Crayola Art and Craft, and similar glues are nontoxic. They are strong enough to hold sculpture together and, diluted with a little water, are fine for pasting paper. Such glues can be used with a brush, a wooden stick, or directly from the squeeze bottle. Add a few drops of food coloring and the paste adds to, rather than detracts from, the completed artwork. Glitter glue, which comes in sparkly colors, also can enhance a child's artwork and is great fun to use.

Buying two ounces of finger paint at a time in a toy store is not a very economical way to shop for an enthusiastic new painter. As an art teacher, I had access to bulk supplies at reduced rates when I worked with my son. There are wholesale school suppliers all over the country, and I have provided you with a list of those I use regularly and feel comfortable recommending. This will help you set up a rich learning environment full of all the supplies your child needs to engage in the creative activities described throughout the book. Please see Appendix 3, a list of art suppliers, at the end of this book. Call their toll-free telephone numbers and order a catalog from each company. You will find all of the materials I recommend in this book and probably discover many others that interest you.

Eventually, storage of your child's many masterpieces becomes a problem. I would no more throw out one of my child's drawings than discard one of his baby pictures. These drawings and paintings provide a priceless record of growth. As you may well imagine, my son did more artwork than most children. Despite the fact that I saved every last one of his pictures, we were not inundated with paper in our city apartment. Most parents encounter storage problems because of poor planning, and solve the problem by throwing art away. This communicates to the child that the work he or she produces is garbage. Even though you want to emphasize the experience of work more than the final product, you denigrate the process by being callous about the product. I have lost count of the number of times students of mine, who spent ages working painstakingly on a single project, have said to me, "You keep it, Ms. Striker. My mother just throws out my artwork." When did tidy houses become more important than children's minds and egos? Never let your child see you throwing artwork in the garbage. That should be his or her prerogative! Planning for art storage does not require anything more complicated than making or purchasing a 20" × 24" portfolio in an art or stationery supply store. I find that one or two will hold a year's worth of work. If you are inspired to create a more elaborate storage system, a handy carpenter can fashion a wooden storage box out of plywood—you could also use an old toy box. Make compartments for each year or season and simply slip each new work of art at the back of the box to keep everything neat and in chronological order. I once heard my son proudly tell a friend, "My mommy has every picture I ever made." Simply knowing that the work is being saved adds enormously to a child's self-esteem.

Susan Richardson of the Historical Society of Greenwich says, "It is most important to store your archives in a safe environment. Avoid powerful sources of heat, damp, and pollution. Don't store anything valuable in attics or basements, or near water sources. Do not hang valuables over radiators, the fireplace, or heat-producing appliances. The ideal is a moderate temperature and humidity, clean air and good air circulation, and not excessive natural or fluorescent light. Light causes fading and damage."

I mount every single piece of art every child creates in my art program in a large elementary school. The art is stored in a portfolio and sent home, with much fanfare, at the end of the school year. It takes many dedicated parent volunteers to coordinate this with me and is (almost) always greatly appreciated by the parents of my students. Parents tell me that pictures that come home in backpacks, folded and wrinkled, often get thrown out, but similar drawings mounted and in an art portfolio get the lavish praise they deserve. One parent, however, sent me a letter chastising me for wasting paper. She complained that, as a taxpayer, she objected to my extravagant use of colored paper. Proudly she recounted the story of how she sat down with her daughter and went through the art portfolio. They removed each piece of art from the colored paper mounting and returned it to me to reuse in the art room. She allowed her daughter to keep a few "special" pieces of art and threw out the rest. I had tears in my eyes as I read that letter, picturing that child, who had been told by her art teacher that art needs to be valued and that colored mats help present it effectively. Her mother taught her that the colored paper she returned to the art room was more valuable than the artwork she had spent a whole school year producing! I'm all for ecology, but I don't see any value in sending a child the message, intentional or not, that any piece of artwork is not worth the paper it is mounted on.

I send the following note home to help the parents of my students encourage creativity.

How to Encourage Your Child's Creativity

1. Be a role model. Instead of saying, "I can't draw a straight line with a ruler," say, "I love to create things." The process of creativity is far more important than the product. If your child sees you taking risks and making things, he or she will follow your model.

2. Don't only hang your child's art on the refrigerator with a magnet. Your child already knows that "real" art is framed and hung throughout the house. Take something that your child creates to the framer and hang it in an important area of your home. You can also have your child's artwork copied as a piece of silver jewelry or printed on a number of household items, such as mouse pads and aprons (see Appendix 2: Art Supplies).

3. Show a clear preference for your child's original work. Let your child know that copying, tracing, and coloring-in of adult art are not creative. Copying is cheating, just as it would be in math. Help your child understand that solving problems while creating a work of art leads to solving problems in all areas of life.

4. Verbalize why you "like" a picture. "Pretty" is not particularly helpful. For example, "the colors are so bright and cheerful, there are straight lines and curvy lines and they look good together, the colors remind me of that day you were so sad," are the kind of phrases that can help your child expand his or her vocabulary. They also reinforce what is already being done on an intuitive level.

5. Visit an art gallery or museum with your child. Look at the artwork and encourage your child to look at and talk about the art without worrying about being "correct."

6. Make holiday cards out of your child's drawings or paintings and mail them to friends and family.

7. Have your children's birthday party guests decorate their own cake, using squeeze tube frosting and candy.

8. Set aside an area of your home that can always be "messy." Put an easel, chalkboard, crayons, paints, glue, and a box of scraps there. Call it the art studio, and encourage daily use.

9. Buy a big portfolio and save artwork. There is nothing more discouraging than working on a picture for two art periods only to have Mom throw it out on trash day.

10. Occasionally buy plain, light-colored things for your child to decorate, such as T-shirts, curtains, sheets, dishes, canvas bags, etc. Use them!

11. Buy a leather-bound blank book for your child to use every day, even when you travel. Use it regularly and it will soon be a delightful record of your child's growth and development.

Ten Cardinal Rules for Teaching Creative Art

1. Let go of your own expectations of how an art project should be completed, and let the child's imagination decide how the art materials will be used. (Instructions can prevent exploration, which is the essence of creative thinking.)

2. Never draw, paint, or write on a child's artwork. (The child's own art is more important than any contribution you may make and it may discourage age-appropriate work.)

3. Never point out accidental similarities to realistic objects. (This can distract from the value of the kinesthetic activity of the project.)

4. Never show a child "how" to draw, or entertain a child by making realistic pictures. (These lessons can quickly become substitutes for creative exploration.)

5. Don't ask "What is it?" or "What are you making?" ("What" it is is not as important as "how" it is being made.)

6. Never give a child coloring books, dot-to-dot, magic paint with water, molds, drawing machines, drawing computers, or similar anti-art toys. (There is no value for a child in completing something another person created.)

7. Never encourage children to participate in art contests or other forms of competition that pit child against child. (Children benefit most from setting their own goals and competing with themselves.)

8. Encourage a child to come up with many different solutions to problems, rather than only one correct answer. (In life there is rarely only one "correct" solution to problems, and sound art experiences can teach children how to solve problems.)

9. Don't scold for drawing on unacceptable surfaces. Offer paper and say, "Oh good. I see you feel like drawing." (Emphasize the positive—your child wants to draw—and provide an acceptable substitute surface.)

10. Do not rush a child to the next level of development. (Each stage is important and there is no advantage gained by rushing through one stage to reach another.)

The following chart, "Art Activity Developmental Norms," is intended for use as a guideline.

Art Activity Developmental Norms

Activity	6–12 months	12–18 months	18–24 months	24–30 months	30–36 months	36–42 months
Drawing	Holds, looks at, mouths crayon	Does tentative scribbles	Draws vertical, horizontal, and diagonal lines Experiments with scribbles Is interested in textures	Does freer, circular scribbles Experiments with many scribble shapes	Connects lines to enclose shapes Names shapes after drawing them	Tells stories about pictures Begins mandala experiments May draw human shapes
Clay or play dough work	Tastes and eats clay	Pinches, squeezes, and pounds on clay	Rolls snakelike coils	Makes clay balls Gives names to objects made and plays with them (cats, trains, snakes, and pancakes are favorites)	Incises decoration on clay and sticks things into it	Produces flat designs with clay Adds on, builds
Painting	Smears paint with hands and tastes it	Does body decorations Makes dabbing movements	Paints lines with a brush similar to scribbles	Continues scribbling development through paint	Paints whole areas	Entire paper covered with areas of paint

CHAPTER 1

Drawing

Scribbles are the building blocks of children's art.
Rhoda Kellogg

From approximately ages one through four, children go through what art educators call the scribbling stage. They enjoy scribbling tremendously, and benefit from enthusiastic support in their endeavors by loving adults. That the
word *scribble* is used so often as a term of disparagement is one indication of
how we fail our children in their quest for knowledge. Scribbling includes all
of the hand and arm movements needed later in writing, and is an essential
activity for all children. Although most adults cannot make any sense out of
scribbles, it is far from a senseless activity. The motor activity that takes place

Jason drawing while sitting in Cookie Monster chair

during scribbling is a good example of children who are engaging in learning that contributes to language development. Arnold Gesell, the noted child psychologist, pointed out that language and social growth are developed through kinesthesis, or body movement. Visualize a child learning about the concept of round, not by having it explained by an adult but by playing circle games, catching a ball, eating an apple, or spinning a hula hoop.

Children scribble purposefully and it represents a growth process. Well-meaning parents and teachers who try to teach a child in this stage how to draw an apple or a face produce only frustration and insecurity. That these marks on a page have any connection to real objects is not what an art experience should be like for a child under the age of four. The child can already "read" pictures and photographs in books and magazines, but it will be a long time before he or she "writes" them in the same sense. Children do not learn art in the same way that they learn to write. A child must be shown what each letter of the alphabet looks like and what it means, and taught how to make it. The same child independently invents each of the scribble shapes that later become letters, and soon discovers, without being shown, how to draw realistic objects. In fact, being "taught" is more likely to interfere with the child's ability to learn. I recommend giving a child a crayon sometime around the first birthday.

The first time you offer a child a crayon, it generally goes directly into the mouth. If you purchase nontoxic, unwrapped crayons, there is no reason to thwart this initial exploration. Offer your child his or her first crayon and demonstrate its use by quickly scribbling a few lines on your own paper and then removing your paper from sight to discourage copying.

The first scribbles can be done by accident. Then the mental connection is made and the child recognizes that his or her arm movements cause the lines on the paper. Interest in scribbling begins at that point. Attention span is short for the beginning scribbler, and the child frequently draws while attention is focused elsewhere. This occurs because the physical action is what is important to the child, not the picture itself. Early scribbles reflect the child's limited physical coordination. The lines generally go back and forth or up and down, and are created by shoulder movement rather than hand or arm movement. As the child matures, coordination improves and the attention span lengthens. Scribbles then include circular lines, and the child commences experiments with all of the shapes in the "alphabet" of scribbles. The following illustration is an example of a child's early scribble.

Child's scribble

First scribbles should meet with the same praise and encouragement that first steps do. Indeed, that is what they are! These two developmental achievements happen at about the same time, and both signal great growth and new potential. Your positive reaction to your child's art helps establish a healthy, confident self-image and adds immeasurably to self-esteem. Because you are accepting of this work, your child is free to progress naturally. Vague compliments such as "very pretty" and "I love your drawing" are value judgments that do not help the child move ahead and grow. In fact, children often will interrupt their explorations to draw parent-pleasing pictures ad infinitum. Criticizing, correcting, and directing art activities cripple the child's efforts and eventually cause the child to stop enjoying art. Many people proudly teach their children to write their names at this time, and the children abandon scribbling to repeat these movements over and over. This should be viewed as interference of development and is akin to the old Chinese custom of binding a child's feet. It looks pretty, and is socially acceptable, but it cripples.

In *The Psychology of Children's Art* Rhoda Kellogg and Scott O'Dell isolate the twenty basic shapes with which all children begin their artistic endeavors. As you look at them, you can see that, combined in different ways, these lines and shapes make up our alphabet. Ms. Kellogg collected and studied thousands of scribbles and is responsible for most of the significant work in this area. I recommend her book to all parents, caretakers, and teachers. From ages one through two, children scribble randomly; then they begin to concentrate on establishing a full vocabulary of scribbles, experimenting with each of these twenty shapes:

· ˙	dot	ᔓᔕ	roving enclosed line
│	single vertical line	⌒⌒⌒⌒	zigzag or wavy line
—	single horizontal line	ℓ	single loop line
\ /	single diagonal line	ℓℓℓ	multiple loop line
⌒	single curved line	ⓔ	spiral line
ⱴⱴⱴⱴ	multiple vertical lines	●	multiple line overlaid circle
≋	multiple horizontal lines	◎	multiple line circumference circle
⫽ ⫽	multiple diagonal lines	⬭⬭⬭	circular line, spread out
⌒	multiple curved lines	♂	single crossed line
⌇	roving open line	◯	imperfect circle

Twenty basic scribbles. Illustrations adapted from *Analyzing Children's Art* by Rhoda Kellogg

All of the world's alphabets were derived from the shapes children experiment with as scribblers. Here you see the title of this book, *Young at Art*, written in English, Chinese, and Japanese. Observe that only the basic scribble shapes are needed to create each letter.

young at Art

年青的藝術

若き芸術家

The words "young at art" in English, Chinese, and Japanese, demonstrating
how all alphabets are derived from the lines in children's scribbles

By age three, after about two years of scribbling, the child begins to notice similarities in completed scribbles to things he or she knows, and will name them. The child is still not setting out to draw something in particular, but notices, after the shapes are drawn, that they share characteristics in common with real objects. Since many different objects share a similarity to a single shape, the objects named, or story told about a single drawing, may change from viewing to viewing. It is therefore not particularly helpful for you to record the picture's name or story for posterity. Many parents and teachers listen to the story a child tells about a scribble and proceed to write the story directly on the picture or to label lines in the drawing with the names of objects they are supposed to represent. An adult's writing on a picture is an unnecessary intrusion into the child's work. It alters the arrangement and composition of lines and shapes on the background that the child has produced. This adult labeling also prevents the child from changing the story or the names of things and discourages the child from reading new things into the shapes at a subsequent viewing. The adult's writing may be taken as a kind of sanctioning of the first story. It finalizes the description and prevents the flexibility and fluidity of thinking that should come naturally at this stage of development.

Most helpful is for you to verbalize for the child just what characteristic in the drawing makes it look like something else. For example, today's "Yes, I can see that your road is very long" can become "That is surely a very long train" tomorrow.

The child recognizes that the drawn line is long, much like a road, a train, or a multitude of other things. It is this mental connection that is of great significance. This use of lines and shapes as symbols for other things is the bridge leading to symbol recognition and formation used in reading and writing. It stands to reason that the more experience a child has in dealing with producing art, the easier learning to read and write will be later on. People who push children to read very early are stealing time from this important prereading activity. The effect is often to make reading more, not less, difficult.

If given freedom to experiment with scribbles, the child, midway through his or her third year, makes an important discovery. By connecting the two ends of a line, a shape is created. The scribbled lines now have a beginning and end and enclose specific shapes. Moving from line experimentation to making round or oval shapes represents an enormous step forward. New possibilities present themselves frequently, and it is a matter of a short time before these shapes become realistic objects. Add dots for eyes and you have a face; radiating lines transform it to a wheel, flower, or sun. If encouraged to develop freely, one of the shapes the child will be experimenting with will be the mandala form, which is usually a circle or a square with a center and radiating lines.

After the child achieves proficiency with lines, he or she can be expected to draw shapes in this progression of readiness:

CIRCLES
Ages 2½–3½
SQUARES
Ages 4½–5½
TRIANGLES
Ages 5½–6½
DIAMONDS
Ages 6½–7½

Giving younger children stencils to trace or patterns to color in won't change human nature. Rushing things and pushing children to do things before they are ready exacts a toll by causing problems in other areas, most notably in the child's self-confidence. The Crayola Crayon Web site, www.crayola.com, states, "Children's creativity is strengthened when they create original works of art. That creativity is stifled and children's artistic competence is compromised when they mindlessly color predrawn pictures."

Mandalas are usually circles or ovals with crossed lines over them. Carl Jung described them as "a search for order." When normal art development is allowed to occur without too much interference or undue outside influence, variations of the mandala come at the turning point in children's art at about age four, after free scribbling experimentation and before representational drawing. Mandalas take many forms and are sometimes difficult for adults to locate in the middle of a scribble. Just as all children, though they share certain simi-

Typical mandala

larities, are quite different, so too are their drawings. The mandala is not always the clearly defined shape that we might expect. It takes on all of the many individual characteristics of the child's personal search through shapes and forms. Though the variations may be great, the basic shape is still there.

Fred's mandala

It seems to me that a parallel development is a shape that looks like this:

It is not technically a mandala by definition, but it is similar in that it has a sense of symmetry through repetition of lines and it conveys a feeling of a sense of order.

The evolution of the mandala into a human being is easy to trace. Dots learned in scribbling suffice for eyes, with the radiating lines becoming the arms, legs, fingers, toes, teeth, hair, and eyelashes.

Adults often wonder where the torso is, and "help" children by talking about tummies, chests, and belly buttons. The child has known where his or her belly button is for two years already and needs no reminder. The circle is really a symbol representing the whole human being and is derived directly from the mandala, which is in turn derived from scribbling experiments. The child who has learned to draw a human being in this self-taught manner retains the ability forever and will probably continue art experiments. The

Ladder mandala

child of the same age who has put together an adult-planned human has learned nothing from the experience. Lessons contrived to "teach" children about such things as human anatomy and facial structure are completely off base. For the preschooler, art is not the vehicle for increasing body awareness, as it might be with seven-year-olds. It is counterproductive to impose subject matter on a child under seven. Communicating your own preference for subject-related art is in no way helpful.

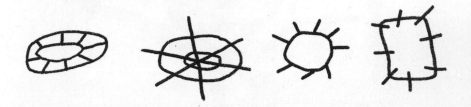

Four mandala variations

The drawings done during this period of development in child art are often called tadpoles since they resemble them. Even this term shows the common thread of misunderstanding running through young children's art. Adults seem to need a label for drawings, even when it is inaccurate and is not intended by the child. Later, when realistic drawing begins, the mandala reappears as windows, suns, wheels, and spiders.

The sunlike mandala is an early example of the many shapes and patterns that children make in their quest for mastery of drawing. Mandala drawings precede the first realistic efforts, which usually come at around age four. Calling them suns or wheels often happens after the drawing is completed. It is retained in subsequent drawings as a "sun" at the top of a drawing, although other shapes are discarded or assimilated. As the child progresses through the scribbling stage, the mandala finds its way into a child's pictures for many years, sometimes into adolescence. I believe this is because it is quickly labeled a sun by an overanxious adult. This label, or adult stamp of approval, is seen as a preference for this form over others that meet with no interest and is retained in a desire to please and to be more "grown-up."

This point in scribbling development is so crucial to the child's normal development that it can be devastating to now rush the process or "teach" the child how to represent realistic objects. The capacity to discover the mandala lies within every child, as does the later need to represent people and objects realistically.

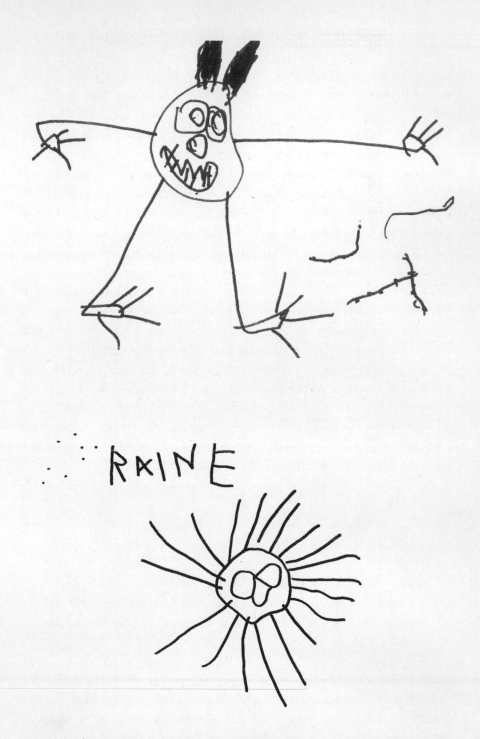

RAINE

Four drawings of humans that demonstrate how an understanding of the mandala
leads to the early drawings of a human

Art educators and psychologists have different theories to explain the psychological meaning of the mandala form children draw. It isn't necessary to read about the many conflicting theories art educators have about the meaning and origin of each scribble. Like walking, all healthy children do it. Indeed, not doing it indicates a problem. The question should be, "How can parents best recognize and assist children in this developmental hurdle?" The answer is to offer as much time as the child needs to pursue art, a place in which to do it that can get messy if necessary, and encouragement and approval. The key words should be "Don't teach." Instead, *let* your child learn.

In my experience, I find that the more parents know or think they know about art, the more harm they are inclined to do. By having fixed ideas, they have a tendency to impose rules prematurely and perpetuate fixed stereotypes about how to draw or make things.

In scribbling, of which the mandala is part, the child utilizes lines. The lines start out freely and progress through an unconscious use of increasing repetition and patterns and, later, enclosed shapes. Children who are kept busy making turkeys and Christmas trees can't concentrate on the evolution of the scribbling process. Communicating to our children that "pictures" are better than the patterns they obviously have an enormous need to do can cause them to abandon art. Most children, in fact, do this when they are not allowed to develop freely. When the child accepts the parent's notions that pictures have to be pretty and that pretty means realistic, the personal search for understanding the world through art ends.

Scribbling can reflect the physical development of a child and provide an emotional outlet. The experience of scribbling, according to Viktor Lowenfeld and W. Lambert Brittain in their book *Creative and Mental Growth* (page 132),

> is mainly one of motor activity. At first satisfaction is derived from the experience of kinesthetic motions, next from a visual control of lines, and finally from the relationship of these lines to the outside world.

Scribbling also reflects the child's personality. A timid child will do light, timid-looking scribbles, while the work of outgoing, gregarious children looks bold and dramatic. The child cannot help but approach art materials in the same way he or she approaches life. Children at this age do not intend to express their feelings through art when they draw or paint, but they inadvertently do exactly that. You can learn so much about a child, by both watching the child at work and looking at the finished art. Two children, in the same stage of development, given identical materials, will make vastly different pictures. A wonderfully sensitive nursery school teacher told me that after she got to know her students, she always recognized who had done a painting without looking for the child's name. I am still sometimes astonished to see the results of two toddlers, sitting side by side doing the identical art project, and coming up with two pictures that look so different.

Scribbling is also an accurate representation of intellectual growth. A school-age child of five or six years who is still scribbling needs to complete this stage before he or she can learn to read or write. Forcing the issue, or encouraging the child to skip this important stage by drawing realistically, causes emotional damage on top of the slow learning. Children of normal intelligence should feel free enough to revert back to scribbling, even after they have started to draw representationally. Most children don't

Two children in the same setting work with the same materials and come up with vastly different pictures

really abandon scribbling completely until age five or six. I have always believed that schools that eliminate art are the ones that have problem readers. Schools where art translates as coloring in adult-drawn pictures with a "neat" back-and-forth hand movement may contribute to some of the problems children have when they learn to read. Low reading scores too often cause these institutions to eliminate art programs and concentrate time and money on reading; the problem may be compounded instead of solved. Too often educators fail to credit scribbling as a significant precursor to reading.

Scribbling is one of your child's most important activities. Interfering with the natural scribbling process by "pushing" your child to draw realistically, or by disciplining a child who may have drawn on an unacceptable surface, can have serious ramifications later. One indication of a problem is that the young child begins to repeat the same shape over and over. It is a sign of self-consciousness about art and insecurity about one's own abilities. It most often happens to children who are "taught" how to draw a picture or write letters, and to children who are "entertained" by watching an adult draw. The greatest disservice we do to the development of our children is to believe that the sooner they decode the written word the better. Early reading and realistic drawing can certainly be achieved, but it is usually done at great expense in other areas of the child's development. The child who abandons scribbling activities may have difficulty learning to write and will almost surely abandon art as a means of self-expression. This signal from a child is not to be taken lightly, since scribbling can affect language development and later reading and writing abilities. If the child under three begins to do small, self-conscious scribbles, in which stereotyped motions such as circles are repeated over and over, it may mean that the child has lost confidence in his or her drawing ability. The parent should look into the child's drawing experience at home and with others. Perhaps a well-meaning grandparent, baby-sitter, or day care worker is prematurely "teaching" the child how to draw or write by providing adult patterns or drawings to color in. This represents a serious impediment to learning and can indicate a problem of self-image that can be long-lasting. I have seen this kind of small, tight, self-conscious drawing in children as young as eighteen months. It always indicates too much adult direction in their artwork and, quite often, their play activities as well. It often means that someone was drawing for the child, or "teaching" the child how to draw. Encouraging a child to write letters too early has the same effect. The child feels secure by repeating the same thing over and over, but this false sense of security blocks further learning and personality development. It is an indication that the child needs to be helped, and that supervision needs to be changed.

Every art teacher will tell you that parental response to a child's work may be one of the most important elements in the child's feeling for his or her work. Therefore, it is better not to ask your child, "What is it?" It is most helpful to focus on the activity rather than the similarity to things you can recognize. You can describe what the child is doing, such as, "I can see you are covering your whole paper with lines," "You sure are working hard," or "Your whole arm is going up and down and so are the lines on your paper." You can describe how a tool is being used. For example, "When you rub the paper with the side of the crayon the line is as wide as the crayon is!" You can focus attention on the lines. While pointing to the line in question, you might say, "You made a zigzag line." You can point out the effects of pressure, as in "Look how hard you are pressing with the crayon. That makes it look very dark." Familiarize yourself with the scribbling "alphabet" on page 27. When you recognize one of these symbols in your child's scribble, exhibit pleasure and offer encouragement. You can contribute to your child's art vocabulary by noting: "Oh look! A diagonal line!"

Color use is another area you will want to comment about: "You used a lot of blue and just a little bit of red." Comparison to other work can also be helpful: "That red hardly shows up at all on the red paper but it looks so bright on the white paper." When trying to think of helpful comments to make, remember that by simply describing the activity or the picture, you are being very helpful because you are providing the child with an awareness of the causes and effects of his or her actions, and you are stimulating language development by adding to the child's vocabulary. Your interest and approval are the two most important contributions you can make to your child's art. Consider the child's level of development when making your comments. "That looks like a house" might be an appropriate comment for a seven-year-old, but it isn't for a three-year-old (even if it *does* look like a house to you). Consider these areas when trying to think of comments to make:

1. How the child's actions affect the picture
2. How color is used
3. The type of line that is used
4. How the work differs from a previous work
5. The way a tool is being used

6. Pressure of the hand on a tool

7. How the child feels while working

Helpful comments give vocabulary to your child's work and validate his or her efforts. For example,

• "Oh, look! You made both straight and curvy lines."
• "Some of your lines are so long that they go right off the paper."
• "I see a fat line right next to a thin line."
• "You must have pressed very hard on your crayon to make such a dark line."
• "The black shape is right next to the blue shape."

Keep in mind that art doesn't have to be "pretty" to be good or to have provided the child with an important learning experience. Encouraging words should therefore not be restricted to "very pretty!"

Comments *not* to make about your child's art:

• "What is that?"
• "Don't do it that way. Do it this way."
• "Why don't you do what Tommy is doing?"
• "Make a picture for Mommy."
• "You naughty boy! Don't draw on the walls."

The very first scribbles should be recognized as a child's first use of a tool of communication, and therefore noteworthy. If you don't get excited about your child's drawing until you recognize something about it, like a face or a house, you are negating much of the value of at least two years of the hard work of scribbling your child is now engaging in. Scribbling is a long learning process, and your child needs your help, praise, and encouragement just as much as he or she did when learning to walk or talk. We are thrilled by the first wobbly step followed by a flop, knowing it becomes well-coordinated walking very soon. The first "mama" sounds so beautiful to our ears, and is transformed into a full vocabulary so quickly. So too, very soon, the first scribbles will become a drawing more to your taste, and, shortly thereafter, letters and words.

Unfortunately, scribbling is a word that has been overused as a derogatory term. Even art educators are often guilty of describing a drawing as "just scribbling" as if it lacks any significance at all in children's art or human development. Parents and teachers often wait out the scribbling stage in anticipation of the emergence of "real" drawings. Too often, the only pictures remaining from childhood are of first attempts at drawing a person. These pictures, saved by parents, come three years after the child's first drawing, but are remembered as "first drawings," perhaps because they were the first that the parent could relate to.

The one-year-old will continue to scribble for about three more years. If it were possible for a child to never draw until age four, he or she would pass through the scribbling stage in a shorter period of time. No matter at what age a child begins to draw, he or she will still have to pass through the scribbling stage before learning to draw or write.

Scribbling Development

After experimenting with mandalas, children make their first attempts at drawing humans, which are based on knowledge of mandala-like shapes.

Somewhere around the age of 4 the child will draw a combination of crossed lines over circles or ovals (called mandalas by Rhoda Kellogg) and other scribbles that show symmetry and a sense of order.

At approximately age 3½ the child connects the two ends of a line to enclose shapes.

Purposeful scribbles become increasingly complex as physical development progresses in the 3- to 3½-year-old.

After the child has completed work, he or she may tell stories about the drawing, which may change from one telling to the next, based on new things the child discovers in the lines.

Children 8 to 12 months of age explore crayons with hands, eyes, and mouth.

The 10- to 14-month-old child moves crayon on paper but attention may be focused elsewhere.

At 14 to 18 months the child recognizes the connection between hand movement and marks on paper. Scribbles may look uncontrolled to an adult.

Children 18 months to 2 years of age do scribbles that are controlled mostly by shoulder movements; they are horizontal or vertical lines which gradually may curve.

Childern 2 to 3 years old do scribbles that include all twenty of the basic scribbles.

The chart on page 39 takes you through the stages of art development, beginning with "tasting" the crayon through the many levels of scribbling experimentation and culminating with the first drawing of a person. That final stage signals reading readiness, as it represents the internalizing of the abstract concept of lines on paper representing something. When your child begins to draw lines that symbolize objects, it is a signal to you that the child will easily understand the concept of letters representing sounds, just as the pictures being drawn represent objects. Our preschools should not be working toward early alphabet recognition. They should be constantly seeking ways to provide engaging scribbling activities and offering opportunities for independent problem solving.

The section that follows offers suggestions for a logical sequence of drawing activities you can offer your child.

Scribble with Black

Crayons have traditionally been the all-time favorite first drawing utensils. It is best to purchase them unwrapped, or to unwrap them before giving them to the child. Large, easy-to-hold, unwrapped crayons encourage children to turn them on their broad sides and to draw thick lines with the broad ends. The box of neatly pointed, wrapped crayons inhibits drawing by encouraging the imitation of the use of a pencil. The paper wrapping is designed to keep the hands clean, a most unrealistic and unnecessary goal for a toddler participating in an art activity. Buy a box of not more than eight colors. A box of sixty-four pointed crayons is more intimidating than anything. Use one, break one point, and the whole box seems ruined. Your wisest investment in crayons would be to purchase a box of sure-grip crayons. They are actually designed for group situations and therefore include several crayons of each of the eight basic colors. This set provides for extensive use, and occasional loss, of the essential colors and does not cause confusion with too many variations of color. Paper should be at least 11" × 14", or at least as long as the child's arm can reach, and it is a good idea to place the white paper on a contrasting dark surface or the black paper on a light surface to delineate the boundary clearly. Children whose work begins to move from the paper to the background may be exhibiting a creative problem-solving thought process or may very simply need larger paper. The sensitive adult will know the difference, as well as know that reprimanding the child can discourage future art activity. It's best to start by offering one color crayon at a time, since color has no meaning to the very young scribbling child and since the goals of scribbling are motor activity and kinesthetic pleasure.

I like to give my students a black crayon and white paper for early scribbling experiments. Black and white provide the strongest contrast possible. It also is the most typical presentation of the written word in books and newspapers. After the child has worked with black crayon on white paper, offer a white crayon and black paper. Try also black "scratch art" paper, that is, white or colored paper that has been coated with ink. Pictures are scratched, rather than drawn, with a pointed wooden stylus that comes with the package. Crayons should always be available (stored together with paper to prevent damage to your home). The child doesn't need an adult to pour or mix crayons, as with paint, and therefore crayons can permit more spontaneous work.

The most effective ways to help the beginning scribbler progress through the scribbling stage with maximum benefits to learning and self-esteem are to do the following:

1. Provide one drawing utensil at a time to help the child focus his or her attention on the process of scribbling instead of the profusion of colors.
2. Verbalize your observations of what the child is doing to help focus attention and reinforce learning.
3. Communicate to the child that his or her efforts are of value.
4. Don't direct, help, provide coloring books, or demonstrate drawing. If you must demonstrate, do so at the child's level; scribble, don't draw a picture.
5. Place a thick pad of newspaper under the drawing to ease a smooth application of the crayon on paper.

The following scribbling activity suggestions will provide you with an orderly sequence of color projects, beginning with black, moving to the three primary colors, followed by the secondary colors.

Allow the child to be well acquainted with one color before moving on to the next. After the child has had considerable experience scribbling with a black crayon, switch to a white crayon on black paper, and then switch to a new color. Coordinate other activities, such as painting, singing, making sculpture, and playing. Chapter 6 pulls together these activities for you.

Scribbling with a Red Crayon

Red is vibrant and a favorite color of many young children. The real learning taking place has to do with kinesthetic pleasure, mental development, the solving of the puzzle of making shapes, and controlling eye-hand coordination. You are most supportive of this activity when you provide one crayon at a time, as this helps the child to focus on what's important. As the child becomes familiar with the materials and the colors, you will naturally make more colors available. I am well aware of how boring or repetitious drawing with one color at a time can appear to an adult, but it is anything but boring to a child under three. Children learn through repetition. They want to hear the same story read over and over, listen to the same song again and again; in the same way, they benefit most by drawing with one utensil until it is fully understood and mastered. When you do offer a change, remember that in a little while the child will be happy to come back to the first material, seeing it with fresh vision.

Learning to recognize and name colors is a useful skill in life, but this is *not* the point of this project. The value of an art experience diminishes when it is viewed as a way to accumulate facts. It is possible to be creative without being able to name colors. Certainly, people who are color-blind and can't differentiate between colors can think in innovative, fresh ways. On the other hand, do not hesitate to offer single colors to a child just because he or she "knows" the color.

The new scribbler is ideally eight to fourteen months old and will enjoy experiencing redness. Noticing all of the red things in the world for a week or so, drawing with red, eating red apples, tomatoes, peppers, and lollipops— even singing a song about red adds to the learning experience. See if you can find the book *Red Is Best* by Kathy Stinson and Robin Baird Lewis. Being forced to color an adult-drawn tomato red in a coloring book or workbook serves to inhibit child-initiated creative activity and doesn't teach the child to recognize red as well as the personalized activities alone do. Don't plan a red experience if your child prefers blue. The child's self-motivation is always the best teacher.

The child may go for long periods without showing interest in drawing, but may make up for it by scribbling on everything in sight at another time. Scolding a child for drawing on an unacceptable surface has the effect of discouraging free expression rather than teaching respect for property. It is best to calmly move in with an acceptable surface, such as a sheet of paper or a blackboard, and as enthusiastically as possible say, "Oh good, I see you are drawing. Here's some paper. If you draw on the walls we'll have to wash them, but we can save a drawing on paper forever!" In no time at all, the child will look for an acceptable drawing surface when the urge to draw hits. Intact egos and a sense of the high value of art activity add to a child's feeling of self-worth. The lure to draw is so strong that children who are not provided with appropriate art materials will be the most destructive and will draw on walls and furniture. You can best teach your child about painting in appropriate places by reading some of the books on the subject (see page 198).

Blue Scribble

Picasso had his "blue period"; now it's your child's turn! Drawing freely with a blue crayon and simultaneously noticing the color blue in the environment produce a very different kind of learning than does the traditional preschool method of giving a child an adult-completed picture to mindlessly color in using a color chosen by an adult. Eating blueberries, observing a summer sky, buying new jeans, picking cornflowers, or playing with a cuddly friend like Sesame Street's Cookie Monster doll are all experiences that best teach a child what blue is.

Many publications widely distributed in schools confuse the issue by suggesting that caps, balloons, kites, or boats must be blue when every child has seen red hats, yellow balloons, green boats, and fanciful, multicolored kites, and knows that this is not so.

At the same time, presenting a confusing array of crayons produces a haphazard learning experience, with attractive colors vying for attention and distracting the child both from the experience of scribbling and from focusing on individual colors.

In time, the child will use an extensive palette and draw realistic pictures, but presenting the materials now and expecting adultlike art is like giving a newborn a knife, fork, can opener, and six cans of food. Despite the provision of nutritious food, the baby would starve to death. Many children's minds are being starved, deprived of the opportunity and encouragement to work within their own capabilities. The option of growing and learning through art is being denied them. In its place the child is given adult art, which no child can digest. I've seen mothers who were still nursing their children give them coloring books! To expect mere babies to produce adult art while still suckling is ludicrous! This premature expectation predisposes children to fail in art and give it up.

Admirers of my Anti-Coloring Books frequently tell me that they offered one to their preschooler. Encouraging a child in the scribbling stage to do a drawing motivated by subject can be as stifling as offering coloring books can be. The Anti-Coloring Books offer stimulating subject motivation for drawings and are intended for much older children. By following the advice I offer in this book, your child should grow up with enough self-confidence to work freely in art, with no adult assistance. Keep in mind that free scribbling is the primary goal of this activity and that learning to identify and label "blue" is secondary. It is a useful skill but is unrelated to creativity.

Yellow Scribble

The look of yellow crayon on white paper is very different than black, red, or blue. Yellow doesn't show up well on white paper, but it usually engages a child's attention, as does white on white. Subtle contrast can fascinate a child. The child observes this and can be assisted by your observations: "Oh look, even when you press very hard the yellow still looks light." Offer brown or black paper next, to allow the child to observe the reverse effect.

Buy or pick a bunch of daffodils to display at home during this period; prepare an all-yellow breakfast of eggs sunny-side up, bananas, and pineapple juice. On a trip to the supermarket, ask your child to pick out all of the yellow items. See if your local library has the book *Yellow Yellow* by Frank Asch or *Hello Yellow* by Robert Jay Wolff. The painting, printing, collage, and sculpture chapters in this book have lots of activities you can use to further focus your child's attention on yellow. Try to keep in mind that while working with yellow your child will learn to recognize and name the color but that is not the major advantage of this activity; free scribbling is. By concentrating on one color you facilitate focusing on its essence, its name, and the effects it produces. You also heighten the child's awareness of objects that are commonly yellow. It is detrimental to suggest that the child draw specific objects yellow. Such a stifling self-conscious use of color is inappropriate for this age level. Children can with no trouble learn to identify colors and to recognize that certain objects are specific colors, while using color freely and without subject connection in their own art.

This activity is extremely enjoyable for toddlers, but is enjoyed by older children too. I frequently declare "yellow week" or "red week" with my kindergarten, first grade, and second grade classes. I always wear that color from head to toe and the school can be in a frenzy of excitement, trying to get an early glimpse of me when I arrive, to see what color we will be using in art class that day.

The entire effect of a crayon drawing is changed simply by using a textured surface. For variety occasionally offer the new multicolored crayons (Chunk-O-Crayon, or a gold or silver one). Let the child's request for more crayons at one time be your signal to offer them.

Scribble with an Easy-Grip Marker

Very young hands may find these felt-tip markers, mounted on a sponge rubber ball, just the right introduction to drawing with markers. They are designed to fit into a toddler's hand and do not require adultlike finger coordination to grasp.

Chunkie Markers are also easy to hold. Since the tip can disappear into the ball, when your child discovers "dots" and proceeds to gaily bang on the paper, it's time to move on to regular felt-tip pens or go back to crayons. Although they are advertised as being for two-year-olds and up, I find them best for very new scribblers as young as twelve to eighteen months old. By age two, your child should be sufficiently well coordinated and experienced in scribbling to be introduced to regular drawing utensils, such as markers and crayons.

Help vary the experience by offering corrugated cardboard to the child who has become accustomed to drawing on smooth paper. Tan cardboard can

Scribbling with an easy-grip
marker on corrugated cardboard

be cut from an old carton, and gaily colored sheets are available through art suppliers.

Many plain white objects are available to be decorated by your child. I regularly purchased undecorated items to be personalized by my son Jason and his friends. Some of them were cardboard lunch boxes, plastic Frisbees, plastic dinner plates, and cups with paper inserts that can be drawn on. Jason made so many plates during his preschool years that we set out fifty on a buffet when we had our housewarming. When he drew all over his scooter I con-

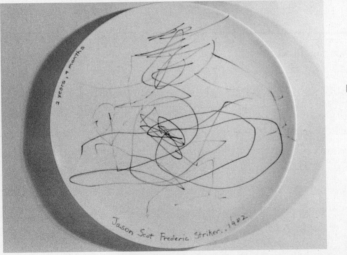

Plastic plate

Cardboard lunch box

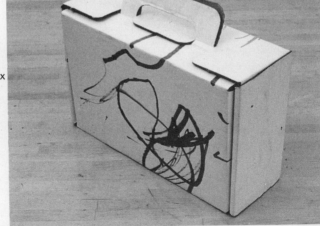

gratulated him for his ingenuity instead of yelling at him. We never had trouble finding it in the playground after that.

Since permanent markers really are permanent, you can use them to decorate clothes as well. At the end of the school year, all of the children in my son's nursery school class helped design an apron as a gift for their well-loved teacher. The apron was sewn from inexpensive white muslin. I made black lines on it to divide the surface. Each child in the group drew in the rectangle designated with his or her name. Although every child did a scribble, each scribble was very distinctive and expressive. The finished apron was very colorful and quite lovely. You'll have to decide for yourself whether permanent markers are appropriate for your child.

Apron created by a preschool class for their teacher

Drawing with Markers

Felt-tip pens or markers are quickly replacing crayons as every child's favorite drawing utensil. The wide assortment of colors are bright and clear, and they flow onto the paper smoothly. Felt-tip pens should never, however, be substitutes for crayons, since these two drawing utensils create quite different effects. Light pressure on a marker creates very intense colors, whereas the intensity of crayon lines are the direct result of the amount of pressure with which the crayon is applied. Colors drawn with felt-tip pens are flat, while crayons can produce a textural illusion.

It's essential to purchase nontoxic, water-soluble markers both for your child's health and the preservation of your home. Buy the large, easy-to-hold size and, as you would when introducing any new material, offer one color at a time, with the others out of sight until the child is familiar with the first one. You will be amazed at the variety one child can achieve with just one marker.

Later on, when the child is more involved in detail work, offer a finer-point marker. Stay away from fruit-scented markers at first, since it is not helpful to have the child confuse art materials with food. Every child will taste markers in any event and nothing can be gained from having the taste

Drawing with markers

Drawing with a brush-tipped marker

buds rewarded. As long as the markers are nontoxic, this exploration of the material, which may disgust you, is actually helpful for the child. You may as well just look the other way. It is a lot more fun to draw with markers than to eat them, and the child will learn this quickly, if you permit the necessary tasting.

Since most markers will quickly dry out when the caps are not replaced, storing them requires the help of a cooperative adult. There are now markers that will stay fresh when left uncovered for twenty-four hours. I have been reasonably successful making children aware of the "click" sound that a marker makes when closed properly, and encouraging them to listen for it.

Scribbling with a Brush-Tipped Marker

The scribbler who will soon be ready to paint may find the transition eased by first drawing with a marking pen that has a brushlike tip. It is similar to the felt-tip pen with which the child is already familiar and the paintbrush that comes next. Since the brush doesn't have to be refilled with paint at frequent intervals, it is simpler for the toddler to use. I like to use Crayola Brush Tips with my youngest students.

Drawing with Chalk on a Blackboard

We already know that scribbling is among the most important activities in which a child can engage. Providing alternative materials that vary tactile experiences and allow an experience in different color comparisons may be all the variety needed to keep interest in this activity strong and the learning that scribbling provides thus broadened. Drawing with one piece of chalk helps the child focus on kinesthetic experimentation, which is the important goal of scribbling. As always, how the drawing utensil is used is more meaningful than how many colors are used.

In addition to drawing on a blackboard, try chalk on black paper, colored paper, or sandpaper and take your child out to draw on the sidewalk; the next rain will wash it away. Chalk is a drier and more powdery drawing utensil than the wax crayon to which most children are accustomed. For this age group I like Scola short, fat chalks, which come in a package of eight sticks, six bright colors and two intense whites. They are the same size and shape as the Chunk-O-Crayon and will feel familiar to the child who has had crayoning experience with them. Other brands also make large, easy-to-hold chalks. Just make sure that white is included in the set you buy.

A child can draw with the end of the chalk, turn it on its side to create broad strokes, and create feathery effects by smudging and smearing. Chalk drawings, when rubbed, disappear as if by magic, unlike crayon, pencil, and marker drawings. Chalk on paper that has been wet with buttermilk or water produces rich, vibrant colors. Given time, space, and material, your child will come to discover all of these special qualities about chalk.

When my son was about three years old, he made a wonderful drawing with white chalk on a blackboard. I had the entire blackboard framed under glass, and it still hangs in a place of honor in my home. I told the reading teacher at school about it when her four-year-old daughter created a "masterpiece" on the very large chalkboard in her mother's classroom. Mom knew how special the drawing was and solicited my advice. Together we removed the metal frame around the blackboard and took the drawing to a professional framer. The framed picture on its chalkboard now hangs in the living room of their home.

Drawing with a Pencil

Scribbling with a pencil differs from drawing with a crayon or marker in that it helps introduce the child to what will be his or her first writing instrument and allows for much more intricate work than crayons allow. This tool should be available when drawing details becomes the child's goal. Always offer pencils all by themselves. It doesn't work to offer a child a pencil and then expect the child to color the drawing in with crayon, since pencil lines are so much finer than crayon lines can ever be. Drawing with a pencil makes the child feel grown-up. It requires that the child draw with the point of the instrument, thereby developing smaller hand muscles. It provides an introduction to light and dark shades and, of course, also comes in assorted colors. Fat hexagonal pencils are easier for young hands to hold than are the regular-sized ones, easing the transition from crayon or felt-tip pen to pencil for very young children. You can also buy rubber pencil grips that slide over a standard pencil and facilitate holding it. Soft lead, though it might smudge, is easiest to draw with. Soft- and hard-point pencils offer variation of lines, with number 7B being the softest and number 9H being the hardest. You can increase interest in pencil drawing by offering both smooth and rough papers. Don't forget colored pencils also come with silver and gold lead.

Turning the pencil over and scribbling with the eraser, thereby eliminating pencil lines, enchants toddlers and will take up as much time and interest as will actual scribbling. Since eraser drawing utilizes all of the hand and eye movements and control that regular drawing does, it is just as valuable an art experience. These "invisible" pictures produce no end product, which may be hard for adults to understand or relate to. But the *process* of work, not the end *product*, is what is important, and it is a very meaningful and enjoyable experience. The child may not have a beautiful product but still may have had a beautiful experience.

Rubbing

Children will instinctively touch objects that have interesting textures, and rubbing them with crayon to preserve the look of the material's surface is a good way to take advantage of the child's natural interest. Rubbing the broad side of a piece of crayon, chalk, or charcoal, or the side of a pencil on thin paper that has been placed over a textured or relief surface helps increase awareness of texture and pattern.

Encourage the child to freely arrange coins, textured fabrics, embossed wallpaper, doilies, geometric shapes, leaves, tree bark, cut-out letters, or any other textured objects under lightweight paper. This is the only project that I recommend newsprint-weight paper for. Rub the paper with the broad side of the crayon. The shape and texture of the object underneath will seem to magically appear, increasing the child's awareness of surface patterns.

After your child has some experience, have him or her join you in the search for appropriate surfaces for texture rubbing on a walk around the house, playground, neighborhood, or classroom. Radiator covers, screens, manhole covers, flowers, tools, some types of wood, stuccos, toys, and bricks are ideal. When the child chooses one that you know is too smooth to work effectively, don't dismiss it. Say instead, "Let's see what happens." Verbalize the experience, helping the child develop vocabulary and a feeling of success, in discovering what "smooth" means, rather than failure at choosing the "wrong" item. If the child produces a rubbing that looks like a realistic object, don't get more enthusiastic about the image than you do about the child's technique.

The natural outgrowth of selecting and arranging objects for rubbings is the introduction of pasting down the objects that have been arranged, as in collage. The rubbings themselves may be saved and cut or torn for later use in a collage. Doing a rubbing is quite the same as making a print; this activity is an ideal introduction to the art of printmaking.

The creative activity comes at first in selecting rubbing surfaces and arranging elements in a composition. Later on the child can experiment with creating textured surfaces to rub. Cut or torn paper collages and string designs are examples of textured surfaces that make interesting rubbings. Rubbing techniques originated in China possibly as early as 300 B.C. Archaeologists often use these instead of photography to preserve carved or incised artifacts. Rubbing plates, available through art suppliers, which are textured sheets of plastic, 8½" × 11", can be used both under a paper and directly on polymer clay. They come in an assortment of textures, including parallel and wavy lines, dots and squiggles.

Drawing with Four Shades of One Color

Although I have consistently recommended buying only the primary and secondary colors plus black and white, for a total of not more than eight colors, I am now going to be inconsistent. Purchase a set of twenty-five (Sanford)

Craypas or twenty-four (Sargeant) pastels. Both brands package these materials to contain four different shades of some colors. With them your child can learn about light, lighter, lightest, medium, dark, darker, darkest. Even pressing very hard with the lightest shade won't equal the effects of the darker chalk, and vice versa. Monochromatic color schemes create a sense of unity in the completed work and easily demonstrate color relationships.

Creative Development in Scribbling

Children over twelve become much more aware of detail and depict depth, correct proportions, and color gradations. For most people artistic development as well as interest in art ends here. It is usually impossible to tell the difference between the art of a fourteen-year-old and an adult.

Children begin to scribble when they are one year old if they are encouraged by their parents. Children experiment with approximately twenty basic shapes, which are the building blocks of later writing and drawing.

Children between the ages of nine and twelve are interested in detail and very conscious of themselves as members of a peer group. Self-consciousness about art begins now. Children of this age group like to work on group projects or on drawings that depict how groups work together.

Toward the end of the scribbling stage children spontaneously draw mandalas, which invariably precede the first attempt at drawing a human form. Mandalas are circles or ovals divided by crossed lines and are symmetrically balanced.

The first drawings of human figures seem to spring from experimentation with the mandala form, therefore the arms and legs branch out from the basic circle or head shape.

Somwhere around the age of seven, children work out a formula that they use repeatedly to depict people and other important aspects of their art. All elements of the art are placed on a common base line. When the base line is inadequate to represent a certain scene, the child may solve this problem by using a fold-over technique.

Between the ages of four and seven children begin to draw other objects they see in the world. These are placed randomly on the page and colors are chosen for emotional reasons rather than for their realistic connection with the objects.

Scribbling is so crucial to your child's development that you will want to encourage it as much as possible.

A roll of paper on a slanted drawing board stored near crayons or markers and always temptingly in view, helps to stimulate scribbling activity.

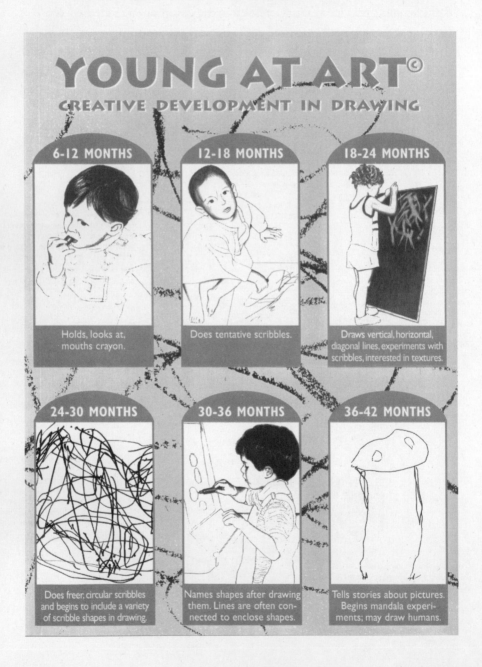

YOUNG AT ART©
CREATIVE DEVELOPMENT IN DRAWING

6-12 MONTHS
Holds, looks at, mouths crayon.

12-18 MONTHS
Does tentative scribbles.

18-24 MONTHS
Draws vertical, horizontal, diagonal lines, experiments with scribbles, interested in textures.

24-30 MONTHS
Does freer, circular scribbles and begins to include a variety of scribble shapes in drawing.

30-36 MONTHS
Names shapes after drawing them. Lines are often connected to enclose shapes.

36-42 MONTHS
Tells stories about pictures. Begins mandala experiments; may draw humans.

A stimulating drawing project is to give your child blank slides to draw on. They are fairly inexpensive and available in camera stores. The approximately one-inch-square drawing space is hardly ideal for this age, but can be managed by an experienced three-year-old. Although I always recommend large drawing backgrounds, this exception to my rule is made because it is well worth the sacrifice. When you've got a collection of them, put them in a carousel and have an exciting child-made art show. The magnified version of the lines and shapes on the projected film or slide gives a dynamic image. The sense of having made the image that is projected over an entire wall gives children a sense of the power art can have.

If you think your child needs more stimulation to draw than is provided by the crayons, pencils, and markers you've been using for three years now, try scratchboard. Scratching out a design with a wooden stylus, a long nail, or an old ballpoint pen on black scratchboard paper is an additional opportunity for children to experiment with interesting materials while providing much-needed time to explore the world of different lines and directions, varying pressures, changing shapes, and new textures. Scratchboard is available in most art supply stores. In addition to black and white scratchboard, there is also a multicolored version, gold and silver. As always, adult direction should come only in the area of demonstrating how to scratch away the black ink, not about what to draw. Comments that will help your child learn will be similar to those made at a scribbling activity: "All of your lines go 'round and 'round, except this one, which goes up and down." The tools are sharp, so this is strictly a "sit-down" activity.

When your child appears disinterested in scribbling it may mean that he or she is concentrating on other areas of development. This may be the time to introduce exciting new drawing materials: a gold felt-tip marker, a Superman pen, or some other novelty drawing utensils. Although toy guns were forbidden in my home, I did permit a drawing gun; the rationale being that it was a toy gun designed to create rather than destroy. It was really a toy gun with a felt-tip pen stuck into the nozzle.

Picking up and using a drawing utensil for the first time marks a very special event in the life of a child. It signifies endless future possibilities: drawings and paintings to be created, poems, stories, and plays to be written.

CHAPTER 2

Painting

Paint is one of the most important materials with which your child can work. When presented properly, it offers endless possibilities for problem solving and an infinite number of opportunities for exploration. Few materials have the potential for learning that paint does. It can be explored and applied with the fingers and hands as a manipulative material. It can also be used effectively with different tools. Paint can be an expressive material, and the child's method of applying it can communicate much about his or her mood and feelings. It can be used with pleasure and explored in depth by babies; at the same time, adult artists can devote their lives to working in this medium. The problem some parents and child care workers encounter with paint is that it does have the potential of making a mess.

Everyone knows that at some point a painting child will paint his or her own body, the furniture, or a wall. That is true, but every child also falls before he or she walks, and yet we don't prevent children from walking because we know they might fall! In fact, we recognize that falling is an essential part of the process of learning to walk. So, too, experimenting with body painting and environment painting is a necessary part of learning about paint. Supervising adults are most helpful when they realize this.

In my art classes for toddlers, I always provided for this phenomenon early in the term by planning a (nontoxic) makeup and body-painting lesson.

By setting aside a place that can get messy (such as a garage, basement, backyard, or tile bathroom), setting out limited amounts of materials at one time, and providing for quick and efficient cleanup nearby, parents can per-

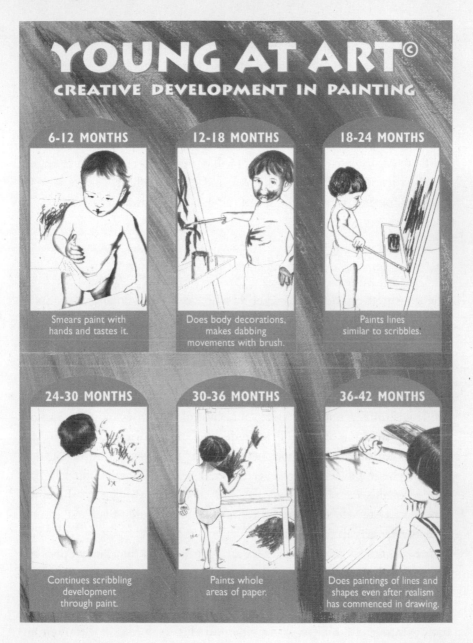

YOUNG AT ART©
CREATIVE DEVELOPMENT IN PAINTING

6-12 MONTHS
Smears paint with hands and tastes it.

12-18 MONTHS
Does body decorations, makes dabbing movements with brush.

18-24 MONTHS
Paints lines similar to scribbles.

24-30 MONTHS
Continues scribbling development through paint.

30-36 MONTHS
Paints whole areas of paper.

36-42 MONTHS
Does paintings of lines and shapes even after realism has commenced in drawing.

mit this kind of exploration without suffering damage to their homes. Yelling or punishing ends learning for the obedient child and teaches the independent child to misuse art as an act of rebellion.

Albert Einstein once said, "Imagination is more important than knowledge."

Many schools in years past eliminated art from their curriculums to make way for science courses. As those stifled children grew into adolescence, we had the most turned-on, tuned-out, rebellious group in American history. So many of these children, as they approached adulthood, seemed almost desperate to express themselves and be heard. It seems to me that an inordinate number of them turned to graffiti and arts and crafts as a vocation, especially those whose parents were against it. Providing your child with the wherewithal to engage in painting activities will not prevent rebellion later on, but it will provide for self-expression now and can give the skill necessary for using art constructively as a means of self-expression always.

Finger Painting with Food

The six- through ten-month-old child who can now sit up and reach out to touch interesting things is as likely to smear applesauce on everything in sight as he or she is to eat it. "Don't play with your food!" does not make any sense for a child this age. It will certainly be a goal for later, but now your child should be doing as much touching and as much squishing of food as he or she wants. This is all part of your baby's exploration of the world. From it, the child learns about the nature and physical properties of food, develops motor coordination, which will soon develop into drawing and writing, and creates a healthy attitude about being allowed to satisfy curiosity. An inexpensive plastic tablecloth or large trash bag under the high chair will help you make this learning experience one about the wonders of the world instead of a premature lecture on tidiness. One spoonful of applesauce on a high chair tray is all you need.

It is simplest to plan this activity *after* mealtime so that hunger does not interfere with the play activity. However, the activity is most effective when it is initiated by the child and encouraged and praised by you, even if it occurs at the most inconvenient times—as it probably will! It is interesting to note that many children who are permitted to explore food with their fingers as infants will pass through this stage in no time and become meticulous eaters later on. As they move on to more sophisticated art materials, having satisfied their curiosity about food, they have established a good background in developing the hand and arm movements needed for later scribbling, drawing, writing, and painting. Food quickly becomes something only to eat. Children learn this best by trial and error and from observing their family

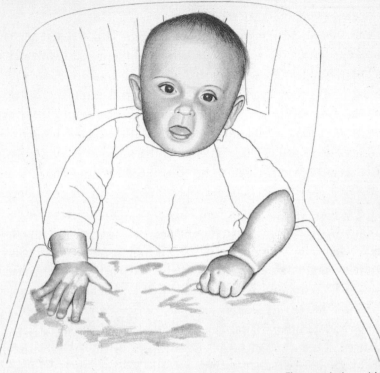

Finger painting with food

members. What they instinctively do when introduced to a new food—looking at it, and touching, tasting, and manipulating it—provides maximum learning and heightens sensitivity to the physical world. I frequently remind new parents to relax. Your baby will not still be smearing applesauce all over the table at his or her wedding!

Babies are as hungry for information as they are for food. Just as it is best to provide food when the child indicates hunger, so it is more effective to wait until the child expresses interest in exploring a material than it is to set up adult-initiated lessons. Chocolate pudding and whipped cream provide delicious alternatives and nice variations of textural experiences. Your child will benefit most from choosing the time and place for these experiences. So, during this short stage of development, the key for parents is to *be prepared*. Providing for, not preventing, such experimental behavior is what good parenting is all about.

After considerable experience with food manipulation, you can switch to finger paint. Children adore finger painting. This is not to say that the activity can be expected to last more than three to five minutes, while cleanup may sometimes take much longer.

No activity points out the difference between children and adults more than finger painting. Very young children delight in messing with and mushing paints on tabletops and paper, and all over themselves. Adults are often mystified by the attraction children have for this medium. Part of every child's early introduction to painting involves paint smearing, paint tasting, and body decoration. Freud called this natural need to mush around the *anal period*, but I suspect the Victorian children he studied were not given many creative art experiences. Parents who do not like the mess of finger paint will discover that, if nothing else is available, children will smear whatever they find, including, as Freud pointed out, their own feces.

Children take great joy when they mess—and are learning—and it should not make adults uncomfortable. Indeed, even by age three or so, many children already find finger painting distasteful. This activity is so valuable for the child who is interested in it that it is well worth the effort on your part. Parents need to provide for this necessary process by providing appropriate materials and a corner of the home that does not have to be kept clean. Sometimes all that is needed is a large, inexpensive vinyl tablecloth.

The most popular brands of finger paint say they are for children over three years of age, but I feel this is much too late for a first finger-painting experience. Most of the value of this activity is lost on three-year-olds, whose approach to art is already well established. It really is essential to introduce and encourage finger painting *well before* the child develops an understanding of "clean" and "dirty" or, worse, a preference for "clean" hands. Since finger painting can be messy, and it is true that young children will approach the activity with glee, the supervising adult needs to prepare for this in advance and set up the situation so that it will not get out of hand. The logical time for a finger painting activity is right before bath time; if you plan carefully for the activity, there is no reason for it to get out of control. Children do so much early learning through manipulation of materials that it is well worth a pair of "dirty" hands! I have found that the ideal spot for a child's first introduction to finger paint is an empty bathtub, with the baby stripped down to a diaper. The child who has already painted with food will be ready for this activity at the age of approximately one year.

You may prefer to confine the child to a high chair. Not confining the child in any way can mean fingerprints on walls and furniture, and an experience that should be delightful and educational may easily be reduced to a tearful failure. It can be fun to finger paint directly on the high chair tray. For this reason I always recommend that parents purchase a high chair with a solid white tray to avoid distracting from the artwork. The finger painting surface should be as large as possible. Large white plastic trays with raised edges to contain the mess are also available. They can be placed on any tabletop or on the floor.

When you work directly on a surface without paper, you can always place a piece of paper over the picture and take a print of it simply by rubbing the back of the paper with the back of a spoon. For work on paper, you can purchase glossy finger-painting paper, cut open a brown paper bag from the supermarket, or use brown wrapping paper. For contrasting textures, also offer bumpy paper.

On a warm, sunny day you can try finger painting on the lawn, particularly if you have a hose or a wading pool nearby. Always remember to wear old clothes yourself! A large roll of paper towels will save your good bath towels.

Of course, finger paint must be nontoxic, as the mouth will certainly be included in the child's first exploration of the medium. This is quite normal and a necessary part of the child's introduction to the new material. The child will learn something about finger paint through tasting it and soon will stop doing so, without the need for reprimand. If this aspect of finger painting troubles you, mix up your own batch of edible finger paint with either flour or cornstarch, some water, and food coloring, or try this recipe:

1 egg yolk
2 tablespoons of water
A few drops of food coloring

Instead of paper, use bread. You can even bake it in the oven and eat it for lunch! Keep in mind, however, that by taking this route you may be encouraging your child to eat art materials. Later on, this can be dangerous. I believe it is best to let the children eat as much nontoxic paint as they need in order to explore the material sufficiently. If you offer this activity after mealtime it may help curtail excessive eating. Bath time is an obvious choice for introducing finger painting. Add some water and food coloring to Ivory soap flakes and mix it until it is the consistency of pudding. Your child can paint directly on bath tiles. The mixture will actually make your bathroom cleaner when you rinse it away.

Present only *one* color of finger paint. For a child under two years of age, color has no significance. Motor activity, material manipulation, and texture exploration are the important aspects of this project. More than one color detracts from concentration on the activity and can cause frustration as the colors merge and turn muddy. Each time the child stops using one color to switch to another the continuity of the activity is interrupted and learning is minimized. Offering several colors serves only the pleasure of the viewing adult; it is not required by the child, who will be enchanted with the activity even if only one color is available. Purchase a one-quart jar of bright-color paint and offer it alone each time you present the activity. Talk about the name of the color. Point out that color each time you see it in the environment. Continue to do so until the jar is empty. The repetition may seem very boring to you as an adult, but children learn from repetition. Just as they will listen to the same song or story over and over until you think you will lose your mind, so too will they paint with one color on plain white paper for what seems like an eternity, always making vastly different pictures. I believe that a simplification of materials presented helps the child focus his or her attention on the task at hand. Pablo Picasso's "blue period" lasted for several years.

Finger Painting with Red

The excitement your child will feel while finger painting is echoed in the first color chosen to present the material—red. Red is a favorite choice of both children and adults. It is a stimulating, exciting color and has been shown to increase blood pressure, pulse, and respiration. Talk about red with your child as you did when the child was scribbling with red. Read *Red Is Best* and *The Red Balloon*, sing songs about red, eat red foods, wear red clothing, and fill the collage box with red papers. In addition to red finger paint, try red bathtub finger paint, which has a soap base, for fun at bath time. See chapter 6, "Exploring Color," for more on this subject.

Finger Painting with Blue, Yellow

When the first jar of finger paint is empty, you can replace it with a new color—blue or yellow. Focus on the second color by completely eliminating the first and remembering to talk about the name of the new color each time you encounter it in the environment. Talk also about what the paint feels and smells like. By providing vocabulary for the experience, you help imprint it in the child's memory.

Refrain from mentioning recognizable objects in your child's creations, even though they may have been made by accident. Many children's artistic development has been stunted because they have been made self-conscious about their art ability by having adult preferences for realism, stereotypes, and art formulas forced on them too early. Finger painting is one medium that practically begs to be free of subject matter, but, even so, some adults impose it on their children.

When my son was about ten months old, he did his first finger painting with paint on paper. I never mentioned the fact that I could clearly see the image of a person, since I knew it was done accidentally. Pointing out unintended similarities to realistic pictures tends to make a child self-conscious while working. Children want to please their parents and will try to again create the image that was praised, therefore missing out on necessary experimentation.

Below is a perfect example of how adults take good experiences and ruin them for children. A nursery school teacher not only cut a child's finger painting into the shape of a turkey, but also drew on it and wrote the child's name across the front of it.

Jeffrey's finger painting cut up into a turkey

After freely experimenting with the materials, the child may have felt that he had done something wrong. Otherwise, why would the teacher have found it necessary to alter his work so as to make it unrecognizable? Any painterly effects the child may have made were totally obliterated when the teacher wrote his name over the front of the picture. Even if the rest of the picture had been left alone, the teacher's addition of the written word would have been enough to alter the design and placement of the original work. This is an all-too-common example of many preschool teachers' lack of knowledge about the value and significance of preschool art; they feel it is acceptable to transform children's art into something recognizable. These kinds of activities are responsible for the sad fact that so many children already believe that they "aren't good at art" or "can't draw" by the time they enter kindergarten. Taking scissors to the completed painting is an attack on the child and his or her sense of self-worth. When a child puts brush to paper, the result is improved development of muscle coordination, increased awareness of his or her capability to experiment freely, and a resulting sense of pride in achievement. Be sure that when you're looking at day care centers and nursery schools for your child, you observe the art on the walls and talk to the teachers about their philosophy. You'll want to avoid those places whose teachers don't encourage your child's development and aren't sensitive to his or her needs.

To provide variety, consider having the children paint on black or brightly colored paper, corrugated cardboard, or sandpaper; on a window, a mirror, or on a sidewalk. T-shirts, pajamas, and socks can be painted with nontoxic fabric paint.

Tempera paint is the best painting medium for young children. It dries quickly and is reasonably washable (although some colors, notably green, will stain fabrics). In most brands, the colors mix well. If you buy colors that do not mix well, change brands. There are new nontoxic acrylic paints available that can be used on wood, plastic, or glass for permanence.

After sufficient exploration of the paint itself, a child will move on to using tools such as brushes. Messing and painting with the fingers will appear to be outgrown. Nevertheless, the child will benefit from the availability of finger paints for a long time.

Occasionally, an activity that was planned differently will turn into a finger painting project. You may set out paints and brushes for a child who has used them for quite some time, only to find him or her smearing paint with both hands. With the child older, more settled, and more experienced, this

Finger painting

kind of exploration is much less likely to get out of hand. The need to confine the child in a high chair and bathtub is eliminated. Periodically the child
will be inspired to touch and manipulate paints. This should *not* be viewed as
regressive behavior by parents or teachers. The child is assisted by your spoken or unspoken approval of this activity. The growing, developing child
brings new skill and more information to this old experience and continues
to benefit from it. The experienced child will find many new things to do
with finger paint: drawing with one finger, scratching with a fingernail or the
handle of a brush, mixing two colors together, making prints by placing a second sheet of paper on the picture, and making finger and hand prints. The
earlier permission to freely explore and "mess around" with finger paints lays
a solid foundation for working with the material in more sophisticated ways.
This would be a good time to introduce "paint scrapers." They give children
an opportunity to experiment with scraffito, which is scratching into the
paint with a sharp tool. This tool has several design possibilities. You can also
use a fingernail or the handle of a paintbrush. I do finger painting with my
kindergarten classes regularly. We usually work as a group, directly on the
tabletop. The children enjoy cleaning the table with sponges afterward
almost as much as they enjoy finger painting.

Many adults have been conditioned to find these activities unappealing.

Even people who offer the materials to children are unlikely to try them out themselves! If you are brave enough to try it yourself, you will be surprised at how much you will learn and how much fun you and your child will have together. I generally discourage parents from letting their children see parents drawing and painting, since it can make children despair of ever equaling their parents' achievements, but since it is practically impossible to make an adult-looking finger painting, why not give this activity a try? It will help you appreciate your child's efforts so much more.

Painting with a Brush

After your child has had considerable experience exploring the physical properties of paint through finger-painting activities, you will want to introduce paint with a brush. Eighteen months of age is the ideal time to do this, but you will know when your child is ready by noticing that he or she really understands the concept of doing things with such tools as combs or spoons. A paintbrush is one of the most basic tools in the child's world, and a child learns so much when using one. One small container of tempera paint (that is thick enough not to drip) on absorbent paper and a one-inch-wide brush are all you need to provide weeks of enchanting fun and a solid education for a toddler.

True learning takes place when a child has the opportunity to work in depth with a material. It is necessary, therefore, to make these simple materials always available. Invariably, all of the parents who have told me that their children were "not interested in painting" kept their paints hidden away and, when it seemed convenient to them, invited the child to paint—only to meet with a negative response. Unlike adults, children are inspired to work by seeing materials. The enticing presence of art materials is very stimulating. It is important for children to have the option to paint every day. When the child is too young to responsibly handle the constant presence of paints and other potentially messy materials, they can be kept in view but out of reach. The child may choose to paint several times a day or not at all for days or weeks. It is okay if the child chooses not to exercise this option, just so long as the choice belongs to the child. Disinterest can be your cue to introduce new colors, different-shaped papers, wider (or thinner) brushes, or new materials.

Presenting a beginning painter with a wide array of colors can interfere with learning. With older children, a broad spectrum may increase creative potential, but the same is not true for very young children. The time that a toddler spends washing or switching brushes and choosing a color takes away from time spent in body movement. The interest in color detracts from the main purpose of the activity, gaining control over body movement and coordination. If you observe a toddler with several colors at an easel, you will most likely see the child methodically move from one to another in a left-to-right or right-to-left progression, frequently stopping to be distracted by the profusion of colors.

If you are a teacher, it is safe to assume that the child has had very little painting experience at home, and needs to start at the beginning, regardless of age. I have offered one color of paint to seven-, eight-, and nine-year-old children who were simply delighted with the opportunity to paint and never expressed any dissatisfaction with the color limitation. The many joys of the full spectrum and the magic of color mixing come much later, after sufficient learning through kinesthetic activity has taken place.

Later, children may use color as a means of creative expression. There are also scientific observations that can be made under the right circumstances. Providing paint in this recommended sequence will in no way stifle creativity, but will provide increased opportunity for understanding the effect of colors alone and in combination. By the time your child is three or four years old, and has worked with paint in depth, several colors can be made available at one time. Do it only if it seems right for the child's interest and experience. Respond to the child's wishes in this matter. If the child remains interested and satisfied working with one color, there is absolutely no reason to rush the issue.

Each color or group of colors can and should be offered in *several* consecutive painting experiences, before moving on to the next. It is helpful when learning about color to experiment with different colors, one at a time and then in groups. I have refined this sequence of activities over many years of teaching. I think it is logical to begin with black and move on to the individual primary colors and secondary colors before introducing multiple colors. Where necessary, I've listed what supplies you'll need in addition to the paint, such as empty containers or extra brushes. Please see chapter 6, "Exploring Color," for more specific directions and for supplementing painting activities with art projects in other media.

Sequential Color Presentation

1. Black, one black brush
2. Red, one red brush
3. Blue, one blue brush
4. Yellow, one yellow brush
5. White (on black paper), one white brush
6. Green, one green brush
7. Orange, one orange brush
8. Purple, one purple brush
9. Red/yellow, empty container, three brushes
10. Yellow/blue, empty container, three brushes
11. Blue/red, empty container, three brushes
12. Color + white, one brush
13. Color + black, one brush
14. Black + white, empty container, three brushes
15. Black/white, empty container, three brushes
16. Red/white, empty container, three brushes
17. Blue/white, empty container, three brushes
18. Red/green, empty container, two brushes
19. Yellow/purple, empty container, two brushes
20. Orange/blue, empty container, two brushes
21. Red/yellow/blue, three empty containers, six brushes
22. Red/yellow/blue/black/white, one palette, nine brushes

Unfortunately, most children encounter painting experiences for the first time when they enter school. These children, who may be three, four, five, or even six years old, must first explore the material in the very same way as an eighteen-month-old. The structure of a school experience places inhibitions on this introductory experience, so your child gains most if you provide him or her with experimental art experiences at home.

It is important to remember that I recommend limiting the number of colors offered to the child with the idea that the first painting experience will be at about age eighteen months, not six years. Nevertheless, if the first painting experience *did* turn out to be at age six, I would make the exact same recommendation. Color mixing and multicolor visual expressions will be best postponed until after the child has run the gamut of kinesthetic experiences leading to the stockpile of information necessary for forging ahead. As with other play, the older child will pass through the various stages more quickly than the younger child will.

It is *never* appropriate to suggest a theme to paint. Children at this age respond to materials, while subject motivates older children and adults. Adults need to remind themselves of this fact frequently when they work with young children. Paint and brush provide all the inspiration necessary!

If at all possible, invest in a decent-weight paper and give the child a chance to truly experience painting, rather than battle with inferior materials. Painting provides additional opportunities to practice similar hand and arm movements learned in scribbling. The scribbling stage in painting usually lasts longer than it does in drawing projects. The child may be doing free, abstract-looking paintings long after representation has begun in crayon. Here again, since motor activity is the goal, providing more than one color of paint will usually result in the colors being mixed together, losing the main point of the project. Remember that it is not what colors are chosen but how the paint is used that is important. In just a little while, the child will be ready for mixing experiments. My favorite brushes for young children are Stubby Brushes. They are easy to hold and come with colored handles. We use the red brush when painting with red paint, the blue brush for blue paint, and so on. They are sold in packages of thirty wooden-handled, natural-bristle brushes in ten different colors to a canister. "Knobby brushes" have easy-to-hold handles like bulbs. If your child's grasp is not strong, you may want to give them a try.

Any child old enough to paint with a brush is old enough to wash the brush out by sloshing it about in a bucket of cool, soapy water. Occasionally, the child will enjoy this activity even more than he or she enjoys painting! Making sure that the bucket is partly filled and nearby is your job. Children can and should learn from the very beginning that caring for materials is essential to creative art activity. After all, you cannot work with a brush that is as hard as a rock. It is a good idea to make a cleanup chore that the child is capable of accomplishing part of every painting experience. Buy fairly wide, flat brushes. Stored brushes must, like people, stand with the hair on top. Use a permanent marker to draw a little face on the brush as a helpful reminder. If the handles are

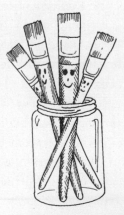

Paintbrushes with faces painted on them to teach proper brush care

too long, cut them off so the child will not poke an eye while painting. No child under the age of four can be expected to take proper care of expensive art materials alone, so follow-up care must be provided by you.

Paper cups and orange juice cans can tip over too easily to serve as paint containers; I like spill-proof, plastic containers for young children. I recommend Childcraft Non-Spill Paint Pots, which have red, yellow, and blue tops for color coordination with the paint. If you are not able to obtain these containers, try coasters, canisters, pet food dishes, plastic food containers, muffin tins, rug yarn caddies, egg cartons, margarine tubs, or shallow jar tops. Vaseline's thirteen-ounce plastic jar is a perfect fit in easel trays. Even empty half-pint milk cartons can be used to store tempera and can be held closed between painting sessions with a clothespin or metal clip. That old training cup with weights at the bottom that helped your baby make the transition to drinking from a cup is a great container for water or paint since it will not easily tip over. The parents of several of my students work at a hospital and save the plastic containers that 4" × 4" sterile gauze pads come in; we use them when we paint at tables. They are squares with flat bottoms and can never tip over. I am told that special containers marked "Ms. Striker's Art Room" sit near both the emergency room and operating rooms. I love Stancups, which are like those paper covers covering drinking glasses in hotels. They are inexpensive and I order a thousand at a time. They can be filled with paint and thrown away, making for a "painless" cleanup. The kind of container you use is not important. For years of teaching, I successfully used plastic food containers provided courtesy of my favorite take-out food store. What is important is being consistent. Having a well-known routine and setting up materials efficiently prevent confusion and spills. Repetition provides the familiarity with routine that frees the child to concentrate on art. The relative advantages of each procedure are described in the following pages.

Standing double easels are nice, since they allow for socializing while painting without inviting the comparison of work that two wall-hung easels do. In my classroom I use four-sided easels, since I have more than twenty young artists painting at the same time. Buy the sturdiest one you can afford and, when considering the expense, keep in mind that working at an easel eliminates the possibility of buying cheap watery paint that will surely drip. Be sure to purchase an adjustable easel that can grow with your child. Some are made of chalkboard, which adds a new dimension. Clear Lucite easels are interesting, but buy one only if you won't be tempted to place a picture behind it for your child to trace. Consider the easel a permanent part of the decor in the child's room and always have it ready with clean sheets of paper so your child can work at will. Unless your child's friend is visiting, keep paints on one side of the easel and drawing utensils on the other. A cork-board can work as a wall easel, with paints sitting on a nearby table or in a shoe box that is affixed to the board.

When making your decision about whether or not to buy an easel, remember that painting on a paper that is placed on the floor or at a paper-sized table encourages the child to walk around and view the work from all four sides. Great masterpieces have been painted on basement floors and at kitchen tables as well as at easels. There is no right or wrong in this matter. The opportunity to work freely, along with your encouragement, means more to the child than expensive supplies ever can. Your child's development will be greatly enriched when he or she has the opportunity to paint daily, and not having an easel should not inhibit you.

Young children quickly forget the thoughts and feelings they had while doing a picture and often cannot recognize their own work. For them the

Double easel

process of work is far more important than the finished product. Many work happily on a painting only to discard it when it is completed. Nevertheless, it is important for parents to show the child how much the work is valued by exhibiting the finished product in the home. The refrigerator door does not compare to that spot over the mantel. Buy a real picture frame for a special picture. Parents can also communicate high regard for the child's efforts by saving artwork. Encourage children to decorate their own greeting cards, gifts, and party decorations. Holiday art means more to a child who has been given time and encouragement to think about the meaning of the holiday rather than to one who has mindlessly colored in or pasted down the teacher's art. The skills and maturity to express these feelings through art will come much later than the preschool years, so keep in mind that gaily colored scribbles provide holiday cheer without inhibiting development.

When paint does stain an article of your child's clothing, use it for a new art project. Paint-splattered T-shirts, jeans, jackets, or sneakers can be very attractive. I once purchased a small black evening bag and gave it to my son when he was four years old. He decorated it with gold paint, and I still use it.

Black

Start by offering one color. Black is a good first choice as it provides maximum contrast on white paper and is the usual manner in which the written word is presented. Children like black and white, so try to forget any morbid associations you may have with the color black. This color limitation should not be forced on a child who has indicated a preference for a different color. Give the color its proper name to help the child learn it and, for the next few days, point out all the black objects you see.

Place the materials to the right if the child is right-handed and at the left for a lefty. Establish predictable work patterns and realistic cleanup goals. Children can slosh a brush around in a can full of water before they are capable of thoroughly cleaning it. They can also learn to cover the paint container at the end of the activity.

I like black paper as much as I like white paper. White on black paper, as with the combination of black on white paper, provides the powerful effect of strong contrast, something young children relate to pleasantly. The child who is used to seeing black on white will find that the reverse creates an

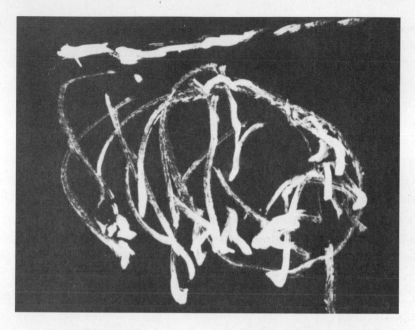

White painting on black paper

interesting visual effect. Scratch-Art makes a dramatic multicolor finger-paint paper that looks great when used with black finger paint.

Red

After working with black and white, remove it and substitute red. Red also creates a vivid contrast with white paper and seems to be a favorite with many children. You declared "red month" when your child was scribbling and finger painting with red. Coordinate painting with a brush with red paint, or with black paint on red paper to coincide with those activities. There are many books and songs to sing that feature red. You can also change the words of other songs to suit the theme. "Mary sat on a red chair, Mary did a red painting" can also transform the classic song "Mary Wore Her Red Dress." After all, creative thinking should carry over to every area, not just be restricted to art.

Keep in mind that the point of concentrating on red is to experience what "redness" means and enjoy it. Do not make your child feel that he or she must learn to correctly recognize and name all the colors in the rainbow to please you. Drills and quizzes can take all of the fun out of learning. Art experiences should always be experimental in nature and should not be reduced to becoming a vehicle for the accumulation of facts.

Blue

What could be more natural than painting with blue paint under a wide blue sky? Painting out of doors frees the child from worry about spilling paint or otherwise messing up the family's home. It is best for the child to wear old clothing, or, if weather permits, no clothing! After all, children are washable! That freedom permits total concentration on art.

The easel can be brought outside, or a large sheet of paper can be laid on the grass or tacked to a tree. In fact, paper is not needed at all. It is great fun to paint on the sidewalk! Add some liquid soap to water-soluble paint and it will adhere to picture windows. (We always preceded window-washing day with this activity.)

Since the child has already experienced scribbling with blue crayon and marker and finger painting with blue paint, he or she probably understands what the label "blue" stands for. You can help expand the child's understanding of the color by talking about the nature of "blue." Blue is considered a cool color, reminding us of cool water on a hot day. Talking about the last time the child swam for so long and got so cold that his or her lips turned blue will help imprint this notion on the child's memory. The book *Kinda' Blue* is good for communicating the effects of blue. Follow up with a nice indoor collage experience with various blue papers (see chapter 6, "Exploring Color").

Yellow

Yellow looks different on white paper than it does on black paper. Painting with a wide brush is quite different than painting with a thin brush.

By providing opportunities for your child to personally experience these differences, you are enriching your child's storehouse of knowledge. At the library, choose *Hello Yellow* and *Yellow Yellow* to read this week. You can sing "The Yellow Rose of Texas" and "Yellow Daffodils." Buy lots of bananas. Scramble up some eggs for lunch. Make a pitcher of lemonade with the help of your toddler. Slice a lemon, dip it in yellow paint, and create fruit prints.

Painting Variations

Given enough time, space, materials, freedom, and adult encouragement, your child will most likely discover some of the following painting techniques completely on his or her own:

- splatter painting
- drip painting
- painting on wet paper
- taking a print from a painting (lay a clean sheet of paper over a wet painting and smooth your hands over the whole sheet)
- folding to achieve symmetrical design
- dry-brush painting (a dry brush will produce a rough-looking textural quality)
- affixing objects to a painting (you'll need glue for this, as an object stuck on wet paint will fall off when the paint dries)
- crayon resist (painting over a waxy design)
- spray painting (a freshly washed, empty bottle of window cleaner or liquid hand soap dispenser works well)
- painting with a feather, feather duster, leaf, or any item not ordinarily considered a painting utensil
- squeeze-bottle painting (you can find good ones in the hair-color section of a drugstore)
- blowing paint through a straw (be sure that the tip of the straw is above, not in, the paint)
- scraffito (scratching into paint with a comb, fingernail, or the back of the paintbrush)
- impasto (applying paint very thickly to the painting surface)

You can encourage your child to seek out new painting utensils with which to experiment. He or she may find twigs, string, shoe polish daubers, cotton swabs, and a multitude of other items around the home that you and I might not consider. I am against using utensils that the child cannot control, such as string. Finger painting and brush painting are still the best. More exotic methods, like spray painting, have the advantage of being stimulating. Just put some watery paint or just plain water in an empty spray bottle, plant sprayer, or liquid soap dispenser.

The process of self-discovery makes the learning experience far more valuable for the youngster than an adult-initiated experience can ever be. Verbalizing for the child always helps him or her focus on what is being learned. Providing vocabulary and encouraging fresh new experiments is your job.

When children begin dripping or splattering paint, sing a rain song, such as "Rain, Rain Go Away" or "It's Raining."

Rain, Rain Go Away
Rain, rain go a-way. Come a-gain a-noth-er day.
Lit-tle (child's name) wants to play. Rain, rain go a-way.

It's Raining
It's rai-ning, it's pour-ing. The old man is snor-ing.
He went to bed and bumped his head.
And couldn't get up in the morning.

You can alter basic tempera in the following ways to vary the painting experience:

- *Glycerin* or *liquid detergent* will help it adhere to slick surfaces like windows, wax paper, plastic, or mirrors (as well as making cleanup easier).
- *Sand* or *sawdust* will make the paint bumpy and gritty.

Drip painting

• *Liquid glue* allows you to affix paper to your picture.
• *Watering* down the paint will make it skip over the wax on a crayon drawing and create a jewel-like effect that fascinates children of all ages.

With your encouragement, your child will think up other interesting alterations. My own son once poured salt in a container of tempera and the paint glittered as if gems had been set in it!

You can further challenge your child's mind by occasionally having round, triangular, or free-form background paper available. Paper with a hole cut out of it creates the challenge of working around negative space. Do not insist that the child use these altered papers if he or she prefers a whole one, but have them available.

Painting with a Sponge

Sponges should always be available for cleanup *after* painting, or for the child to use for the occasional spill. Ideally, the spontaneous child will be curious about other ways to use a sponge. It is up to you to encourage experimentation with the sponge. Dabbing it on the paper creates prints, smearing it creates streaks, squeezing it releases blobs of paint. Assist your child by describing what he or she is doing and what the results are. The project will help him or her become more aware of texture and able to create its illusion. Don't tell your child that there is only one way of handling the sponge. This actually lessens learning and diminishes the possibility of discovering other techniques of using paint with a sponge; self-discovery adds helpful information to the child's ever-growing storehouse of knowledge. Children learn most in an open-ended situation in which experimentation is encouraged and adult approval expressed.

You can buy a plastic container with a sponge top, intended for moistening postage stamps, in a stationery supply store. Fill it with watery paint.

Blowing Paint Through a Straw

Every child who ever drank milk or juice through a straw eventually figured out that funny things happen when you blow out instead of suck in. The resulting bubbles and noises are a source of delight to children everywhere.

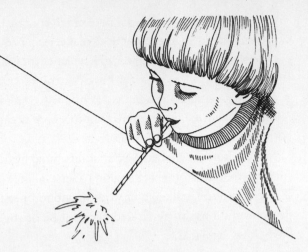

Blowing paint through a straw

They should be your cue to pull out the paper and food coloring and let the child experiment with using his or her breath to control the flow of color.

Be sure that your toddler understands that the straw should be above, not in, the paint and that he or she should be sure to blow out so as to avoid ingesting the paint.

Painting with a Roller

Painting with a roller is great fun for a child, particularly for a child who has seen Mom or Dad paint the house. Toddlers can help paint the house, too. If you are not ready to delegate the responsibility, allow him or her to paint with water. Rollers provide an opportunity for the painting child to use large-motor skills rather than the small-motor skills used with a paintbrush. It reinforces the concept that a picture does not have to be realistic to be valuable and provides a whole new art experience through simple materials used in a new and innovative way. My son became fascinated watching a carpet installer use a roller to flatten new carpet. When I suggested that he could paint with a roller, he was hooked! Over a period of several months, he did many varied works with a roller and only one color of paint at a time.

Rollers, or brayers as they are also called, are versatile tools. The dry, clean roller can be used by an imaginative child as a toy, like a car or steamroller. It can also be used (without paint) like a rolling pin on clay. Brayers are most frequently used to spread ink on a palette in preparation for printing. Professional roller artist Sig Purwin has given descriptive names to some of the strokes or rolls that he uses, including the "edge bounce stroke," the "pivot/swivel roll," the "up/down drag roll," and the "wiggle roll." I mention them because they seem to express the many variations available in this medium. You and your child can create your own with tempera paint in a shallow baking tin.

You can also try wrapping yarn around a roller before painting to create interesting surface patterns. Textured rollers are also available through craft supply catalogs and stores. A paint-covered brayer can roll over an oil chalk or wax crayon drawing for an interesting resist effect.

Painting with Complementary Colors

No color combinations are more vibrant than complementary colors. They include red with green, orange with blue, and purple with yellow. These three sets of colors are opposite each other on the color wheel and are not chromatically related to each other. When mixed together they create a neutral grayish or brown color.

Children benefit enormously by being given these colors in pairs. If they do not mix them together the effect is dazzling. When they do mix them, the neutral color immediately softens the effect. Either way, the child is experimenting and learning. It is not helpful to say, "Don't mix. The colors will get muddy." It is much better to let the child learn through experiments and set his or her own goals. The paint containers suggested in the next three projects work toward that end. Telling the child not to mix the colors prevents the kind of learning that was taking place the day I heard one of my students excitedly say, "Oh wow! Look at that, I made brown!" Thinking his painting was getting muddy, I was tempted to intervene just as he made his discovery. "Muddy" is a value judgment. Some people prefer neutral colors and some prefer intense colors. It is not fair to force your preferences on the child and it is not helpful to set limits on how much may be learned, but you may occasionally offer challenges as an alternative. "I see that you created brown yesterday when you mixed red with green. I wonder what it would look like if you didn't mix the colors." Another challenge is "Have no white paper show-ing through." The child, though, should be setting his or her own goals as much as possible.

Red and Green

Perhaps one reason that red and green have come to symbolize the Christmas season is that the two colors together seem to vibrate with the same intensity and excitement that the holiday season brings with it. Give your child two brushes and equal amounts of red and green paint in a pet food dish. You may have an old divided baby food dish that will work as well (the weighted bot-tom will help prevent spills). Remind the child that the red brush is for the red paint and the green brush is for the green paint. You can cover the brush handles with red and green tape or self-adhesive paper to serve as reminders, or buy Stubby Brushes, which come with colored handles.

You may find that this is the right time to make your child aware of traffic rules: red light means stop and green light means go. You can play a running game with your child and a few friends. The traffic director gets to say, "Red light!" and all the runners must stop and stand very still until they hear the "Green light!" signal to go. Read *One Mitten Lewis* to add to the fun of the activity. Vary the game by using sheets of red and green paper instead of words. This will help the children learn to identify colors as well as learning some traffic rules that will keep them safe.

Yellow and Purple

Like all combinations of complementary colors, this one is vibrant and intense when it is not softened through mixing or by white paper showing through. To help your child experience the intensity of these colors when they are not mixed, offer them in containers that do not encourage mixing, providing separate jars for each color—no extra brushes, mixing containers, or mixing surfaces. On another occasion, provide the extra brushes and con-tainers, which will lead the child naturally to color mixing. The manner in which materials are set up helps determine what will be learned and can also prevent spills and confusion if done efficiently. Let your budget guide you. If you can afford spill-proof paint pots with one brush for each container and a sturdy easel, buy them. I feel they are the easiest to work with. If you do not have them, use whatever you can find. Be consistent, however, as repetition provides the familiarity with routine that frees the child to be concerned only with the production of art.

Blue and Orange

An old book titled *May Horses* by Jan Wahl, illustrated by Blair Lent, is about two "splendid horses" named Blue and Orange and the little boy who goes off on an imaginative flight with them. Blue and Orange look like streaks in a painted sky and can be the inspiration for painting with these two colors. It is fun to think of the color on the brushes as having a life of their own and, with the story as inspiration, a child can have the experience of painting with two flying horses instead of two brushes. If your library or bookstore does not have a copy, you can improvise and make up a story of your own based on the theme. I also like *The Orange Book* by Richard McGuire. It is illustrated in orange and blue as well and should be easier to find.

The two-fisted approach is the typical response of a young painter when first offered two colors at one time. Young children sometimes seem to use their entire bodies to do things that adults would do with a slight movement of the wrist. It is no wonder that the excitement of the introduction of two colors requires the involvement of both hands in the initial exploration. The use of spill-proof paint pots, without a palette or empty container, inhibits mixing, so be sure to offer this color combination at another time when the child will be encouraged to mix. In this way the child can have the experience of observing the tension that two complementary colors have when used together with blending, as well as seeing how, when mixed, the effect is softened by the addition of a neutral color.

Painting with Two Primary Colors
to Create a Secondary Color

Red, yellow, and blue are called the primary colors. It is from mixtures of these that all other colors are derived. The new colors produced by these combinations are labeled secondary colors and include green, orange, and purple.

• Blue and yellow make green.
• Red and yellow make orange.
• Red and blue make purple.

In order to provide a child with the stimulation that personal color mixing experiences can provide, you need to limit the palette to certain specific colors and provide utensils that simplify and encourage the logistics of creating new colors. If a child starts painting with the full spectrum and only one paintbrush with some muddy water, some of these discoveries will still be made. Colors can be mixed directly on the page, and all children do some of that kind of experimenting. Since learning becomes accidental, it is not enough to make that the only available alternative. I believe the child benefits more from being assured of having certain color-mixing experiences through proper planning by you.

I offer several suggestions for painting procedures in this series of projects. You will need to find and perfect the one that works best for you, the family or school budget, and your child. Spill-proof paint pots with one brush for each container, lots of disposable aluminum pie pans, high-quality paper, and a sturdy easel are my favorite materials.

I have found it best to give a child one container and one brush per color, and to encourage him or her to "keep the blue brush in the blue paint, and the yellow brush in the yellow paint." Using Stubby Brushes with colored handles is a big help in the beginning. They are easily available wherever school supplies are sold. The child can put a little of each color into either side of an aluminum pie pan and mix it with the extra brush, which now becomes the "green brush."

When working with groups of children, such as in a playgroup or class, this becomes the only way to assure that each child gets pure colors and a chance to create new ones. No preschool child can or should be concerned with washing a single brush before each dip. It is far too distracting. The spill-proof containers are my favorite choice to offer children of this age. They come with covers that allow you to store paint without having it dry up. The tops come in colors so that you can coordinate them to the paints you are offering the child. They are available from most craft suppliers.

Small plastic jars are ideal for small hands, and pouring is a simple and enjoyable way for your child to experience color mixing. If you fill two empty clear spice jars, medicine bottles, or other small containers with very small amounts of paint to which water has been added to simplify pouring, your child can manage pouring by him- or herself to create the new color. Prepare the work space efficiently and cover the table with newspaper so that the child does not worry about spills. You will find that simply mixing colors and pouring paint back and forth between containers is a fulfilling art experience in itself. It does not necessarily have to be followed by a painting experience.

Yellow and Blue

When children begin to show an interest in mixing colors, it is essential for you to make sure, in advance, that the colors you offer will not turn into "mud" when mixed together. Different procedures and setups than those offered with complementary colors will encourage, rather than discourage, the mixing of colors. To encourage color mixing, I like to start with blue and yellow. In almost all brands of paint you are assured of a fairly nice green resulting from the mixture. The book *Little Blue and Little Yellow* by Leo Lionni is a classic and the best available book on color mixing I have seen. Take advantage of its availability to motivate the activity. I keep two pieces of cellophane, one blue and one yellow, stored next to my copy of the book. Childcraft also makes Lucite "color paddles" that aid in explaining the concept of color mixing. Unable to find any book as magical as this one for teaching about mixing red and yellow to create orange or red and blue to create purple, I simply transform *little blue and little yellow* to both *little red and little yellow* and *little blue and little red* when reading this book to my students.

No book, demonstration, or lesson can equal the moment when magic occurs. Blue and yellow mixed together on the paper or in an empty container are mysteriously transformed into green. The discovery opens up a whole new world of possibilities.

Yellow and Red

After yellow has been presented with blue for several consecutive painting experiences, remove the blue and replace it with red. Yellow and red is a safe bet—even the least expensive brands of tempera will produce a fairly lively orange. After the child has created his or her own special blend of orange, creative painting can continue uninterrupted. By supplying one brush for each of the three colors, you simplify the mechanics of dealing with the problems of the materials, thus freeing the child for creative work.

Pads of paper are made to function as disposable palettes and are available in art supply stores. Traditional palettes work just as well, but they have to be washed after use, and I am against anything that will discourage you from letting your child paint. The more efficient and simple your painting procedure is, the more likely you are to encourage frequent painting experiences, thus giving your child a chance to maximize benefits from painting. The child can use the brush that is in a certain color's container to place that color on the palette. Then the child can take a brush from the container of extra brushes and use it to mix the paint with another color on the palette. That same brush can then be used to paint with the new color.

Red and Blue

Red and blue should make purple, but some of the very inexpensive brands produce a very muddy shade of it. Try this combination out yourself before sharing it with your child. You may want to add a little white to the blue first. Keep the container covers handy so that you can store the paint to use on another day. When you do paint, always provide one brush per color. It takes a professional to manage this color-mixing business all with one brush, and even a pro usually uses a whole handful of brushes at one time.

Tints and Shades

It is astonishing to note how quickly children understand that hundreds of variations of one color still remain that color. Light blue is blue, as are turquoise, navy blue, and the multitude of tints and shades in between.

You may also want to try giving your child a color plus both black and white, or just black or white.

One Color plus White

A tint of a color is any color lightened by the addition of white. If you start with white and gradually add more and more color to it, you can best demonstrate this principle of altering a color. Muffin tins, egg cartons, or rug yarn caddies, which look like muffin tins but are clear plastic, all work well for this activity. I prefer the Styrofoam egg cartons over the cardboard variety, since they don't absorb as much paint. Put the color on one side of the container and the white paint on the opposite side of it so that the child can use each of the sections in between for a different tint. Provide one brush for the color, one brush for the white, and some extras for the new colors.

One Color plus Black

After lightening a color with white, the child will now benefit from experimenting with learning to darken that same color with black. The result is called a "shade" of that color. Put the color on one end and the black diagonally across from it on the opposite side of the container. Use the empty sections in between for mixing various shades of the color. When the child is involved with painting in tints and shades of one color, plan drawing and collage experiences that also concentrate on tints and shades of one color. A handful of crayons, pencils, or chalk of various shades of blue, for example, enrich and expand the learning taking place in painting experiences. Coordinate these activities for the time when you offer one color of paint plus black and encourage mixing.

Painting with Multiple Colors

Painting with many colors is a different kind of experience than painting with just two colors. Several colors together present a seemingly endless number of possibilities for color mixing. The possibilities for success as well as disaster are increased with the addition of each new color. The child who has been offered paint in the controlled manner recommended in this book has had a very thorough introduction to color mixing. Such a child approaches the full palette with all of the skills and confidence necessary to make good use of it. Just as a child learns one letter of the alphabet at a time, and soon is putting them together and writing words, so too should the child study one color at a time before embarking on experiences involving combinations of colors. If one color equals one letter of the alphabet, then a five-color palette is like a novel! The confident, experienced young artist will now be able to

Painting with watercolors

work with watercolors, despite the fact that there are so many colors so close together in the paint box.

Watercolor sets are my least favorite painting material for this age because the profusion of colors so close to each other and the necessity for constantly cleaning the brush can be distracting. Nevertheless, the compact unit travels well and we always took one with us on trips to assure uninterrupted access to painting experiences when we were away from our easel. At least try not to introduce it until the child is an experienced painter.

You can facilitate painting now through the careful and thoughtful presentation of quality materials and by generously offering words of encouragement. You and your child will now find that working with many colors was well worth the wait. The in-depth study of color and paint provided your child with a solid background and many skills that will last through a lifetime of enjoyment through art!

CHAPTER 3

Printing

The need for a broader form of communication than the single original painting could produce was the impetus which spawned the art of printmaking.
—Gerald F. Brommer, *Relief Printmaking*

Whenever multiple images can be made from one master, or original, the technique is called printing. It is any process when an image is transferred from one surface to another in one unique print or in a multiple edition of prints. There are four different traditional techniques for making prints. They are the relief process, incised process, lithography, and stenciling. With the exception of lithography, I have set forth some modified versions of all of them that are appropriate for preschoolers. The relief process is cutting away part of the surface of a block so that the desired image to be printed stands away from the surface. The incised process is exactly the opposite of relief printing. In this the printing areas are grooves that have be cut away from the surface to carry ink or paint.

Lithography is based on the natural antipathy of oil and water. The image is created on a stone or plate with a greasy crayon. When a layer of ink is applied to the surface, the ink adheres only to the greasy areas.

The stencil process consists of cutting areas of specially treated paper away and applying paint through the open areas. Sad to say, we find ready-made stencils far more than we find children creating their own. They are easy and fun to do, so try this technique with your child. Linoleum and woodcut printing is not an appropriate medium for preschoolers, since it involves carving with sharp tools, but looking at books illustrated with them is a good introduction. You'll find *A Gardener's Alphabet* and *Miro in the Kingdom of the Sun* listed in chapter 9, "Books About Art for Children." Children love making finger, foot, and lip prints. They can be observed in any playground by sticking shells, rocks, and toys in wet sand to create prints of them. At painting time, every child sooner or later discovers hand-prints or sticks a piece of paper over a painting and creates a monoprint, which is different from other prints because only one impression can be made. Prints take on some of the character of the material being printed from, adding to its fascination for children. Printing is a form of repetition and children love repetition. When printing is discovered and fascinates the child, the subject can be expanded for the child through additional printing experiences. You will also find it the perfect time to read *Emmie and the Purple Paint* by Dorothy Edwards and Priscilla Lamond and other books in chapter 9.

Fingerprinting

Your baby's first print was probably made in the hospital's delivery room, when the doctor or nurse made a print of the sole of baby's foot. The first time a child notices that his or her dirty finger leaves marks on a towel or a wall or muddy feet track up a clean floor is a good time to get out an ink pad (or some washable paint in a saucer) and show the child how to make marks on a page with the tips of his or her fingers. A finger probably made the first print, so this is an excellent way to introduce the art of printing. It is quite a different experience from finger painting and should come after considerable experience with the more kinesthetic approach of finger painting. Lip prints on the window, on the mirror, or on paper with chocolate or Mom's lipstick will delight the child, and may be the impetus for this project as well. If the child suggests footprints, remember that the paint can be slippery. It's safest to try making them while seated in a chair, or with two hands being held by one or more adults. Consider reading a book about footprints. There are several on chapter 9's booklist. *Footprints in the Snow* is good for now, since it is geared to very young children. Of course, footprints don't have to be made with paint. Making and observing them in the sand, mud, or snow can be a delightful and enlightening experience. If your child is very free and you are not at all finicky, he or she can crawl through the paint!

Body parts are ideal subjects for printing since they reveal delicate textures and intricate patterns. The back of the hand as well as the palm of the hand, the nose, and the knee create surprising effects. This project appeals to the child who has not yet outgrown the need to paint his or her body. Cleanup will be complicated if you are unprepared but will be part of the enjoyment of the experience if you are.

To create a handprint, show your child how to paint the hand with a brush or paint a hand with a paintbrush. The first time, help the child press his or her hand on a piece of paper. Remind your child not to move the hand. When the hand is lifted, you will have a handprint. To create a fingerprint, you will want to have a water-soluble, nontoxic ink pad. Press your child's finger on the pad, then demonstrate how to print it on the paper. With my youngest students, I always chant "Dip and print, dip and print, dip and print," to help them learn the process of first inking before printing. That was the inspiration for the song "Dip and Print" that you will find in chapter 10, "Songs About Art."

In the elementary school where I now teach I have started a handprint tradition. Every child in kindergarten does one handprint on the wall of the main hall. I wait until they have gotten to know me and are comfortable enough with me to let me paint their hands. It has become a tradition, and as the children grow they always enjoy getting down on their hands and knees to try to fit their big hands on the little handprints they made when they were in kindergarten. It is special to their parents, too. I simply write the child's name directly on the wall in permanent black marker. I use acrylic paint, and a parent volunteer stands ready with a bucket of soapy water and paper towels. I hold the child's wrist firmly and paint the child's hand with a 2" brush. I remind them to spread their fingers and not move at all, but to let me pull their hand away. I then give them a sheet of paper with a poem on it to make a second handprint on to take home to the family.

Found-Objects Printing

You have a print when there are many identical, original images made from one master. Move on from hand- and fingerprints to printing with a variety of small objects. A small square sponge, an old toothbrush, bottle caps, plastic forks, discarded costume jewelry, corks, the rubber soles of outgrown sneakers, erasers, cardboard tubes, and a multitude of other household discards can be dipped in thick tempera paint or painted with a brush and pressed on a piece of paper to create prints of interesting repeat designs. Children should feel free to dab, smear, roll, or otherwise use the objects to create interesting effects. It can be stifling if an adult has strong expectations about how prints are to be made. These "dab-only" instructions limit the amount of learning that can take place.

Food Printing

Certain foods and plants are ideal for printing. Cut some vegetables in half, dip in a saucer of paint, or paint the cross section with a brush—the real treat will be visual rather than gastronomical. It is exciting to discover hidden designs in food. Try cabbage, mushrooms, green peppers, and oranges. Potatoes don't have to be incised to create a relief print. They make interesting circular and oval designs when simply cut in half. Vegetables give a clear print when fresh and crisp. There is no need for you to waste food in order to do this project. The discarded stems of carrots, broccoli, and other vegetables may be saved and later put to use in the interest of creativity. Why not prepare a salad with your toddler? The experience will then include creative food preparation as well! *Gyotaku* is a Japanese art of fish printing. It was originally used by fishermen who used it to prove their prowess after their catch had been cleaned and cut. All you need is a fish, some newspaper, rice paper, or newsprint, and nontoxic paint. Simply apply paint to the fish and roll it carefully on the paper. The fish can be thoroughly washed and eaten. You may prefer to invest in a rubber fish made specifically for this purpose and available through art suppliers (see page 268).

Rubber Stamps

You may think I'm splitting hairs, but I detest the idea of giving children rubber-stamp pictures. However, I think giving them letters, numbers, or geometric shapes is fine. At first glance they may seem very similar, but they are actually vastly different. Little pictures can easily become substitutes for a child's drawing, while geometric shapes become building blocks for original designs. Rubber or sponge alphabet and number stamps are sufficiently abstract to be acceptable for a preliterate child while having the added advantage of providing familiarity with letters. If you are concerned with quality, you may wish to order high-quality sets from Toys to Grow On (see page 270).

Printing with rubber
alphabet stamps

The same company also makes stamps of geometric shapes. You can also carve your own set for your child, using erasers and a sharp X-Acto knife.

Glue Prints

Simple white glue can also be used to make a print. The child can squeeze glue onto cardboard and allow it to dry. The next step is to roll the brayer back and forth and then over the glue design. I use a strong plastic cafeteria tray on which to roll the brayer back and forth when applying paint to it. Rice paper or newsprint is then placed over the cardboard and rubbed with the back of a spoon.

Collagraphs

Your child can also make a print from a collage he or she has made. Pasted buttons and cardboard scraps make wonderful surfaces to print from. These are called collagraphs. *Look at the Moon* is a book fully illustrated with collagraphs.

Printing with Clay Shapes

Children can roll clay with a rolling pin and use a pointed wooden stick to cut shapes out of it. Allow the clay to thoroughly harden, paint it with tempera paint, and press it facedown on a piece of paper.

Styrofoam Tray Prints

The Styrofoam trays that meat and fruit often come packed in can be gouged with a stick, covered with a thick layer of paint applied with a brayer, and used as a master for prints. Simply place a sheet of paper over the painted and incised tray and rub it with the back of a spoon. Lift the paper off to reveal your print and learn about mirror images at the same time. This technique is a variation of incised printing woodcuts. Art suppliers provide polystyrene foam sheets for this purpose.

Stencils

Stencil paper is heavyweight and waxed and can easily be cut by a pre-schooler. It is easiest to fold and then cut into the fold to create openings in it. Unfortunately most children don't encounter stencils unless they have been cut out already, because it is so tempting for some adults to give them ready-made shape and picture stencils. Your toddler can cut simple shapes out of a stencil, dip a sponge in tempera paint, and dab it over the opening to create an image on construction paper.

Technology

Children today take photocopy machines and scanners quite for granted. Most young children have had an experience observing one of these machines and therefore understand the principle of multiple copies. If your child hasn't observed a copy machine in action, have him or her do a drawing on white paper with a black felt-tip pen, place it in the machine, and let the child press the buttons to activate the machine and see the art reproduced. Encourage experimenting with printing on different colors of paper and reducing or enlarging the image. Before the invention of copying machines, woodblock prints and etchings were the only way an artist could make multiple copies of work.

Photography

Photography is a relatively modern method of creating multiple prints. Most young children are familiar with cameras after being photographed themselves. I know that I could count on my son to smile at the camera as soon as he saw me aim it at him, even as young as six months old. You can let your child take one or two shots from each roll of film you use, and create a delightful scrapbook together. Invest in a roll of Polaroid film for a very rewarding activity! One of my favorite photos of myself was taken by my son when he was about five years old. The top of my head is cut off and the angle he photographed me at is not the most flattering, but whenever I come across that picture I smile. I don't see myself when I look at it; I still see Jason's shining eyes, big smile, and pride in his accomplishment with the camera.

There is sun-sensitive paper available that creates prints and requires no camera, inks, or brayers. You simply place objects or paper scraps on it and expose it to the sun for two or three minutes to create a print of the silhouettes of the objects. Plain water sets the image permanently. As a teacher I couldn't plan a lesson that depended on whether or not it was sunny so I was delighted to discover that the paper works perfectly well under a sunlamp.

Computer Art

It is likely that your child will be exposed to computer art during the preschool years. Computers are tools, just as surely as crayon or paintbrushes are tools. Apply the same criteria to computer art games that you apply to traditional art projects. If the child is manipulating the lines and colors and solving problems, it's a good program. Working with computer "clip art" is the technological equivalent of coloring in coloring books.

CHAPTER 4

Paper

Working with paper is a wonderful way for children to be exposed to the concept of making and changing things. Altering paper is something children can easily do in a variety of ways; crumbling, tearing, and pasting are mastered quite early. These skills pave the way for later, more controlled alterations such as cutting, folding, adding to, and removing from. Paper should be available in great quantity to provide for experimentation without fear of reprimand.

Tearing Paper

Tearing a sheet of paper into two pieces may seem like a simple skill to you, but it requires quite a bit of coordination. On their first try, children frequently try to hold the two ends of the paper and pull it apart with brute strength. It takes time to learn just how to hold the paper so that it will tear easily, and learning this will instill a child with a feeling of accomplishment. Unfortunately, too often children get to try this out only on their expensive books or your important papers. Many parents therefore view it as a destructive activity and put a stop to it. Providing for this need with an interesting variety of papers is the more helpful form of supervision, and one that stimulates learning.

Don't tear clouds, Easter bunnies, trees, or flowers. Tear paper! Offer different varieties of papers such as newspaper, which tears easily, construction paper, tissue paper, old envelopes, junk mail, color catalogs, and old magazines.

Tearing provides a great release of energy. And, like almost everything children do, it contributes to muscle development. It is a project in and of itself and doesn't necessarily need to be followed by a collage experience, although you will probably want to save the paper in your collage box. Cut paper has straight, hard edges while torn scraps are ragged and appear softer; you can help your child make these observations.

Hole Punching

Hole punchers fascinate children. Simply punching holes in plain paper seems uninteresting to adults, who have a tendency to contrive unnecessarily cute projects to justify the activity. Too often hole punchers are offered with yarn and directions to "lace up" some adult-conceived project. Punching holes out of paper makes the child aware of negative space and aids in confident mastery of the tool. You can help by holding the completed work up to the light or over a contrasting color paper and talking about the effect. You can also help by holding the paper for the child, who may need both hands to squeeze the hole punch closed. The child may suggest saving the remaining circles to paste down in a collage. They are small and difficult to handle, but if you lick the tip of your finger you can easily pick them up. They can be dropped into globs of glue that have been painted thickly on the background.

Cutting with Scissors

One reason that children find cutting so difficult is that adults try to convince them that they have to cut out something like a heart or a circle. Early cutting should not involve cutting along a line. Just making cuts in paper is quite an accomplishment for a toddler.

Later, the child will want to cut chunks out of the paper; much later, specific shapes. In any case, it's up to the child to set goals, not the adult. At some point in the child's life, he or she will draw a shape of his or her own and be self-motivated to cut it out. This, and only this, should be the child's first experience in cutting along a line and will probably not occur, regardless of age, until after three years of free-cutting experiences. Because of the high motivation and the fact that the experience is personalized, learning is rapid. For beginning cutters, there is no correct way to hold scissors. Whatever is

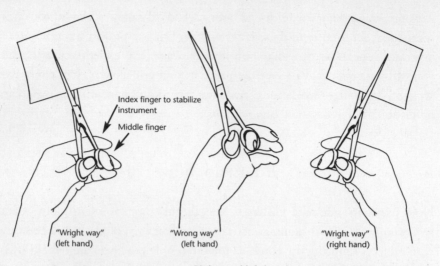

Right- and left-handed scissors holding instructions

most comfortable for the child is the correct way to hold them. They may need two of those little hands to control scissors, which is fine. If the child is frustrated in his or her efforts to cut, you may want to show the child this way to hold scissors, which gives more control. Incidentally, this is an easier way for lefties to cut as well. Left-handed children should be provided with left-handed scissors, or the new kind of scissors that are designed to be used with either hand. Since some nursery schools may not have them, you may want to buy an extra pair to send in with your school-age left-handed child. The child who holds a pair of scissors with two hands can make decorative cuts in the paper if an adult holds the paper. Since you want to be nearby while your youngster works with scissors anyway, this is not a problem. Many people don't allow young children to handle scissors, or they holler the ominous "Be careful!" as a child approaches them. This serves no useful purpose and only makes the child feel inadequate and unworthy around new tools. "Be careful" really means "be scared." More useful would be directions like "Touch the point very gently. It is sharp," "Hold the scissors with the point facing away from you," or "If you walk with scissors and fall on them you could get hurt."

Let your child use scissors as soon as he or she expresses interest in doing so, even if the child is very young. As always, good parenting means taking the time to supervise exploration, not prevent it.

Blunt scissors are safe, but your child will most likely be inspired to cut by seeing you use adult-sized, pointed ones. Children don't want imitation scissors any more than they want to play with a red plastic telephone—they want the real thing! For very young children, large scissors are easier to manage with two hands, the usual first cutting position. It is easier to cut with the sharper blade than with the dull "safe" blade of many children's scissors. Under your extremely close supervision, perhaps even while holding the child on your lap, let the child work with the tool that inspired interest in the skill. By all means buy your child blunt scissors to experiment with while you are busy elsewhere. But first try them out yourself. Some are so safe that they don't cut anything at all! This is no way to teach a child about cutting. The best children's scissors that I know of are plastic, with metal-edged blades, and are made by Fiskars. All of the teachers in my school district tested everything on the market and we agreed that Fiskars was best to work with. They meet all of the U.S. safety standards yet they cut very well. They can be used effectively by left- and right-handers and are available in most school-supply catalogs. They cost less than two dollars a pair. Fiskars Paper Edgers come with a variety of interesting curved blade shapes and should extend the amount of time a child retains interest in cutting paper.

Cutting is a satisfying and significant experience in and of itself. The preschooler does not necessarily want to follow up the activity with pasting cut shapes in a collage. Most adults plan cutting as an adjunct to pasting, but the two experiences are very different to the preschooler. Cutting can be an absorbing experience, but the intrusion of pasting materials and information will distract from it.

Collage

William Seitz of the Museum of Modern Art said:

> No mode of creation is more direct or naturally arrived at than the accumulation and agglomeration of materials found close at hand.*

Collage, from the French verb *coller* ("to paste"), is a picture made by pasting paper, fabric, and other materials to a flat surface. Collecting and arranging the objects in a collage encourages children to look at mundane objects in fresh new ways.

---

*Quoted in *Gloria Vanderbilt Book of Collage*, page 110.

For preschoolers, any valuable collage experience must be nonrepresenta-
tional. Many adults feel that pictures must be of realistic objects, but this is
not at all the purpose of art for a child under four. Art is expressing oneself,
experimenting with new ideas and materials—doing your "own thing" with
given materials and developing meaningful skills.

Children learn more when an activity has personal meaning for them.
They will usually spend more time and become more involved in pasting
shapes they have chosen or made themselves than pasting adult-made shapes.
Keep in mind that for the very young child, making or collecting materials
should actually be planned as a separate activity from the actual pasting. The
child who cannot yet cut will enjoy choosing random scraps and will create
new ones by tearing. Presenting a child with such items as teacher-made
apples, turkeys, and pumpkins infuses the activity with artificial and distracting adult significance that has no meaning for the child. Scraps that are prepared by an adult should be geometric or free-form shapes, not pictures. The
real value of this activity is that the child has solved the problem of how best
to affix one piece of paper to another. On the very same day my son brought

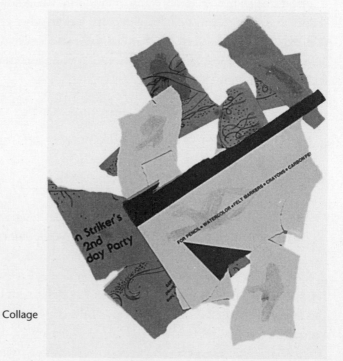

Collage

a fruit collage home from a playground birthday party with six pieces of adult-made fruit pasted on it, he also did this collage, which he made from the extra invitations to his second birthday party. It includes layer upon layer of pasted papers and kept him absorbed in his work for a long time.

Begin with simple paper collage experiences, gradually adding more elaborate materials onto a cardboard background. A white vinyl plastic glue can be used directly from a squeeze bottle or thinned slightly with water and poured into a shallow container for use with a brush. That awful library paste that you remember using when you were a young child is, thank heavens, obsolete, because of the invention of nontoxic polymer emulsion glues (such as Elmer's Wilhold, Sobo, and Crayola Art and Craft), which adhere paper and other materials permanently to backgrounds and dry clear. Glue sticks are great, but it is not realistic to expect a toddler to put the cap back on, and these sticks don't last through the night without tops on them. Pasting with fingers is impossible. Children will at first experiment with smearing great globs of glue on the shapes as well as on the background, but they soon become more adept at pasting. Criticism of overuse of glue is not helpful at this time, since it serves to prevent a necessary exploration of what stickiness is. The child who has had a chance to explore glue and use it freely, without adult reminders about "wasting" it, will surely use too much at first, but will gradually come to an understanding of how this material works best and will become proficient at pasting. As always, don't teach; let the child learn.

Pasting is a complicated skill that, when attempted too early, can drive many children to tears. One- and two-year-olds want to affix papers and they want to squeeze out great globs of paste, but coordinating the two activities is overwhelming. The child loses sight of his or her goals while becoming involved with the materials. The completed work will often be so completely covered with paste that it serves only to frustrate the child and tear down his or her self-esteem.

Remember that it is impossible to explore textures when your fingers are full of paste. Be sure that brushes, sticks, or squeeze-bottles are available for applying the paste. Children adore squeezing paste out of them all over everything in sight. I take advantage of their enjoyment in this activity by also filling squeeze-bottles with thinned-out tempera paint, for a free-painting experience. Painting with squeeze-bottles helps children fulfill their need to experience this activity. When they are finished with it, they tend to control the squeeze-bottle better and not use quite so much paste.

In addition to squeeze-bottle painting, another natural follow-up project includes an exploration in smooth- or soft-textured objects. You will need satin, cotton, acetate, some fur or fake fur scraps, and all of the other smooth or soft objects you and your child can find together. The child can make a collage by pasting a variety of textured papers and fabrics on cardboard. Since many of the objects suggested here are quite heavy, consider using a cardboard background that is strong enough to support the weight of the objects plus the glue. My local framer saves scrap mat board for me. He is happy not to have to pay to have it carted away and I have elegant sculpture bases for my students at no cost.

Assemblage

Perhaps assemblage, or relief sculpture, which is attached to a flat background, is the natural outgrowth of collage experimentation. Styrofoam pieces, straws, boxes, wood scraps, and shells are ideal for introductory assemblage materials. Cardboard, wood, or blocks of Styrofoam make good, stable backgrounds. Assemblage is a bridge leading naturally from collage to sculpture: art in three dimensions. Paste is, at first, handled as if it were paint. There is no need for the child to paste neatly at the outset, since working is what is important, not the final piece of work. By using too much and then too little, the child learns best how to paste.

Do not present extravagant, adult-chosen materials and instruct a child to "paste them down." To have a valuable art experience, the child should participate in choosing and collecting the materials, and the collected material should have some common characteristic for the child to focus on and learn about.

Red Collage Experience

Plan a treasure hunt. Looking for all of the different red papers the child can find will make the point that there is a great variety of tints and shades of red that are red nevertheless. Small patterns in which red is the predominant color also qualify. Don't use patterns of realistic objects such as trees or houses, since children sometimes feel that the object is important and they will try to cut or tear around it and make it into a substitute for their own work. Shiny and dull reds, light and dark reds, and small and large red scraps all add variety and interest to the collage and help expand vocabulary as well.

Blue Collage Experience

Collecting a wide variety of plain blue papers in various shades of the color can also be the subject of a treasure hunt. Shiny, dull, bright, light, medium, and dark all help to provide variety. A large blue sheet of paper or cardboard can be the background. The child who has drawn with blue crayons and markers, and painted outdoors with blue paint on a sunny day, will find this indoor, rainy-day experience an enriching one. Find an old blue box or bag for storing all of the blue papers.

Don't think that because the child has already drawn and painted in blue or done a collage exclusively in another color that this will seem boring. The subtle nuances of shade and color are more readily evident in a monochromatic color scheme than in multicolor combinations. Working with this wide array of blue papers will increase the child's sensitivity to the effects of varying purity, intensity, and value.

Yellow Collage Experience

Right about now you are probably rolling your eyes and saying, "Here she goes again." You may be bored stiff working with only one color at a time, but your child won't be. The world is full of wonder for young children, and what seems repetitious to you is not for a child. It can be very exciting for a child to find a piece of yellow paper where no one else noticed it, and the child who discovers a multitude of yellow in a small collection of old papers has learned an unforgettable lesson. The fun and excitement this kind of learning provides keeps the flame of curiosity burning and opens a child's mind and eyes to future educational possibilities. It would be logical next to do an all-green collage, a purple collage, and an orange one as well, without having overdone the experience. A multitude of shallow, onetime art experiences can never equal the value of one experience studied and worked at in depth. Parents and teachers often make the mistake of changing art projects for children frequently. That keeps life interesting for the adult but deprives children of the education they derive from the simple, basic projects. The "back to basics" movement so popular in education circles talks about reading, writing, and arithmetic, but long before children get to that they are scribbling, painting, pasting, and sculpting. Those are the real basics that contribute to the mental and physical development that makes the others possible later on.

One creative activity often inspires another. While engrossed in a pasting experience, my two-and-a-half-year-old son spontaneously began to sing these lyrics to the tune of "Skip to My Lou":

> *Glue, glue, stick my glue*
> *Glue, glue, stick my glue*
> *Glue, glue, stick my glue*
> *Stick my glue, my paper.*

Staplers, tape, paper clips, rubber bands, string, ribbon, even thumbtacks—all of which are similar to paste in that they cause two objects to be affixed to each other—may also be discriminately used to enhance the experience of fastening two things together.

Helpful comments you can make include pointing out how the glue is being used, how the papers or fabrics relate to each other and the background. Nothing more profound is needed than a simple description of what the picture looks like. Don't feel foolish saying, "The blue shape is next to the red piece" or "The black piece of paper is far away from the red piece" or "Look how part of the blue piece covers part of the brown piece." By merely describing what the collage looks like, you help provide vocabulary and heighten awareness. "Very pretty" doesn't mean as much as simple descriptions. Really looking at the child's work is required, and both you and your child will benefit.

With sufficient familiarity of the materials serving as a firm base, young children often spontaneously discover surprisingly sophisticated collage techniques. They may "reinvent" the collagraph or combine print, which can be made from low-relief paper or cardboard. A collagraph consists of a background that has a design built up on it, as in a collage. It is possible to ink the surface and create a print of the collage on another sheet of paper. Photo montage, which is a collage made from photographs, is another possibility. Like children, professional artists frequently combine drawings and paintings in collage. Double, triple, and quadruple exposures made by toddlers trying out cameras can have the same effect as collage. Tearing and remounting pasted papers is called decollage.

The next few projects suggest categories of things you can offer the child to help focus attention on visual or textural qualities. These experiences help the child to understand basic perceptual concepts, such as similarities and differences of shapes, colors, texture, and weights.

Arrange Tape

Using precut pieces of tape on paper is an excellent way to introduce the pasting concept to the young child who is not quite ready to handle paste. Inexpensive masking tape is all the child needs, but tapes are available in every color of the rainbow if more elaborate materials appeal to the child. Choosing the colors and studying color contrast add to the learning experience. Transparent tape can be lots of fun to work with, too. Prepare a dozen or so pieces, short enough not to tangle too easily. A few masking tape and self-stick label experiences are enough to whet the child's appetite for pasting.

Design with Stick-on Circles

Another perfect prepasting activity many children will enjoy utilizes self-stick labels from the stationery store. They are available as circles, rectangles, stars, notary seals, and a multitude of other shapes. There are also many stickers on the market, such as rainbows, smiling faces, animals, and cartoon characters. They unnecessarily perpetuate the notion that art projects are best when they are realistic. Stay away from them and stick to geometric shapes. Also steer clear of sticker sets that have patterns for the child to follow.

Prepasted shapes that "magically" stay where they are placed provide an introductory pasting experience without tears. You will need to show the child how to bend the backing paper to make the sticker pop off.

Begin by presenting the child with multicolored various-sized circles one day, squares another, triangles another, and a combination of all of the shapes only well after the child is familiar with each individually. As always, with a child under the age of four, showing the child how to put shapes together to make a realistic object is counterproductive. Many children will do so to please an adult, but in so doing they miss out on developing the problem-solving skills involved in doing the child-motivated work appropriate for this age level. You can buy circles, squares, and rectangles easily. If you can't find triangles, precut your own by cutting squares in half on the diagonal. Make crayons or markers available later on, to add the variety of mixed media. Try also self-stick notes, which come in square and rectangular shapes. They are a little easier to handle than stickers and are therefore good for beginners. Self-stick letters are a lot of fun and good to use after the child has done the project several times. As an added bonus, they help increase familiarity with the letters. Even the gold stars you probably remember from your childhood now come in the self-adhesive variety.

Another variation on this theme is to have plain paper scraps and a sticky background. Bemis-Jason Corp. makes something they call Quick-Stick, a large sheet of brightly colored adhesive board. It's intended as a bulletin board, but I cut it into smaller sheets and give it to children with some paper scraps that adhere to the background with the slightest pressure. It's not cheap, but is endlessly reusable and can be recycled as a bulletin board when the child moves on to more sophisticated pasting projects. A similar self-stick background is available as a refill for scrapbooks and is available in variety and/or photography supply stores. It comes covered in clear acetate, which, combined with the scrapbook, makes it an ideal material for preserving your child's art. Flannel boards can also be used with geometric shapes of flannel, instead of the corny cutouts that are usually packaged with them.

My students at Young at Art regularly made collages using the postagelike stamps that came with offers for joining a book club. Consider also buying envelopes of inexpensive foreign stamps. (Just make sure they still have glue on the back and weren't used previously, for your child's health.) Watch your mail for Easter Seals and, to further provide your child with interesting art experiences, why not buy fifty or so one-cent postage stamps for use in collage?

My son loved stickers and worked with them almost obsessively for several weeks when he was about two years old. Just when I built up a huge collection of circle stickers in assorted sizes and colors, he completely lost interest in doing sticker art. I brought the stickers to my class of seven-year-olds. They were so delighted that they begged me to bring them in again when we met the following week. Again in the third week they clamored for more stickers. Children of all ages enjoy and benefit from working with simple materials and my seven-year-old students progressed quickly from doing work indistinguishable from a two-year-old's to incorporating the circles into elaborate representational art.

Collage Box

You will want to have your child help with assembling a collage box, since collecting the materials is as important as is pasting them. Begin by buying a package of colored construction paper and putting it in a cardboard or plastic box. Together you and your child will gradually add different kinds of fabric, corrugated cardboard, tissue paper, cellophane, wrapping paper, cotton batting, textured wallpaper samples, and junk mail items. Help your child choose papers in a variety of colors and contrasting textures. In my classroom, I keep twenty-six different labeled collage boxes; one is marked "patterns," another says "bumpy papers." I also have a wide variety of sandpaper, several boxes for wrapping paper, and a shoe box full of scraps of yarn. I have five hundred students passing through my room making art projects every week, so you won't need to have quite as many collage boxes as I have!

Every home needs a collage box to be added to regularly and used frequently. Modern technology has made a wide array of papers available for use or reuse in art. The list of possible materials is almost endless: old envelopes, wrapping papers, junk mail, old greeting cards, magazines, tickets, wallpaper sample books, prints or reproductions of great art, old doilies, and maps. Scraps of corrugated cardboard (which is also available in colors), sandpaper, precut fabrics, velour-finish paper, and old lace add textural interest to the collage box. Scraps that are approximately 3" × 3" are the easiest to handle. After a birthday celebration, iron the discarded wrapping paper and save your old party streamers.

For collage, children love metallic papers, colored tissue, fluorescent paper, fabrics, metal, leaves, and simple patterned gift wraps and wallpaper. Stripes, dots, checks, and small overall patterns are much better than patterns that include pictures of realistic objects. The latter invite children to use the commercially printed art as a substitute for their own. Buttons, leaves, twigs, and sequins usually find their way into a well-stocked collage box. Throw in a feather once in a while, just for fun! Keep your eyes open at tag sales, bazaars, and thrift shops for old, inexpensive picture books. The cut-up pages make excellent collage material. Be sure to ignore the pictures and cut out only areas of color. Fabrics are more difficult to use than paper. They can easily be pasted but are difficult to alter. It takes adult hands to cut or tear most of them. Although you will occasionally want to use fabrics and cardboards to enrich texture exploration, keep in mind that assorted papers are easiest to manage and closer to the real meaning of the collage medium. Don't offer the entire collage box at one time or you will overwhelm the child.

It is easy for collage projects to deteriorate into pointless junk collections. The child who is simply presented with extravagant adult-chosen materials and pastes them on a background to please an adult is not having a valuable art experience. By not participating in the preparation of a project, the child misses out on one of its major advantages. Encourage the child to add found objects from nature or from around the house to the collage box regularly. Since collage materials are most often obtained at no cost, you can use the money you save to purchase good, strong background boards. The weight of the materials combined with the glue can cause warping if the background isn't substantial enough. Use illustration board or cardboard, which can be found in laundered shirts and discarded boxes as well as in art and stationery stores. Shallow box tops make excellent backgrounds for collages that become assemblages.

Collage doesn't involve a child emotionally as deeply as drawing or painting can, but it does provide for the child to use his or her abilities at selecting and arranging materials and can produce an increased awareness of the tactile world. Your enthusiasm for new materials can be "catching" and may stimulate interesting collage activity, but children should never be coerced or forced into using materials. Nature walks and shopping trips can be planned periodically to replenish the collage box, and children should actively choose new materials. Craft catalogs, which often offer bad ideas for formula art projects, nevertheless are gold mines of collage materials that will excite your youngster.

Children constantly hear "Don't touch." A better and far more helpful approach to the issue would be to capitalize on the child's natural interest in touching everything in sight by planning an experience in touching. In addition to using hands for examining, touching, and discovering, the child can now use his or her hands to create things. Put out a collection of bumpy and rough-textured objects for the child to choose from. Look at, touch, and talk about them with the child. Most children like to hold things to their faces when they are learning about what they feel like, probably because the face is more sensitive than the fingertips. You can suggest other ways to explore the

Bumpy-texture collage

materials, such as touching them while the eyes are closed, rubbing them together to listen to the sound they produce, and touching them with the toes instead of the fingers.

Include such items as sandpaper, tree bark, and corrugated cardboard. Burlap and other open-weave fabrics enrich the experience, because when they are superimposed the patterns created by the weave are changed to create new patterns.

Collage of Transparent Materials

The colors of transparent material are altered when placed over each other. During the time your child is experimenting with color mixing through painting, you can help reinforce learning by offering colored tissue or cellophane in the same colors with which the child is painting. As these papers are superimposed, new colors are created as if by magic. Multiple layers of the same color appear darker than single sheets. As the child arranges the papers, your observation about what is happening helps to clarify learning. Small World Toys (see Appendix 3) makes a pair of eyeglasses with moveable red, yellow, and blue lenses. Playing with them also helps the child understand and remember color-mixing facts. Childcraft makes color paddles; red, yellow, and blue sheets of Lucite that demonstrate color mixing. You can duplicate this inexpensively with three sheets of colored cellophane. There are many books you can look at with your child that deal with colors and how they change. See chapter 9, "Books About Art for Children."

Collage serves as an excellent transition between two-dimensionality and three-dimensionality. It bridges the gap between drawing and painting on flat surfaces and sculpture.

Sculpture

We live in a three-dimensional world, and sculpture is art in three dimensions. There are two main types of sculpture: sculptures from malleable materials and from building constructions. To create with malleable materials, such as play dough or clay, portions of it are removed. Building constructions involve adding on. These two sculpture categories teach children the math concepts of addition and subtraction better than any other techniques I have ever seen.

Manipulative Materials

Clay is an exciting medium and children can enjoy and learn from rolling, squeezing, poking, removing from, adding to, mashing, pounding, pressing, pulling, cutting, and otherwise manipulating and shaping the materials.

Most children begin by tasting clay. Since tasting is part of the introduction to the material, the clay must, of course, be nontoxic. For this reason, it is probably best to start with play dough, since all of the ingredients are edible.

I always bought commercial Play-Doh in the "color of the week" (more on that in the color curriculum chapter) but my son's favorite nursery school teacher, Colleen Colbert, had a better idea. She and her students mixed up their own, using this recipe.

3 parts flour
1 part salt
1 part water
1 tablespoon oil per cup of flour
Optional: food coloring
Optional: 1 teaspoon alum (a salt of potassium and aluminum)
    per 2 cups flour, to preserve the mixture for about six months

Another edible recipe you can offer the child who is still using the mouth for learning is this very nutritious variation, provided by Kathy Knudsen.

1 12-oz. jar peanut butter
6 tablespoons honey
3 cups powdered milk

Of course, making the play dough was as much fun as playing with it. I have always found that the teachers who did lots of work before the children came to school were never the great teachers they appeared to be; the teachers who set the stage for the children to do their own work are the great ones! All you have to do is premeasure the ingredients; your child will enjoy putting them all together to make the dough.

The following poem is from *I Wish I Had a Computer That Makes Waffles* by Dr. Fitzhugh Dodson. We always recite it before playing with play dough. If I forget, the children never fail to remind me.

I play with my play dough;
See what I make!
I play with my play dough:
I make a cake.

I play with my play dough;
I shape it and mold it.
I play with my play dough;
I bend it and fold it.

I poke it and punch it;
I roll it and scrunch it.
With a squeeze and a pat,
I squash it down flat!

Dr. Dodson's book is wonderful, with modern nursery rhymes about every-day things like calculators, zippers, and computers. I have read it to thousands of children over the years, all of whom loved it. We know that "Ring Around the Rosie" referred to people dying in the bubonic plague. Why not recite rhymes that, as Dr. Dodson's book does, refer to taking trains, using calculators, and flying to the moon?

Bread dough is also ideal for sculpture experiments before baking. Keep in mind, however, that encouraging the eating of art materials now can set a precedent that can be dangerous later on. You may want to simply switch a chronic play dough and clay nibbler to plasticine or moist clay, both of which taste awful, even though they are nontoxic. Plasticine is easy to handle if kept fairly warm and can be kept for years in plastic bags. If the warmth of holding the clay in your hands for a few minutes is not enough to soften it, put it on a piece of aluminum foil and place it on a warm radiator or a sunny windowsill for a few minutes. Buy one color at a time since there is no way to separate colors after they have been combined and since manipulation, not color, is the goal of the experience. You'll want to switch to Model Magic or beeswax when color mixing becomes the child's goal.

Play dough is a good introductory material for the very young child, but there is no substitute for moist clay. I have included play dough with clay, though the combination is not really correct since the two materials are so vastly different. As Naomi Pile said in her book *Art Experiences for Young Children,*

> Many teachers confuse clay, which is a sculptural material, with dough, and bring kitchen tools like rolling pins, knives, and cookie cutters to the art area. These tools are better confined to the housekeeping areas where play dough, a substitute for real dough, can be used. Play dough or salt dough is for cooking; clay is for sculpture.

The above quote should end with an "amen." Despite play dough's real value as an early manipulative material and an introduction to cooking skills, it is too often misused as a substitute for clay. I like play dough for the twelve-to eighteen-month-old child, but the child who begins working with it at that age will be ready to graduate to a genuine art material, like moist firing clay, within a year. Play dough simply doesn't have the wide range of possibilities that clay has. Clay's potential is so great, in fact, that some people devote their whole careers to working with it. Play dough, on the other hand, permits only shallow exploration and invites the use of tools. I would add that cookie cutters and other molds of realistic objects are three-dimensional equivalents of coloring books. They interfere with the child's efforts to explore and learn. For the preschooler, clay experiments are the three-dimensional equivalents of scribbling. *Don't* expect the child to make recognizable objects, and *do* praise the efforts made at manipulating and controlling the material. Presenting adult-directed projects, such as leaf ashtrays and characters formed with molds or cookie cutters, has no value compared to the long-term experience of working regularly with the earth. In these days of preference for natural materials, what could be more natural than moist clay from the earth? Working with clay helps develop hand and finger motor coordination and builds muscle dexterity. It is an ideal medium for heightening texture awareness and offers many opportunities for scientific experimentation. Clay is literally mud, and mud, sand, and water are basic learning materials.

It is understandable that some parents and teachers are reluctant to bring a material like mud into their homes and classrooms. If you can't provide for clay experiences in your home, do so in your backyard or at the neighborhood park. Clay does require a little more know-how and work on your part than play dough, but the effort is well worth it. The following tips on working with moist clay should allow the first-time user success.

Purchase either the Gordon or Jordan brand of firing clay, even though you won't be firing it. It dries hard without being fired so that you can save completed sculptures. Unlike so-called self-hardening clay, moist firing clay can be revived if it dries up and therefore can last forever. Don't throw away your old, covered, plastic diaper pail, which is an ideal storage container for moist clay. Keep the clay overnight in a sealed plastic bag in the closed plastic container. When it is a perfect consistency, cover it with a damp terry-cloth towel before replacing it in the plastic bag, to help retain its moisture. A good consistency for clay is one a child can manipulate fairly easily, without being too watery. Young children will need moister clay than adults, but it should not be so moist that it gets sticky. When it gets too moist, simply place it on newspaper and allow it to drain and dry out. Since newspaper absorbs the moisture from clay, the child cannot work with clay that has newspapers under it. You will need a durable tabletop such as a clay board or a vinyl placemat. If the clay sticks to the work surface, lift it by running a wire under it and out the other end. Instead of washing the table, which will make it "muddy," scrape off the excess clay with an old ruler, ice-cream stick, or tongue depressor.

Clay is the most economical art project imaginable; one box of it should last throughout childhood. Should the clay dry out, don't throw it away. It can be made like new very easily. To recondition clay:

1. Place the clay on a thick padding of newspaper on a drop cloth made of heavy-duty plastic, and break the clay up into small pieces with a clay hammer. (Your child will probably enjoy this activity as much as any sculpture project.)
2. Put the small clay pieces in a plastic container and add enough water to cover the clay. Cover the container securely and stir once daily for several days until the clay is the correct consistency. If the clay becomes too sticky, spread it on a thick padding of newspaper to absorb the excess moisture. Remove it carefully from the newspaper so that pieces of it do not stick to the clay.

Appropriate questions help the child focus on his or her experiences with clay and clarify what he or she is accomplishing. Your comments should focus on the way the child is handling the clay rather than on the relative beauty of the object being made. Helpful comments clarify for the child what is being learned: "Oh my! The more you roll the clay back and forth, the longer your coil seems to get" or "My goodness! When you pound your hand on the clay, it gets flatter and flatter" or "Oh! I see that you are scratching and poking the clay with your finger. It makes a decoration on the clay." Describe what the child is doing and be generous with "What a good idea!"

It is essential that you recognize how important free, regular exploration of clay is to your child's intellectual and creative growth and appreciate the value of the emotional release it can provide. Don't assume that he or she will become bored if offered the same material every day. Repetition reinforces learning and with each new experience learning is added to old to form a firm foundation for future three-dimensional art experiences. The *child* should be growing and changing, not the art materials. Clay should be temptingly available to your child daily to provide an in-depth exploration of one of the most basic of materials. Clay satisfies a child's natural need for tactile pleasure, provides for a release of tension, and responds clearly to the child's actions.

Although you may want to offer kitchen tools to the child who is working with play dough, they don't help a child learn about clay. Working with tools can serve as a barrier that separates the child from the material, thereby discouraging manipulation of it. When working with clay, a sculptor's best tools are always his or her hands! Much later on, genuine modeling tools can be offered occasionally, but only after the child has had considerable experience learning directly about clay. These include wooden sticks with which the child can incise designs, plastic knives for cutting and trimming, and wooden or rubber pallets for smoothing. You can encourage the child to improvise by using common household items as clay tools. Some children may use tools as hammers, cut decorations with them, or use them in other fresh ways that you and I haven't thought of. "How else can we use that?" is a helpful comment. Designs can be incised with old combs or sticks. At about the age of three, the creative child becomes interested in sticking things into the clay. Feathers, ice-cream sticks, stones, straws, and other items can be made available then.

Clay with decorations stuck in it

Squish, Poke, and Pound on Clay

The very young child who is exploring clay for the first time handles the clay and learns about it by observing the changes that occur as the clay is handled. Noting these changes becomes the focus of the art experience at first. It is an important means of growth and soon the child will be able to make the changes in the clay purposefully. Clay exploration contributes to cognitive and emotional development, adding immeasurably to the child's maturity.

After looking at, tasting, poking, and squishing clay, youngsters quickly move on to banging on it. This activity corresponds to a similar stage when the child is banging on toys and trying out hitting friends and family. Drums, xylophones, and toy hammers are favorite toys of this age group. Clay can be banged on with the fist or the palm of the hand, providing direct physical contact with the material. The child may also want to bring toy hammers or other objects to the clay table to use at this time. Pounding on clay can allow for a release of tension. After all, hitting clay is acceptable; hitting Mommy isn't. At the same time, these simple, introductory experiences are providing opportunities for free exploration and experimentation.

Making Clay Coils

Children discover how to roll clay coils very early on. They may begin naming these clay shapes and engage in dramatic play with them somewhat earlier than they name their drawn and painted shapes. Art educator Viktor Lowenfeld, who was an early innovator of modern art education, felt that this is because the clay has concrete shape, as do the objects the child is reminded of. The child who is getting interested in using a toilet will certainly notice a similarity to feces and label his or her clay creations "doody" or "poop."

Making clay coils is not an activity that you teach to a child; it is the normal outgrowth of in-depth exploration of the material. Supervising adults are most helpful when they simply observe what the child is doing and describe it: "As you move your hand back and forth the coil gets longer and longer" or "I see you've made one fat coil next to one thin coil." To the child who is pushing a coil along and saying "Choo choo," you can say, "I see that your coil is long, just like a train."

Making clay coils

Sculpture

It can be inspiring to observe just how powerful an instinct all children have to build things. They will arrange shapes in space and construct mysterious and wonderful three-dimensional things out of next to nothing. They need to touch and learn as much as possible from everything they encounter in the environment. These children need encouragement from us if they are to grow up to be the architects, engineers, inventors, builders, and social leaders that this world requires. They also need appropriate work space and some simple materials. Strong glue is a good beginning. In no time the child will be ready for a hammer (a real one, not a red plastic one) and some nails. A three-year-old can nail scraps of wood together with the enthusiasm of a great modern sculptor, mold and sand clay like an old master, and twist covered wire into shapes that seem to take on a life of their own.

Children who are encouraged to work with sculpture materials will learn about the nature of three-dimensional form as they do. Children who never even hear the word "sculpture" will nevertheless conduct their experiments in constructing when building with blocks or piling up rocks, and they will successfully and happily fulfill their instinct to model with mud or wet sand instead of clay.

None of these strong urges to control and construct that all children are

born with are satisfied through working with molds or other imitative projects that carry out an adult's notion of cute pumpkins, pretty Christmas trees,
sweet Easter bunnies, and the like. Such activities squelch curiosity, discourage experimentation, and stifle inventiveness. They ignore the child's natural
need to touch, explore, and make independent discoveries about basic materials.

Pumpkins don't always have to become jack-o'-lanterns with two triangle
eyes and a mouth. Give a pumpkin and some nontoxic acrylic paints to a
child and the results may surprise you! Painting a three-dimensional object
provides a good transition activity between painting and sculpture.

Take into consideration these three basic sculpture categories when planning a well-rounded program in three-dimensional experience for your preschool child:

1. Modeling with manipulative materials
2. Constructing
3. Wire sculpture

Painting a pumpkin

Constructions

Many different types and combinations of objects can be attached together to form interesting constructed sculptures. Save your empty film cans, boxes from your groceries, wood scraps, used straws, packing material, and other things you are used to throwing away. Full-strength vinyl glue will hold even wood scraps together. I pour mine into a disposable container the night before I plan to use it so that it is "tacky" for my students. We use tongue depressors to apply it. Children have a strong instinct to build, and arranging shapes in space is an important activity for young children since they learn so many different things from it. Both blocks and constructed sculptures involve building with objects that are already completed.

Box Sculpture

Cardboard boxes are ideal to use when creating constructed sculptures. They are lightweight, simple to paste together using nontoxic polymer vinyl glues, and can be painted with tempera paints. You will probably collect enough in one weekly trip to the supermarket to make a decent-size piece. You can also save gift boxes after holiday or birthday celebrations. Groups can be encouraged to work together on large box sculptures as a means of contributing to cooperative social interaction. A group of ten students of mine built an entire "city" out of boxes and took up half our classroom. One boy who was not in the mood for group work solved his dilemma by building the "suburbs." The book *Changes* by Pat Hutchins is a great book about all the possibilities of building with blocks.

Pipe Cleaners

I hesitated to include pipe cleaners in this book at all. Children inevitably encounter adults who can't help turning them into stick figure formulas, which then become substitutes for child art, as they have been for generations. When working with pipe cleaners, it is essential that the supervising adult give up any preconceived notions of pipe cleaners as stick figures, bug antennae, butterfly wings, or other trivia.

Pipe cleaners are highly flexible materials that have a potential similar to

Box sculpture

wire sculpture. But, unlike plain wire, the cloth cover renders them safe and easy for preschoolers to manipulate. A similar material, Twisteez, is brightly colored wrapped telephone wire; it is sometimes available from the telephone company and has recently been marketed commercially. You may want to staple the first pipe cleaner or Twisteez wire to a cardboard base to facilitate work for the child. You can avoid using the staple, which can scratch little fingers, by poking two holes in the cardboard and weaving the wire in and out and twisting it to firmly attach it to the cardboard.

The artist David Smith described his early wire sculpture as "a drawing in space." For the scribbler, the drawing in three dimensions will parallel flat drawing development (see "Art Activity Developmental Norms" chart, page 23). The major advantage of working with pipe cleaners and wire sculpture is that it helps the child translate flat drawing into three dimensions and begin to understand the possibilities of sculpture. Sculpture projects help children learn about space and their personal relationships with it. They also teach science and math concepts. Sculpture is the best way to address the spatially gifted child's learning style.

CHAPTER 6

Exploring Color

This chapter demonstrates how to integrate stories, songs, snacks, drawing, pasting, painting, and sculpture activities to teach children the art and science of color. It does so through varied activities in order to address the different learning styles we all have. Since many children will look at picture books long before they are exposed to art in any other format, it is crucial for the quality of the illustrations to be outstanding and the stories compelling. Great books can inspire early art activities and set high aesthetic standards. There can be no doubt in any reader's mind that Harold's purple crayon is magic. *Little Blue and Little Yellow* remains the most poignant and effective vehicle for teaching color mixing. I have made two additional versions of it; one for *little red and little yellow* and one for *little blue and little red*, with apologies to Leo Lionni.

You do *not* need to be "talented" or "artistic" yourself to nurture children's creativity. You may, however, need to readjust your expectations and recognize the fact that art is an ideal format in which children can exercise problem-solving skills and engage in critical thinking.

Color skills and concepts can be introduced and reinforced, or even repeated, since they are essential to a child's development. The sequence of color-related projects that follows provides the means to give children a solid foundation of art experiences upon which to build a lifetime of meaningful art exploration. It also involves giving the child the confidence, skills, and enthusiasm to carry out any art activity in a manner that is appropriate to his or her age and grade level.

Learning to recognize and name colors is a useful skill in life, but should *not* be the only point of a project. Knowing how to create colors by combining other colors is a useful art skill, but not an end in itself. The value of an art experience diminishes when it is viewed as a way to accumulate facts. It is possible to be creative without being able to name colors. Even people who are color-blind—and cannot differentiate between colors—can think in innovative, fresh ways. The following list of color concepts and skills is intended as a guide for the parent or teacher, *not* as a list of definitions a child should remember. The list represents the kinds of experiences children should be exposed to in order to help them build the skills necessary to fulfill goals they set for themselves.

Color Concepts and Skills

□ *Analogous Colors*—Colors next to each other on a color wheel.

□ *Color Mixing*—For a child, the experience of blending colors can be full of excitement and discovery.

□ *Contrast: Light and Dark*—While not necessarily being able to define the term, children should be aware of the polarities that exist in nature. When two things are together, they may intensify each other while showing their differences. Lessons in the effects of light and dark on each other can only add to this understanding.

□ *Cool Colors*—The colors on the blue side of the color wheel that are usually associated with water, sky, and foliage.

□ *Monochrome or Monochromatic Color Scheme*—A color scheme limited to tints and shades of one color.

□ *Primary Colors*—The basic colors from which all other colors can be made by mixing. Red, blue, and yellow are the primary colors in painting.

□ *Recognition of Complementary Colors*—Red/green, orange/blue, purple/yellow. The complementary colors are those pairs of colors that appear opposite each other on the color wheel, and contrast most strongly when used in combination. They neutralize each other when mixed, creating gray or brown.

□ *Secondary Colors*—The colors created by mixing equal portions of two primary colors. Purple, green, and orange are the secondary colors in painting.

□ *Shades*—Gradations of a color made by mixing with black.

□ *Tints*—Gradations of a color made by mixing with white.

□ *Warm Colors*—The colors on the orange side of the color wheel that are usually associated with earth, sun, and fire.

The following sequence of activities, designed to explore colors, offers children a chance to freely create and express themselves without caring about right or wrong and a step-by-step introduction to skills and concepts in a context relevant to the children's needs and interests. First we explore individual colors in depth. When we move on to working with pairs of colors, first we work with complementary colors that children do not mix. Then we move on to analogous colors and encourage mixing. We read Leo Lionni's *Little Blue and Little Yellow* before mixing yellow and blue to create green. These activities culminate with several projects that make use of the full spectrum. By then, the child has developed an understanding of the effective use of color and has sufficient technical skills to handle a full palette with aplomb.

Here is a quick and easy guide to a logical sequence of related projects.

Experiencing One Color
Black/White
Red
Blue
Yellow
Purple
Green
Orange
Brown
Gray
Silver
Gold

Experiencing Two Colors/Complementary Colors
Red/Green
Yellow/Purple
Orange/Blue

Experiencing Multiple Colors
Primary Colors
Warm Colors
Cool Colors
Fluorescent Colors
Red, White, and Blue
Multiple Colors

Color Mixing
Tints/Shades
Blue + Yellow = Green
Red + Yellow = Orange
Red + Blue = Purple

Throughout this book I have encouraged you to coordinate information on a given subject and present it to children in a variety of ways. Concepts should be explored on many different levels to be fully understood and to take advantage of children's many different learning styles. I have prepared the following charts for you to save you the time and trouble of reinventing the teaching of some art concepts by indicating songs, games, food, literature, and multimedia art projects in some of the basic art concepts. I think that once you have acquired the habit of teaching your child this way, it will be easy for you to coordinate learning activities on other subjects as well. When you have decided on the subject you would like to present to your child, simply locate the chart of that subject, gather your materials, and let your child start exploring.

Black and White

Individual Colors:	Black	White
Concept	Recognizing and naming colors	Recognizing and naming colors
	Contrast	Contrast
	Painting	Painting
	Modeling	Modeling
Materials	White paper	Black paper
	Multicolor finger paint paper	Black chalkboard
	Black paint	White chalk
	Black crayon	Toothpicks
	Charcoal	Scratchboard
	White round and rectangular stickers	Wooden stylus
		White sheet
	Paper towels and soapy water for hands	Cotton balls
		White glue
		White Model Magic
		Styrofoam
Book	*Ben's Trumpet*, Rachel Isadora	*Animals in Black and White*, Phyllis Libacher Tildes
Snack	Raisins and black string licorice	Marshmallows
Song	"Baa Baa Black Sheep," "Black"	"I Spy White"
Games	Cover pointer fingers with black and white finger puppets and recite with appropriate	Dress up like a ghost and try to scare each other

	Black	White
	hand movement "Two little black and white birds sitting on the hill. One named Jack and the other named Jill. Fly away Jack, fly away Jill. Come back Jack, come back Jill. Two little black and white birds sitting on the hill. One named Jack and the other named Jill."	
Drawing	Draw with black crayon on white paper Draw with a stick of charcoal on white paper	Draw with white chalk on blackboard or black paper Use a wooden stylus to scratch picture into scratchboard
Painting	Finger paint on multicolor finger paint paper with black finger paint	Paint with white tempera paint on black paper. Use a white-handled Stubby Brush
Collage	Read Ben's Trumpet and do a sticker collage using both round and rectangular white stickers on black paper Do a collage with black and white newspaper scraps	Dip cotton balls in white glue and stick them on black cardboard
Sculpture	Experiment with black play dough	Experiment with white Model Magic Build a sculpture out of white Styrofoam. Each piece can be glued or connected with a toothpick

Primary Colors

	Red	Yellow	Blue
Concept	Understanding lines Scribbling Recognition and naming of colors Painting with a brush Expressing emotions Pasting	Recognition and naming of colors Painting with a brush Expressing emotions Creating a highlight	Recognition and naming of primary colors Painting with a brush Expressing emotions Pasting
Materials	Red Stubby Brush Red self-adhesive stickers White paper Red paper Red play dough Red scraps in assorted shapes	White paper and yellow paper Yellow tempera paint Yellow Stubby Brush Yellow play dough Yellow felt pennants on sticks	Blue scarf Visual aids: paintings in one color, especially from Picasso's "Blue Period" Blue tempera paint Blue Stubby Brush

	Red tempera paint Scissors Red scarf Paste	Black acrylic paint Black marker Yellow self-adhesive stickers	Blue crayon Blue marker Blue play dough
Book	*Red Is Best*, Kathy Stinson	*Yellow Yellow*, Mark Alan Stamaty *Goodnight, Goodnight*, Eve Rice	*New Blue Shoes*, Eve Rice *Kinda' Blue*, Ann Grifalconi
Snack	Strawberries	Bananas, lemonade	Blueberries
Song	"Are You Ready for Red?" "Today My Color Is Red"	"Give Me a Yell for Yellow" "Y-E-L-L-O-W"	"Lavender's Blue"—old English nursery song "Little Boy Blue"—nursery rhyme Songs from the album *There's Music in the Colors,* by Willy Strickland and James Earle "Blue" "Look Blue"
Games	Sing and do the things indicated by the following: "Put the red scarf on your head, on your head Put the scarf on your head, on your head Put the red scarf on your head Until it's time for bed Put the red scarf on your head, on your head Put the red scarf in the air, in the air . . . And leave it about a year . . . Put the red scarf on your nose, on your nose . . . Put the red scarf on your ears, on your ears . . . Until your birthday nears . . . Put the red scarf on your back, on your back . . . And give it a little whack . . ."	Sing the song "Give Me a Yell for Yellow" and march to the music while waving your pennant	Dance with blue scarves, making up directions as you go along: "Shake the blue scarf" "Run with the blue scarf" "Jump over the blue scarf" "Wave the blue scarf" "Exchange blue scarves with your neighbor"
Drawing	Draw with a red crayon or marker on white	Put only one yellow sticker on the white page and	Do a drawing with a blue marker or crayon

	Red	Yellow	Blue
	paper or draw with black marker on red paper	complete the drawing using only a black marker. The yellow sticker becomes the highlight of the page	
Painting	Do a painting using only red paint on white paper. Use a red-handled brush	Use yellow paint on white paper and then try it on black paper Create a painting on a yellow felt pennant using black acrylic paint	Paint with blue tempera on white paper. Use a blue-handled brush
Collage	Use red self-adhesive circle stickers on white paper, red stars on black paper	Use yellow stickers on black paper Do a collage of yellow scraps in assorted shapes, sizes, and a wide variety of yellows	Do a collage using a variety of blue scraps in assorted textures
Sculpture	Mix up a batch of red play dough with which to experiment	Play with yellow play dough	Experiment with blue play dough *Optional: If you choose to read *Yellow Yellow*, make a yellow hat according to the directions in the book. The child can wear it while painting and marching to the song

Secondary Colors

	Green	Purple	Orange
Concept	Recognition and naming of colors Painting with a brush Pasting Drawing	Recognition and naming of colors Surrealism Drawing with hard utensils Painting with a brush Pasting Expressing emotions	Recognition and naming of colors Drawing with soft drawing utensils Painting with a brush Pasting Expressing emotions
Materials	White paper Green tempera paint Brushes Water Green envelope or shopping bag	Purple crayons White glue White paper Purple paper Purple tempera paint Black tempera Facial tissue	Orange tempera Black paper White paper Water An orange Orange-handled brush Spill-proof paint

		Red and blue tissue paper or cellophane paper scraps Red and blue Model Magic	container Facial tissues A pumpkin Orange chalk Orange paper Orange stickers or scraps
Book	Spring Green, Valerie Selkowe and Jeni Crisler Bassett The Big Green Pocketbook, Candice Ransom and Felicia Bond	Harold and the Purple Crayon, Crockett Johnson A Picture for Harold's Room, Crockett Johnson	The Big Orange Splot, Daniel Manus Pinkwater
Snack	Green seedless grapes, cut up to prevent choking	Purple seedless grapes Grape juice Grape jelly on cracker	Oranges or clementines
Song	"Then You've Seen Green"	"Purple, Urple Goo"	"Orange Is an Orange"
Game	Dance and move to the song: "Boom, boom went the little green frog one day Boom, boom went the little green frog. Boom, boom went the little green frog one day And he hopped, hopped, hopped away."	Draw a magic purple circle, using Harold's crayon, or use purple hoops. Sing: "We're walking in a circle, We're walking in a circle, We're walking in a circle, and Now it's time to stop Hopping . . . Crawling . . . Running . . . Skating . . ."	Sit in circle, pass an orange as long as music plays. Whoever has orange when the music stops "wins." Keep playing until every child has "won"
Drawing	Read Green Wilma by Tedd Arnold and do an all-green drawing	Draw with Harold's "magic" crayon Draw with blue and red chalk and blend with a scrap of facial tissue to create purple	Draw with black markers on orange paper Draw with orange chalk on black paper
Painting	Read Spring Green use a green-handled brush to paint with green tempera on a different shade of green paper	Paint with purple tempera on white paper Paint with black paint on purple paper	Use a brush with orange paint on white and/or black paper to paint or do printing with a fork Paint with black tempera or acrylic paint on a pumpkin
Collage	Read the book The Big Green Pocketbook. Go on a treasure hunt, collecting only green collage material, and put them in a green	Collage of red and blue tissue paper or cellophane paper craps	Use orange stickers or paste various orange scraps on white or black paper

	Green	Purple	Orange
	envelope or bag. Make a collage using your green treasures		
Sculpture	Experiment bending and twisting three green pipe cleaners that are attached to green cardboard	Play with red and blue Crayola Model Magic, which, when mixed, create purple	Use orange play dough to experiment with Help an adult carve a pumpkin. Paint it

Reflective Colors

	Silver	Gold
Concept	Increase perception of the world around us Painting with a brush	Recognition and naming of colors Painting with a brush Drawing with various hard utensils
Materials	Silver and black tempera paint Brushes Child-size mirror Black and white paper Aluminum foil Silver paper scraps Glue Silver crayons Silver glitter	Metallic gold tempera Brushes White or black paper Metallic gold crayons and pencils Gold paper White sun visor White glue Gold self-adhesive stars Gold wire Gold glitter
Book	If I Weren't Me . . . Who Would I Be? illustrated by Pam Adams	King Midas and the Golden Touch, Nathaniel Hawthorne
Snack	Wrapped Hershey's Kisses	Honey golden graham crackers and/or candy wrapped in gold foil
Song	None available	None available
Game	Move and study your reflection in the mirror. With your partner, pretend one of you is the mirror. Other child moves and "mirror" reflects movements	Play Midas Touch tag: every person who is touched by the "sculptor" turns to a golden statue
Drawing	Draw with a silver crayon on black or white paper	Draw with gold crayons or gold-colored pencils on black or white paper
Painting	Read the book If I Weren't Me . . . Who Would I Be? Look at the reflective surface. Imagine yourself in the picture. Paint with tempera on mirror or use silver paint on black paper	Paint with gold paint on black or white paper and then try painting with black paint on gold paper
Collage	"Paint" with glue and sprinkle silver glitter on the glue	Do a collage of self-adhesive gold stars on black paper Decorate a white cardboard sun

		visor with gold glitter. "Paint" it with glue and sprinkle gold glitter in the glue
Sculpture	Crumble, twist, and combine pieces of aluminum foil into a sculpture	Use gold wire to create a wire sculpture

Neutral Colors

	Brown	Gray
Concept	Recognition and naming of colors Painting with a brush Expressing emotions Increase perception of the world around us	Mixing colors Painting with a brush
Materials	Scissors Mud Water Brown paper bag Brown fabric Paper scraps Brown paint Box tops Corks Brown teddy bear White paint Crayons Paste Mural paper Brushes	Black and white tempera paint Brushes White paper Gray paper Gray stuffed animal
Book	*The Big Brown Bear*, Gustaf Tenggren *Brown Is a Beautiful Color*, Jean Carey Bond	*Why Opossum Is Gray*, Janet Palazzo *The Old Banjo*, Dennis Hasely
Snack	Graham crackers and prune juice	
Song	"It Makes Us Think of Brown"	"My Little Grey Pony," Diller Quaille "Little Gray Mouse," Charity Baley, words by Marian Abeson
Game	Group play with brown bears: sit in a circle and take turns making up things to do— "Kiss the brown bear" "Shake the brown bear" "Hug the brown bear" "Throw the brown bear up in the air"	Play with stuffed Babar or other toy elephant

	Brown	Gray
Drawing	Draw on brown paper bags with brown crayons and markers	Draw on gray paper using black and white chalk
Painting	Paint with dark brown paint on butcher paper or brown shopping bags Do brown tempera footprints on a long roll of brown mural paper	Mix black and white paint to create several shades of gray. Paint on gray paper
Collage	Make a collage using brown paper, yarn, and fabric scraps in assorted textures, shapes, and sizes	Do a collage using varied examples of gray paper
Sculpture	Manipulate mud to create mud pies or mud sculptures Use corks in brown cardboard box tops to create a shadow box sculpture	Glue gray rocks together to create a sculpture

Fluorescent Colors

Concept	Fluorescent colors Pasting Painting with a brush Drawing
Materials	Fluorescent crayons or chalk Fluorescent stickers Fluorescent tempera paint Fluorescent construction paper Black construction paper Black tempera paint Brushes White glue White paper Blank masks Black hoop Black yarn Small traffic cones
Book	*The Neon Motorcycle*, Thomas Rockwell and Michael Horen
Snack	Peanut M&Ms Kiwi fruit
Song	None available
Game	Toss black hoop over fluorescent-colored Styrofoam or plastic traffic cones
Drawing	Use fluorescent chalk or crayons to draw with
Painting	Paint with black tempera on white paper, leaving blank spaces and allow to dry. Fill in blank areas with fluorescent paint
Collage	Use self-adhesive fluorescent stickers on black paper Use fluorescent paper scraps and glue on black paper
Sculpture	Combine large fluorescent beads and black wire to create a mobile

Complementary Colors

	Red/Green	Yellow/Purple	Blue/Orange
Concept	Complementary colors Painting with a brush Pasting Drawing with hard utensil	Complementary colors Painting with a brush Pasting Drawing with hard utensil	Complementary colors Painting with a brush Pasting Drawing with hard utensil
Materials	Red and green tempera Red Christmas ornaments One brush per color White paper Scraps of red and green wrapping paper Red and green pencils Evergreen wreath	Purple tempera paint Yellow and purple marker White paper Purple paint Yellow scrap paper Yellow sponges Purple cardboard Purple food coloring Yellow crayon Hard-boiled egg	Orange paper scraps Blue chalk Blue paper Blue tempera paint Orange paper Orange Twisteez and/ or pipe cleaners Blue cardboard
Book	*One Mitten Lewis*, Helen Kay	*Hello, Red Fox*, Eric Carle	*The Orange Book*, Richard McGuire
Snack	Strawberries and green seedless grapes	Banana and seedless purple grapes	Blueberries and orange or clementine slices
Song	"Red, Yellow, Green Light" "Crayon Neighbors"	"Crayon Neighbors"	"Crayon Neighbors"
Game	"Red light, green light"—children move and respond to leader's signal: red means "stop," green means "go"	Play with yellow and purple balloons	Play with orange and blue balls
Drawing	Draw with red and green pencils on white paper	Draw with yellow and purple markers on white paper Draw on a hard-boiled egg with yellow crayon and dip in purple food coloring solution	Draw with blue chalk on orange paper
Painting	On white paper, paint with red paint and green paint. Cover the entire sheet of paper; no mixing	Paint with purple paint on yellow paper	Paint with blue tempera paint on orange paper
Collage	Paste scraps of red and green wrapping paper on white paper	Paste a variety of shapes, sizes, textures, and color variations of yellow paper scraps on a sheet of purple paper	Paste a variety of orange scraps on a blue sheet of paper
Sculpture	Decorate an evergreen wreath using red ornaments	Create a construction out of small scraps of yellow sponge on purple cardboard	Use orange Twisteez or pipe cleaners to create a wire sculpture. Mount on blue cardboard

Warm and Cool Colors

	Warm Colors	Cool Colors
Concept	Warm colors Painting Drawing Pasting	Cool colors Painting Drawing Pasting
Materials	Scrap of suede stretched over four sticks that have been tied together at the corners Scraps of paper in red, orange, and yellow Glue Red, orange, yellow toothpicks or sticks Small branches Hole punch Red, orange, and yellow chalks Red, yellow, and orange paint Brushes	Blue and green paper scraps Blue and green tempera paint Brushes
Book	*Indian Paintbrush*, Tomie dePaola *Musicians of the Sun*, Gerald McDermott	*The Painter and the Wild Swans*, Claude Clement *Northern Country Night*, Daniel San Souci *Dawn*, Uri Shulevitz
Snack	Warm tomato soup	Pistachio ice cream
Song	"The Bonfire," Estonian folk tune, words by Frances Ford	"Old Jack Frost," Moselle Renstrom
Game	Play "hot potato using a warm, red baked potato	Play a variation of "hot potato" using ice cubes made with blue food coloring
Drawing	Read *Musicians of the Sun* and draw large balls of color with warm-colored chalks Blend chalks with facial tissue in a movement outward from the center, to create the feeling of rays of the sun	Do a collage on blue paper, using a wide variety of blue and green paper scraps
Painting	Read *Indian Paintbrush*. Do a painting on suede, just like the main character in the book did. Use the "colors of the sun," as in the story, to create your picture	Print with geometric sponges using blue and green paint
Collage	On yellow paper, create a collage Use red and orange scraps	Do a collage using blue and green paper
Sculpture	Create a 3-dimensional mandala using red, yellow, and orange Model Magic and adding warm color sticks to radiate out of the center	Create a snow or ice sculpture

Multiple Colors

Concept	Drawing with both hard and soft drawing utensils
Materials	Chunk-O-Crayons
	Red, yellow, blue, green, purple, and orange tempera paints
	Scraps of paper
	White glue
Book	*Oh, Were They Ever Happy!* Peter Spier
Snack	Fruit salad
Song	"There's Music in the Colors"
Game	Play with water using containers
	Pitchers and funnels made out of red, yellow, blue, green, purple, and orange—plastic
Drawing	Draw with a multicolor Chunk-O-Crayon on white paper
	Draw with multicolored chalks on the sidewalk
Painting	Using one container and one brush per color, do a painting using red, yellow, blue, green, purple, and orange tempera paint
Collage	Paste red, yellow, blue, orange, purple, and green feathers on cardboard
Sculpture	Assemblage using assorted colors of scraps, such as sponges, blocks, bottle caps

Multiple Colors

	Primary Colors	Red, White, and Blue	Rainbow
Concept	Drawing with hard utensils Pasting Painting with a brush	Utilizing art to convey a message Abstract art Pasting Painting with a brush	Multiple colors Painting with a brush Drawing with hard utensils
Materials	Red, yellow, and blue crayons Paste White paper Crayons 18" × 24" white paper Brush for each color Water Sheer scarves: red, yellow, blue Blank slides	Red and blue scrap paper White background paper Scissors Blank flags Paste Red, white, and blue acrylic paint Optional: Package of precut self-adhesive metallic stars Red, white, and blue tempera paint Red-handled brush Blue-handled brush Red and blue crayons Empty boxes	Red, yellow, blue, orange, green, and purple tempera paint with a little liquid soap mixed in Brushes with coordinated color handles Background paper White glue Water Twelve-inch ribbons in red, orange, yellow, blue, green, and purple
Book	*Color Dance,* Ann Jonas *Adventures of Three Colors,* Annette Tison and Talus Taylor	*Stars and Stripes: Our National Flag,* Leonard Everitt Fisher	*A Rainbow of My Own,* Don Freeman

Snack	Red, yellow, and blue jelly beans or fruit salad made of bananas, blueberries, and strawberries	Blueberries and strawberries with shredded coconut on top	Fruit salad
Song	"Just Three Colors," words and music by Joe Raposo	Any John Philip Sousa marching songs	"Sing a Rainbow," Arthur Hamilton
Game	Using transparent red, yellow, and blue scarves, dance and wave scarves in the air	After creating a flag, march in your own parade	Play with a prism, catching light in it
Drawing	Draw with red, yellow, and blue crayons	Do a drawing using these symbolic colors: white—faith; red—courage; blue—strength Use a red and blue crayon on white paper	Draw with red, yellow, green, orange, purple, and blue crayons and draw with multicolor Chunk-O-Crayons
Painting	Paint on large white paper. Use red, yellow, and blue paint with a color-coded brush for each color. Use extra brushes and empty containers for mixing	Paint with red and blue acrylic paint on blank flags	Paint on your window, using all of the colors. Use a separate brush for each color
Collage	Do a collage on white paper using red, yellow, and blue scraps	Do a collage using red and white paper scraps on a blue background. Add stars if you want Place red and blue scraps on white paper until you are pleased with the arrangement. Add stars if you want.	Do a collage on cardboard using ribbons in red, yellow, orange, blue, green, and purple
Sculpture	String red, yellow, and blue beads on yarn or pipe cleaners	Build a sculpture using empty boxes. Paint the boxes red, white, or blue and allow them to dry before gluing them together	Build with multicolor Legos

Tints and Shades

	Red	Blue
Concept	Drawing with soft utensils Pasting Painting Mixing Colors	Drawing with hard utensils Pasting Painting Mixing colors

Materials	White paper Black tempera paint Red tempera paint White tempera paint Red background paper Red and pink scraps Assortment of pink and red chalk Pink erasers Brushes Glue	White paper Blue, black, and white tempera paint Brushes with blue, black, and white handles Water Pencils in many tints and shades of blue Blue scraps Blue sponge Glue
Book	*First Pink Light,* Eloise Greenfield	*The Great Blueness and Other Predicaments,* Arnold Lobel
Snack	Watermelon	Blueberry yogurt
Song	"Pink Elephants on Parade"	"Blue" "Look Blue"
Game	Dance, waving a variety of red transparent scarves	Dance, waving a variety of blue transparent scarves
Drawing	Do a drawing using a large assortment of pink and red chalk	Do a drawing using a large collection of pencils in various tints and shades of blue
Painting	Make tints of red by starting with white and adding a small amount of red to create pink. Create a shade of red by adding a small amount of black paint to red. Do a painting in tints and shades of red Hold your brush in your hand and "paint" in the air, trying to get the feel of moving your arm from your shoulder instead of just moving your fingers Paint a large "scribble," creating enclosed shapes wherever the lines cross. In each shape, paint a different tint or shade of pink	Demonstrate how to make tints of blue by mixing it with white (hint: add small amounts of blue to white paint rather than vice versa) Read the first twelve pages of *The Great Blueness and Other Predicaments* (can be read in stages, with the related color being explored as it is in the story). Look at pictures from Picasso's "Blue Period" and read *Kinda' Blue.* Do a painting on white paper using only a blue paint that you have created Paint with a blue-handled brush Demonstrate how to make shades of blue by adding small amounts of black paint to blue Execute painting using only blue, black, and white paint
Collage	Do a collage using a collection of pink and red scraps in assorted shapes and patterns	Do a collage using assorted tints of blue scraps on a blue piece of paper
Sculpture	Do a construction by gluing pink erasers together and mounting on cardboard	Glue together scraps of blue sponge

Color Mixing

"Color Mixing Adventure" by Susan Striker

For a color adventure that's rich and lush,
All you need is paint and a brush.
To create an orange that's warm and mellow
Add a touch of red to yellow.
Mix together red and blue
and you'll have a purple hue.
Blue and yellow mix up to make green,
The coolest color you ever have seen.
Add white to any color, here's a hint
Now you've gone and made a tint.
Add black to a color and what have you made?
That darkest of color is called a shade.
Red, yellow, and blue together make brown.
We're finished now, you can put your brush down.

	Blue + Yellow = Green	Red + Yellow = Orange	Red + Blue = Purple
Concepts	Analogous colors	Analogous colors	Pasting
	Color mixing	Overlapping	Overlapping
	Overlapping	Color mixing	Color mixing
		Expressing emotions	
Materials	15" × 18" (or larger) background paper	Red and yellow paint	Red and blue tempera
	Blue cellophane and yellow cellophane	15" × 18" (or larger) background paper	12" × 18" background paper
	Crayon or pencil for each child to write his or her name	Three brushes per child	Three brushes, one with a red handle, one with a purple handle, one with a blue handle, and one empty container
	Paste	Red and yellow tissue paper scraps	White background paper
	Paste sticks	Empty cups	Red and blue tissue or cellophane
	Blue and yellow crayons	Yellow and red chalk	Red and blue chalk
	Sheer blue and yellow scarves	Sheer red and yellow scarves	Facial tissue
			Sheer red and blue scarves
Book	*Little Blue and Little Yellow,* Leo Lionni	*Red Socks and Yellow Socks,* Joy Cowley	*The Red Horse and the Bluebird,* Sandy Rabinowitz
		Reread Leo Lionni's *Little Blue and Little Yellow,* substituting red for blue and orange for green	
Snack	The child can pour a touch of blue food coloring into lemonade	Fruit salad made with oranges, red apples, and bananas	Fruit salad of strawberries, blueberries, and purple grapes, cut up to safe sizes

Song	"Then You've Seen Green" "Orange Is an Orange" "Bein' Green," Joe Raposo		"Purple Urple Goo"
Game	Read *Color Dance* and dance with sheer blue and yellow scarves	Read *Color Dance* and dance with red and yellow scarves	Read *Color Dance* and dance with sheer red and blue scarves
Drawing	Read *Little Blue and Little Yellow*. While drawing with crayon, overlap yellow and blue on paper to create green	Choose either black or white paper to draw on with red and yellow chalk, blending the chalk with tissue to create orange	Draw with red and blue chalk and blend it with a tissue to create purple
Painting	In a large mixing bowl, mix one or two quarts of water with blue food coloring, and another with yellow food coloring. Fold Dippity Dye paper and dip in one color, then the other, to create some green areas. Open and allow to dry	Paint an orange blob on child's paper in advance. Read the story *The Big Orange Splot* Using orange tempera paint and an orange-handled brush, complete your picture, which started as an orange splot, as you see it in your mind's eye Choose either a black or white sheet of paper to paint on. Use the red brush for red paint, the yellow brush for yellow paint, and the orange brush for creating orange paint. Mix red and yellow in the empty cup	Sing "Purple Urple Goo." As the song suggests, "take a gob of red paint and a gob of blue" and mix together to create purple Use the red brush for picking up the red paint, the blue brush for picking up the blue paint, and the purple brush for mixing and painting with Read *The Red Horse and the Bluebird*. Use one brush to paint with red, a second to paint with blue. Use a third brush and the empty container to mix purple
Collage	Hold blue and yellow cellophane up to the light. Slowly overlap until you create green Arrange scraps on background paper and paste in place, using a wooden stick and white glue Read relevant portions of the book *The Adventures of Three Colors*. Paste blue and yellow cellophane on blank acetate sheets and have a slide show	Do a collage using yellow and red tissue paper. Be sure to overlap to create orange Read relevant portions of the book *The Adventures of Three Colors*. Paste red and yellow cellophane on blank acetate sheets and have a slide show	Do a collage of red and blue tissue paper or cellophane, overlapping the scraps to create purple Read relevant portions of the book *The Adventures of Three Colors*. Paste red and blue cellophane on blank acetate slides and have a slide show
Sculpture	Work with blue and yellow Model Magic and combine to create green	Experiment with combining red and yellow Model Magic to make orange	Mix red and blue Model Magic to create purple

CHAPTER 7

Exploring Shapes and Art Concepts

Learning to differentiate between circles, squares, and triangles and then learning their names is a complicated business. It helps to work with only one shape at a time, perhaps in assorted colors, textures, and sizes. Talk about the name of the shape, compare various sizes, demonstrate the quickest, neatest pasting technique, and let the child experiment freely. In the next few days, point out the shape when you see it, not mentioning the myriad of other shapes you see so as to avoid confusing your child. Mastering one shape at a time is a reasonable goal for any preschooler. You don't need to talk about making realistic objects out of these shapes. What the child needs is to look at, touch, name, and work with shapes, while at the same time experimenting with the properties and possibilities of paint, drawing utensils, sculpture materials, paste, and paper.

Circles don't always have to be wheels, buttons, and flower centers. It's okay for a circle just to be a circle. Let your child explore the meaning of circles and see the differences between big and little ones, light and dark ones. A simple reminder of how to paste them on the paper is the only explanation needed. After the activity is over, offer your child a round cookie and mention that it's a circle just like the paper circles on your paper. Point out the full moon that evening and that the buttons on Daddy's shirts are circles, but when the child is working, paper is paper, not the moon. Adults need to understand that a circle is as real and as important in and of itself as it is when it's part of something recognizable. Consider using a circle as background paper when you repeat this project and when painting. Read a book about circles like *Round and Round and Round* by Tana Hoban. There are very few books that concentrate on a single shape. You can be selective and read relevant portions of books that focus on the shape you are exploring with your child.

Sing a song or make up your own story about circles, play with balls, and end playtime with "Ring Around the Rosie." All of these activities help children experience the essence of roundness. Their aesthetic sense is challenged by the wide variety of colors, sizes, and textures that can be arranged in the most effective manner, within the boundaries of a circular sheet of paper.

As we guide and nurture our children, it is important to keep in mind their unique talents and styles of learning. There are children who grasp concepts more readily when engaging in physical manifestations of those concepts, while others are visual or auditory learners. "Ring Around the Rosie," bouncing balls, and blowing bubbles, painting on round paper, or having a hole cut out of a sheet of paper and having to work around it are different ways to experience the concept of "round." In preparing this curriculum of shapes, I include several different activities that are designed both to reinforce learning and to address different styles of learning.

Howard Gardner, Ph.D., of Harvard University, has helped us see that people have not one, but multiple intelligences. Our levels of intelligence in each area affect the way we learn. Through his work we know that there is musical intelligence, bodily kinesthetic intelligence, logical-mathematical intelligence, linguistic intelligence, spatial intelligence, interpersonal intelligence, intrapersonal intelligence, and naturalistic intelligence. To teach concepts thoroughly and address each child's learning style, we must permit exploration through more than one technique. A child may see a circle and hear one described, but may also need to walk in a circle, read a story that is circular (with the end coming back to the beginning), and roll a ball to fully grasp the concept. The charts that follow present shape facts and some basic art concepts in ways that meet all facets of our children's multiple intelligences to maximize learning. Based on what we know about how children learn, the traditional teaching techniques of offering children adult-drawn shapes to trace, color, and cut out are the least likely to achieve success. It is amazing how many preschools nevertheless persist in perpetuating this ineffective style of teaching.

Keep your focus on the shape facts listed on pages 140–41, but don't think

Multiple circle experiences

that a child who can already differentiate between shapes won't benefit from engaging in a wide variety of multimedia experiences. These activities provide in-depth understanding, not merely superficial learning.

Shape Facts

□ *Amorphic shapes* are fluid and free-form and not related at all to geometry.

□ *Circle* is a single curved line that is equally distant from a point at the center.

□ *Concentric shapes* are different-sized shapes on a plane with the same center—picture a circle within a circle within a circle.

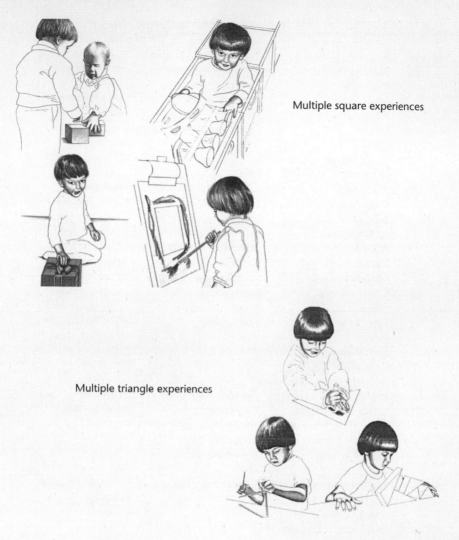

Multiple square experiences

Multiple triangle experiences

□ *Geometric shapes* are regular forms such as circles, squares, triangles, and octagons.

□ *Oval* resembles an egg or an ellipse.

□ *Positive shapes* are the images in a picture; negative spaces remain empty.

□ *Spiral* coils continuously circle around a point, in curves that increase (or decrease).

□ *Square* has four equal sides and four right angles.

□ *Star* is a flat figure having five or six points.

□ *Triangle* is a geometric figure with three sides and three angles.

Geometric Shapes

	Circle	Square	Triangle
Concept	Geometric shapes Drawing with hard drawing utensils Painting with a roller Sculpture: adding on	Using geometric shapes Painting with a brush Pasting Sculpture: adding on	Geometric shapes Painting with a brush Pasting Drawing with hard utensils
Materials	Balls Bubbles Round drawing paper Ritz crackers Paint rollers Round foam Round cardboard sculpture base Water tub Triarco Mr. Button Badge parts Round stickers Hoops Cloth or large pipe tunnel Pizza rounds Cardboard circles Self-adhesive round stickers	Square paper with a square cut out of the center Scraps of wooden blocks Paste Square-tip brush Tempera paint Square scraps of colored paper, wallpaper, wrapping paper, etc., in assorted sizes and colors Square-shaped stacking plastic containers Water Graph paper	Triangular scarf Paint White triangular paper Triangle music instrument Triangle paper scraps in assorted colors, sizes, and textures Crayons Styrofoam cone Feathers, pipe cleaners, straws, etc. Triangle-shaped felt Twelve-inch dowel
Books	*Round and Round and Round*, Tana Hoban *Painting the Moon*, a folk tale from Estonia retold by Carl Withers	*The Square Ben Drew*, Peter Barrett *The Box Book*, Cecilia Maloney *Draw Me a Square*, Robin Suprane	*The Greedy Triangle*, Marilyn Burns
Snack	Eat Ritz or other round crackers Oranges, grapes, or other round fruits can be observed before eating as well	Saltines and a box of juice	A slice of pizza or nachos
Song	"The Wheels of the Bus" "Dip and Print" "A Circle"	"That's a Square"	"The Triangle Song," an old song with words added by Marjorie Atkins (Alyn and Bacon, 1963, *This Is Music*) Play a triangle
Game	Stand in a circle, holding hands. Recite "Ring Around the Rosie, pocket full of posies, ashes, ashes, all fall down," at which point the children all fall down. The second	Draw a square area on the floor. This is the "stamping room." Children stamp to the sound of a drum when they are in the stamping room. A circle on the floor becomes the jumping	Water play with funnels Play with a marble chute Using a triangle scarf, one person hides his or her face. Sing "Where

verse is "The cows are in the meadow, huddled all together, thunder [as children pound on the floor mat], lightning, lightning [shake hands in the air], and they all jump up."

Crawl through tunnel

Sit around the circle on the floor and sing "The Wheels of the Bus," doing hand movements appropriate to the words

Produce a "magic ball." Demonstrate that it can become heavy, small, cold, wet, slippery. It can change into a snowball, balloon, bubble, etc. Pass it around and tell the children what the "magic ball" is doing

Pretend that your finger is a crayon. Draw circles in the air. Now pretend that your nose, toe, elbow, etc., is the crayon. Draw circles in the air

Pretend that the group is a balloon. Blow it up. Keep blowing until the balloon gets too big and bursts, and everyone can fall down

Use your whole body to draw a circle: spin, roll, etc.

room. After you have completed the triangle unit, a triangle can become the tiptoe room

Four children can hold hands and become a circle or a square

Children can arrange child-size cartons on the floor to become trains that they can "ride," cities, and houses, safe places to protect them from sharks in the "ocean"

On the square, which was drawn on the floor in advance, have the children march on the line to the beat of a drum, going faster and faster, stopping when the music stops. Emphasize how we change direction at each corner, while when we march in a circle we never change. Suggest that the children find corners of their own bodies, such as knees, elbows, heels, noses

Let four children become one square

Pretend that your finger, elbow, toe, nose, etc., is a pencil. Sharpen the pencil and draw squares in the air

Play tag with square being "safe"

Build with square blocks

Play hopscotch

Play with square shapes such as beanbags or pillows, and sing songs that have children touch different parts of themselves. For instance: Put the square on your head on your head, put the square on your head on your head, put the square on your head until you go to bed. Put the square on

Is Suzie, Where Is Suzie" and when you sing "Here I am" the hiding person uncovers his or her face

To the circle and square already on the floor, add a triangle, which becomes the tiptoe room. Or draw three triangles on the floor. One is to skip to, one you gallop to, the third you hop to. The children can make up more ideas about how to reach other triangles, which you can then draw for them. (If you can't draw on the floor, use tape or yarn to outline the triangles.)

Create an obstacle to climb on or over. Reach the end and be handed the stick to ring the triangle. (Children should not climb holding the stick, for safety's sake)

	Circle	Square	Triangle
		your head on your head. Put the square on your toe and let the cold wind blow, put the square on your toe on your toe (or "and wave it to and fro"), etc.	
Drawing	Draw on a large round piece of paper. Follow up by drawing on a piece of paper that has a round hole cut out of it. Draw on round paper to create badges	Do a drawing on graph paper	Draw on a large piece of triangular paper
Painting	Paint with a roller on very large paper. Read *Painting the Moon*. Children paint using light colors on one side and dark colors on the reverse. Dip the ends of a cardboard toilet paper or paper towel roll in paint and print with it	Paint on a sheet of square paper that has a square cut out of the center of it. Print with square scraps of sponge	Paint on triangular piece of felt. Add a dowel to it to create a pennant
Collage	Do a collage using self-adhesive, colored circle stickers	Do a collage of square scraps made out of papers in assorted colors, sizes, and textures	Paste paper triangles precut out of assorted colors, sizes, and textures
Sculpture	Roll clay "snakes". Go on a treasure hunt to find only round things. Paste bottle tops, coins, cardboard tubes on a round cardboard base	Glue square scraps of wood to a base. Optional: Allow the glue to dry and paint it when it is finished	Stick pipe cleaners, feathers, or straws into a Styrofoam cone

After your child has experienced circles, squares, and triangles individually, present all three shapes together in an integrated unit.

Geometric Shapes

	Oval	Holes	Amorphic
Concept	Utilizing wax resist. Pasting. Painting. Drawing with hard utensils	Negative space. Cutting. Drawing with hard utensils. Painting with a brush. Pasting. Printing	Modeling. Painting with a brush. Amorphic shapes. Painting with a brush. Working with a group. Pasting
Materials	Hard-boiled eggs	Self-adhesive	Large white mural

	Crayons Precut paper ovals in assorted sizes and colors Water Food coloring Plastic eggs Craft items (pipe cleaners, feathers, straws, sticks, etc.) Styrofoam egg	reinforcements Paper Hole puncher Crayons Tempera paint Water Brushes Cardboard toilet paper rolls Items with holes in them (keys, toilet paper rolls, paper clips)	Paper Blank white puzzles Brushes Tempera paints Roll of mural paper Elmer's glue Old puzzles Amorphic-shaped white paper Amorphic scraps in assorted colors, textures, and sizes Optional: glitter, pin backs
Book	*The Easter Egg Artists,* Adrienne Adams	*The Very Hungry Caterpillar,* Eric Carle *Fly Hoops Fly,* Yutaka Sugita *Holes and Peeks,* Ann Jonas	*Jigsaw,* Miriam Moss *The Little Red Ant,* Yvonne Hooker
Snack	Townhouse cookies and/or hard-boiled egg	Cheerios, Froot Loops, Swiss cheese, donuts, bagels	Potato chips
Song	"Stretch Out a Circle"	"Peek-A-Boo Holes" "Dip and Print"	"Bob the Blob"
Game	Hide plastic eggs and have an egg hunt Stand in a circle, holding hands. Stretch it out to become an oval Play with floating, plastic eggs in a tub of water	Play with items that have holes in them such as strainers, colanders, funnels	Childcraft Space Wheels, amorphic-shaped plastic building blocks with slits in them to connect to each other
Drawing	Draw on a hard-boiled egg with crayon. Dip in food coloring that is a different color than the crayon used. Leave in the color long enough to give the shell a strong color	Draw on a large piece of paper that has a hole cut out of the center	Draw on an amorphic-shaped piece of paper
Painting	Paint on a giant oval sheet of paper	Paint on a large sheet of paper that has a hole cut out of it	Do a painting on a large amorphic sheet of paper Cut a long roll of paper into a puzzle. Give each child a separate piece of the puzzle to paint. After paint dries, each child adds his or her own puzzle piece to complete the puzzle
Collage	Do a collage using	Use a hole punch to create	Glue old puzzle pieces

	Oval	Holes	Amorphic
	precut paper ovals in assorted sizes and colors	holes in paper. Use the paper with holes in it, and the punched-out holes in a collage	together with Elmer's glue. Optional: decorate with glitter. Paste a pin back on the back of it
Sculpture	Add craft items to Styrofoam egg shape	Build a construction using cut cardboard tubes that come in toilet paper or paper towels	Pretend your friend is clay. Mold it

Geometric Shapes

	Stars	Spirals	Hexagon
Concept	Pasting Painting	Making mobiles Cutting paper Recognizing and naming geometric shapes Utilizing geometric shapes Creating geometric shapes Positive/negative space Informal balance: asymmetry	Hexagon
Materials	Self-adhesive stars and/or "glow-in-the-dark" star stickers Black paper Fluorescent, gold, or silver tempera paint Black tempera paint White paper Silver bristol board stars (available at party supply stores) Silver glitter Star cookie cutter White paper circle, to fit in the center of a star Hole punch	Scissors Round construction paper Hole punch Yarn 12" × 18" drawing paper Doodletop (spinning markers)	Paper, precut in hexagons Markers Tempera Brushes Glue
Book	*Laura's Star*, Klaus Baumgart *Wynken, Blynken and Nod*, Eugene Field *Twinkle, Twinkle Little Star*, Iza Trapani *Star Light, Star Bright*, Karen Davis	*Spirals, Curves, Fanshapes & Lines*, Tana Hoban *Hooray for Snail*, John Stadler *House for a Hermit Crab*, Eric Carle	*Buzz, Buzz, Buzzing Bees*, Gene Fulks and Zena Bernstein
Snack	Homemade star-shaped cookies, shaped with a	Fruit by the Foot Twizzler licorice	Nabisco Oysterettes

	star cookie cutter, star fruit		
Song	"Twinkle, Twinkle Little Star"		"Baby Bumble Bee"
Game	Sit in a circle and pass a large star around the group as you sing "Twinkle, Twinkle." At the end of each song, the person who is holding the star stands and pantomimes how he or she is a star. The children guess what the child "shines" at. Each child who performs receives a sticker to wear that says that he or she is a star. No child may perform twice, so if a child who has already had a chance is holding the star at the end of the song, the star goes to the next child in the circle who has not yet performed. Awards might read: "I am a star. I can sing" or "I am a star. I can play baseball." Any child who is too shy to perform can be awarded a star that says "I am a star. I am modest (or humble)"	Play "Follow the Leader" holding hands (or hips) and create a spiral shape of people. Do an about-face and repeat out of the spiral Play with Slinky toy	Draw a hexagon on the floor, which represents a beehive. One child is "queen bee," covers his or her eyes, and counts to six. During the counting, children run out of the "hive" to pick a flower. They must get a flower and return to hive and be "safe." After counting to six, queen bee can "sting" (tap) any child who is not safely in the hive. The child who is stung becomes the queen bee. If no one is stung, the queen repeats his or her turn.
Drawing	Draw on white circle paper, and paste completed drawing in the center of a star. Punch a hole in the top of the star and hang it in the window or on a Christmas tree	Using a spinning marker to create your drawing, hold the marker over the paper and spin like a top	Draw on hexagon-shaped paper
Painting	Use a squeeze bottle of Elmer's glue to paint a design on a silver star. Place star on a sheet of paper that has a fold down the middle, but has been opened.	Paint with tempera on a large, precut spiral of paper. Allow to dry and paint the other side. Hang from the ceiling	Paint on hexagon-shaped paper. Paint a ready-made papier-mâché hexagon box

	Stars	Spirals	Hexagon
	Sprinkle glitter on the star. Use the fold in the paper to catch excess glitter and pour it back into the container On a large star shape, paint with black tempera. Allow black paint to dry and fill in other areas with fluorescent or silver or gold tempera paint		
Collage	Do a collage of self-adhesive gold or glow-in-the-dark stars on black paper	Begin with a round piece of paper and cut a continuous line into the center. Punch holes and hang things from them using string	Do a collage of precut hexagons in assorted colors and sizes
Sculpture		From a large, precut circle, cut a spiral, punch holes in it, and hang things from them to create a mobile	Build a construction using several ready-made papier-mâché boxes

Art Concepts

	Lines	Texture
Concept	Lines Wire sculpture Drawing with hard utensils	Texture awareness Drawing with hard utensils Pasting Painting
Materials	Twisteez wire or pipe cleaners Markers Lined paper Cardboard Yarn scraps Tempera paint	Box Various textures, such as sandpaper, cotton, sponge, lace, coins Unwrapped crayon Corrugated cardboard Sand play dough
Book	*The Lines are Coming,* Hans-Georg Rouch	*Is It Rough, Is It Smooth, Is It Shiny?* Tana Hoban *Pat the Bunny,* Dorothy Kunhardt
Snack	Breadsticks	Apple butter, applesauce, creamy peanut butter, and crunchy peanut butter
Song	"Long and Narrow"	
Game	Jump rope games	Texture puzzle Experiment with the sense of touch with a "texture box," a closed box of all kinds of things to touch that you can't see. An

		opening for small hands is cut in the side of the box. Include lace, sandpaper, cotton, sponge, etc. Try to guess what you are touching
Drawing	Draw straight, curvy, and zigzag lines on lined paper	Draw on sandpaper or corrugated cardboard with crayons Do a texture rubbing on newsprint using the side of a crayon over various textured objects such as screen, lace, coins, flocked wallpaper scraps
Painting	Paint with string that is dipped in tempera paint	Paint with a sponge on paper
Collage	Do a collage using yarn scraps on cardboard and a squeeze bottle of glue	Do a collage of bumpy-textured items such as tree bark, sandpaper, and corrugated cardboard
Sculpture	Shape Twisteez wire or pipe cleaner	Add sand to play dough to change its texture and model it

Art Concepts

	Transparency
Concept	Transparency Painting Pasting Drawing with hard utensils
Materials	Acrylic paint Lucite cup or bottle Clear acetate Permanent markers Blank slides Slide projector Tempera paint with liquid soap in it Glue
Book	*The Adventures of Three Colors,* Annette Tison and Talus Tayler
Snack	Rock candy, clear glass of water
Song	"Transparent"
Game	Play with Childcraft color paddles Play with water
Drawing	Draw with permanent markers on clear acetate or slides. Project slides on screen
Painting	Paint on Lucite cups or baby bottles with acrylic paint Paint on the window with tempera that has liquid soap mixed in it
Collage	Cellophane scraps on acetate, pasted with white glue and a brush
Sculpture	Do a three-dimensional construction out of scraps of Lucite

CHAPTER 8

Birthday Parties and Group Activities

If you are like many mothers, you faced the pain of childbirth bravely, but fell completely apart at the thought of planning your offspring's first birthday party! Birthday parties not only celebrate your child's birth; they are also ideal opportunities to let your child know just how special and loved he or she is. That fact is often lost in the day-to-day routine of our busy lives. Taking time out to make a fuss over your child, giving gifts and a party, can serve as an all-important reminder.

Many parents tell me that they skipped having a party on baby's first birthday because the baby "didn't know" it was his or her birthday. That first year is the most important in establishing the child's sense of self-worth, and having a fuss made at birthday time is just one way of doing so in a positive manner.

As we all know, however, at any age that "fuss" can easily backfire, and birthday parties can deteriorate into noisy melees that end in tears and exhaustion. This may happen, despite all of your planning and hard work, because attention was paid to the wrong issues. When having children's birthday parties, adults often focus their attention on preparing food, baking cakes, shopping for favors, setting elegant tables, and buying partyware. Children do not come to birthday parties to eat, however, and the birthday cake is frequently left over, ground into your new carpet, or used as a missile. At Young at Art, all of the children decorated their own birthday cakes. They were very proud to see the completed cake when the birthday song was sung. This activity has more meaning for guests than does eating a cake that Mom

slaved over in the kitchen for two days! We set two cakes out on low tables, surrounding each with one tube of frosting for each child. Tops were thrown away before the children arrived, to prevent choking. The completed cakes were whisked off to the kitchen, where one was cut up and ready to serve, and the second had candles added to it and became the cake we used for the birthday song ceremony.

For any birthday in the family, buy or bake a plain cake. Instead of offering one that was decorated by an adult, give your child the whole cake and a few squeeze tubes of ready-made frosting. Forget the traditional roses and let your child enjoy squeezing and smearing the frosting. You can forego the expected birthday message so as not to intrude on the child's creation. If you have planned a party, consider giving each child his or her own cupcake to decorate—and then eat. Of course, any excuse is a good one for a party; it doesn't have to be anyone's birthday. In my art classes, cake decorating was one of the favorite projects. We didn't plan it only to celebrate a birthday. I encouraged the children to think of outrageous occasions to celebrate before I allowed them to eat their cakes. We declared holidays in honor of such occasions as the fact that school would be closed a week from Tuesday or that Tommy hadn't teased his sister for five hours (he was in school all of that time). Once we turned it into an event to welcome a new child to the school. Many years later he told me how welcome that coincidental event made him feel. My son's friends could usually count on a dessert-decorating experience when visiting our house.

As you plan a party, keep these tips in mind:

1. Have a realistic understanding of the attention span of the age group to be invited, and plan each activity accordingly. Plan on twice as many activities as you think you will need.
2. For children under the age of ten, parties should be limited to ninety minutes.
3. Expect to spend less than ten minutes sitting at the table eating birthday cake.
4. Alternate active games with quieter activities.
5. Provide individual freedom within the structure of each activity you have planned.
6. To provide continuity, plan all activities around one theme.
7. Have one adult to supervise every seven children. Make sure that each assisting adult understands that this is not a time for socializing with other adults, but a difficult job and serious responsibility. Also, let them know that their job is to facilitate children's activities, not to do things "for" the children.
8. Do not feel that you will hurt children's feelings if you don't invite your child's entire class. Twenty-five or thirty children is too large a group to socialize with casually. You will have to be much more authoritative to manage such a large crowd, and this detracts from the fun of the party. The children know quite well who their special friends are and these are the children that will have the best time at a party. The "class clown" will be even more disruptive at your party than in the classroom, and should only be included if he or she is a good friend of your child.
9. As the years go by, don't feel that each subsequent party has to be more spectacular than the last and different from all of the other children's parties. The fact is that children will feel most relaxed and comfortable if some aspects of the party are predictable. Being unique is not as important as keeping in touch with the purpose of the party—saying "I love you and I'm glad you were born!"

Children are happiest when they are busy and productive. Adult entertainment, no matter how proficient it may be, requires passive participation. Active participation is most enjoyable for young children. The best children's parties consist of activities that children can do themselves under the supervision of an interested adult, but not totally directed by an adult. Art, movement, and song activities can channel excitement and energy into creative expression. Children want to be active and participate at parties, and spending energy planning constructive activities for the guests is your best investment. This philosophy is the foundation of the success of a Young at Art party, and begins by including the birthday child in decision making from the earliest stages of party planning. I feel very strongly that the opening of gifts is not a constructive activity and should be saved for after the guests have gone. Advance discussion of this issue with all but the very youngest of children should suffice. Including the birthday child in the planning of the party is an important factor in the party's success. If the party begins with the birthday child crying because he or she wants to open gifts, and you won't allow it, the party has no place to go but down!

Format

All parties, no matter what the theme, can follow the same format. They should have a beginning, a middle, and an end. The beginning should be designed to make children feel welcome at the party and familiar with each other and their hosts. The middle should include both active and quiet games that *all* children can participate in and that have no "losers." These can be chosen from the following categories, and most should be coordinated with the theme of the party.

1. Songs
2. Drawing
3. Painting
4. Pasting
5. Sculpture
6. Games
7. Story time
8. Cake and juice
9. Good-bye song

Preparation

Preparation is the key to a good children's party. All of the real work must be done long before the first guest arrives. During the party, the adults should be free to interact with the children, observe, and enjoy the party.

Unfortunately, most hosts spend their preparation time doing all of the wrong things! Making a fancy cake in the shape of this year's most popular character is a waste of time. It will take you hours to bake and decorate, but the guests will devote about ten seconds to admiring it (if, indeed, anyone notices at all) and five minutes (maximum) to eat. You would be better off obtaining the simplest, least expensive cake available and devoting your time and energy to facilitating a cake-decorating activity for the children.

At Young at Art we often gave three birthday parties in one day, so it was essential to be well organized and do all of the planning in advance. We made a "party box" as soon as we booked a party. Each item on the list went into the box as it was readied. At party time we took the box off the shelf and set up a party in no time. We all knew that the quicker we could set up everything we needed, the longer our break would be between each party. I once returned to work after major surgery, having forgotten a scheduled party until the doorbell rang and I found twenty-four children at the door. It was so easy to take the box and set up the table that the family never even knew what had happened. I asked each child to blow up his or her own helium balloon to save me a few minutes, and they loved it. No one ever realized that this activity was not part of my repertoire. They also didn't notice that I gave the whole party without assistants to help me and they didn't seem to notice that I was not fully recovered from my surgery. I could never have done it if everything weren't completely ready for me.

I had a checklist at Young at Art that we meticulously followed while preparing for a party. It took years of giving three birthday parties a day to perfect. I consider it my "secret weapon." Here it is!

1. Type the names and addresses of each child on your invitation list on a master for Avery address labels (we used #5160) or use computer software available through Avery. Type the names in a larger type size than the addresses, and you can use them as name tags for the children to wear at the party as well. Or you can make separate name tags using only the child's name, written in large letters in the color of his or her group, as we did at Young at Art. Put the birthday child's name in the

first space on the grid. This list will become the addresses on your party invitations as well as the thank-you notes and identify each child's party favor. Typing the list may seem like a lot of work at first, but will save you lots of time and aggravation before it's all over.

2. Photocopy or print out at least five copies of the list on self-adhesive labels. You will need one for each of the projects you are planning, one for the invitation, one for a thank-you note, one on a blank sheet of paper that will be painted on, and one for each party bag.

3. After all of the names are typed, divide the party list into four equal color-coded groups by putting a colored dot to the left of each child's name. Save one step in this process by color-coding the master list and then copying it in color. The color-coding helped us keep the groups organized. For example, it allowed us to say things like "Everyone in the red group, please come up and decorate the cake."

4. Put address labels on the party invitations and mail them.

5. Put one color-coded name and address label on every child's shopping bag.

6. Put one label on each party project.

7. Take the cellophane wrapping off all the party items you plan to use, such as cups, plates, napkins, tablecloth, etc. Make one "birthday cake set" per child, which includes one party hat, one plate, cup, fork, and folded napkin per child. For each child on your list, make a stack that includes the plate, napkin, and fork. You will be able to walk around the table only one time, setting one "set" and one cup at each place to accomplish a fully set table. Make three or more extra sets, so you will always have handy replacements for mishaps and can accommodate the occasional uninvited sibling who unexpectedly arrives ready to party. You may also want to have some sets ready so that you can graciously offer a slice of birthday cake to parents or caretakers who stay or come early to pick up their children.

8. If T-shirts are one of the party favors, stuff each shirt with newspaper or cardboard so that the drawing done on the front of the shirt won't bleed to the back.

Do a party box correctly and you could pick it up and give your party on the moon if you wanted to. A completed party box contains:

1. One filled-out party invitation pasted to the outside of the box (just in case you forget whether you invited the group for Saturday or Sunday or for 2:00 or 2:30 P.M.)

2. One birthday cake "set" (see #7 on previous page) for each guest plus at least three extras
3. One birthday crown for the party child
4. One party hat for each guest
5. One book of matches
6. Candles
7. Bottle(s) of juice
8. Tablecloth(s)
9. Garbage bag(s)
10. Roll of paper towels
11. Balloons/yarn/rubber bands
12. One disposable helium tank
13. One cake knife
14. One box of crayons per child
15. One ready-to-decorate party project per child
16. Appropriate art materials for decorating the party projects
17. One party shopping bag per child
18. One squeeze tube of colored cake decorating icing per child (with the tops removed and discarded to prevent choking)
19. Old newspapers
20. Marshmallows and/or sprinkles to enhance the cake (optional)
21. One sheet of paper per child (plus a few extras)
22. Water-soluble paint
23. One brush per child
24. One spill-proof cup (for water) per child

Children love frosting cakes and can do so with a rubber spatula. Squeeze-tubes of frosting to decorate a cake can be freely used by any age child. It is important not to impose adult expectations of how the finished cake should look. Scribbling freely all over the cake is a lot more fun than mastering the art of rosettes. Indeed, the cake doesn't even have to look pretty! For this activity, preparation includes:

1. Bake or purchase one plain, eight-inch frosted cake per eight children.
2. Purchase one squeeze-tube of frosting per child in a limited assortment of colors. Limit the colors to control jealousy and keep the project simple. It is best if the children can concentrate on the cake decorating without worrying about using a multitude of colors.

3. Remove and discard the icing caps before the guests arrive so that no child can choke on one.

4. Before the party begins, place candles and matches in your pocket or on a high shelf, out of reach of the children but handy for you.

5. Unwrap all of the packages of paper plates, napkins, etc., long before the party begins.

6. Make a tray ready for the cake slices. Unless your party is very small, your guests should decorate more than one cake. Only one, however, is required for the birthday song ceremony. The others can be cut into slices and set out on the tray long before cake time and then served as soon as the birthday song is over. This will prevent bored, squirming children from ruining the party while waiting for you to cut and serve the cake. When you do pass out cake slices, give the birthday child the first piece and praise the child who gets the last piece for being so patient.

7. Save your environment and preserve your sanity by having a pot of soapy water and paper towels nearby for hand washing. This will avoid trips across your home by scores of children who have frosting all over their hands.

Food

Children are rarely very interested in eating at a party; they are too excited. That excitement is best channeled into physical and creative activities. Excited children can easily choke on food, so the less food there is, the better. Unlike many adults, children eat to live, not for entertainment. Don't count on consumption of food as a meaningful part of the festivities of a children's birthday party. Limiting food purchasing and preparation to juice or milk and cake is a good idea. At Young at Art, we only ate during cake time seated at the table for the safety of the children. I did not allow any finger food to be brought in.

Entertainment

You may also be tempted to spend large amounts of money on an entertainer for the children, but children prefer to entertain themselves! Young children become quickly bored and start squirming after twenty minutes, even when at the circus. Children would rather ride an elephant than watch a grown-up do it, children would rather run around and act silly than watch a clown do so, and most children prefer being the center of attention than watching a magic show. Keep this fundamental fact of life in mind when planning your party. If you decide to have a magician or clown, this can never be the only planned activity at a party. Group sing-alongs, games, art activities, and story time should be included in your plans.

Party Activities

I loathe most party games. They all seem to have only one winner, leaving most of the guests feeling like losers. They also leave too much down time, with unsupervised children who are no longer interested in the game since they have lost, with nothing to do while they wait for the winner to be chosen. Games should be fun for all participants to play from beginning to end. Activities like that are hard to find. As you choose activities, remember to alternate active and quiet activities.

Musical chairs is a typical example of a game that can quickly turn into a wild melee. I have often seen children pushing and shoving to get a seat, and this can cause injuries and tears. There is nothing to learn except aggressiveness from that game. I have created my own version of it that I call Musical Paints. It was the favorite party game at Young at Art and I continue to use it with my elementary school students. I used to restrict it to kindergarten, but after those children came back as first graders and then second and third graders, wanting to know when we would play Musical Paints again, I kept expanding my repertoire. Children never seem to outgrow their enjoyment of this game.

You will need to do some preparation for this game, but I promise you it is well worth it. In addition to having one color paint and one brush for each child, you will need a crayon or pencil for name writing for each child and a CD or tape player. Newspaper on the table is always a good idea.

1. Remove all of the chairs from the party room and set the tables in a long row or a large circle.
2. Put one sheet of paper at each place that has a child's name written on it in pencil or permanent marker.

3. Place a *different* color tempera paint with a brush in it at each place. (Remember, in addition to the basic colors you can combine colors and add black or white to colors to create new ones.) I recommend mixing the colors long before the day of the party and storing them in tightly covered plastic containers.

4. Place a picture of an arrow facing to the right under each container of paint. (I make one big arrow in black on white paper and make one photocopy for each child.)

5. Before beginning the game, announce "story time" and read a music-related book to the group. (See chapter 9. If possible, choose a piece of music to play that echoes the theme of the book.)

6. Explain the rules to the children while they are still sitting in a group, then again after they have found their own papers at the table.

7. Children do not begin painting until they hear the music begin. They paint with that color as long as the music continues and must stop the very second that the music stops (even if they are in the middle of painting a shape).

8. The child puts the brush back in the paint, picks up the paper with both hands, and listen for directions. "Move one color to the right (in the direction of the arrow). Do not begin painting again until the music begins to play."

9. "When the music begins, paint for as long as you hear the music, then stop painting as soon as the music stops."

10. Repeat steps 7, 8, and 9 until all of the children have finished painting. Children may choose to skip any color that they don't like by waiting at the color for as long as the music plays without painting. I always ask the children that if they choose not to use one color they should fold their hands on the table as a signal to me that there is no problem that I have to stop the game for, but that the child is not painting by choice. A child who completes a picture may wait for the music to stop playing and then step away from the table to place his or her work on a drying rack or clothesline and take another paper before returning to the table.

Since everyone who plays Musical Paints has done a complete, multicolored painting to take home from the party, *everyone is a winner*. An elegant touch is to include a colorful mat or picture frame, with Plexiglas instead of glass, in the size of the paper, to include in your guests' party bags. The children have also enjoyed good literature and fine music. Most important, they have learned the advantage of flexibility and fluidity of thinking by stopping, not when they are finished, but when the music stops. You will want to plan this activity early enough so that the pictures will dry before the party ends. If you have lots of help, someone can be assigned to the job of taping the dry pictures into the mats or putting them in the picture frames and placing them in the child's party bag. (Hint: children love drying their paintings with a hair dryer.)

Artist's Scavenger Hunt

Another art-related game you can play with the children is a scavenger hunt. Give each child a plastic art portfolio with a bottle of glue, a sheet of cardboard, and a packet of cards with clues written on them. (Prereaders' clues can be in pictures instead of words.) Hide art materials and when all of them have been found, the children can do a collage or assemblage project using what they have found. The art project, unused materials, and the portfolio become party favors! Ideas for collage and assemblage materials are recommended in this book throughout the Paper and Sculpture chapters.

Simple Simon Is an Artist

We also play Simple Simon with movements suggesting art ideas:

1. Draw in the air with your finger.
2. Throw paint.
3. Squeeze the glue.
4. Paint with two brushes at one time.
5. Paint with your nose.
6. Make handprints on the floor.
7. Point to something purple.

Statue

Playing Statue is another way to keep your party activities in keeping with your art theme. You can show slides of great statues on a white wall before playing the game, to ensure that children understand how to pose for statues.

Children move to music and must "freeze" as soon as the music stops and resume moving when the music begins. Polaroid photos that can go home in the party bag add a wonderful dimension to this game.

Magic

At one party we gave at Young at Art, magic was the theme since the parents had hired a magician to entertain the children for a portion of the party. I fastened sequined gold stars to paintbrushes to transform them into magic wands. I demonstrated color mixing by giving each child two colors with brushes in them and one empty cup with a magic wand in it. We placed each of the two colors on different sides of the empty cup and, while saying "artacadabra," the children mixed magic new colors using their magic wands. All of the guests enjoyed a project creating magic that can be believed!

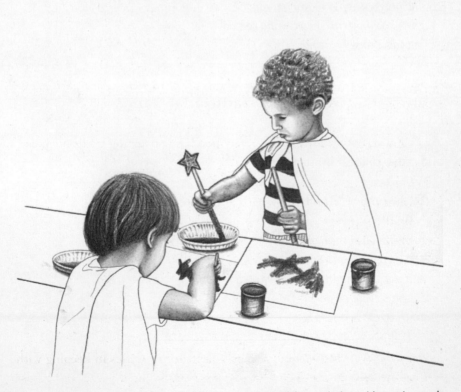

Artacadabra, painting with magic wands

My Paint Brush (by James Earle and Susan Striker)
My paint brush is my magic wand
Artacadabra skibbidy boo
I love to paint with my magic wand
Artacadabra skibbidy boo

I dip it in yellow, I dab it in red
And orange is saying "hello" instead
There's so much my magic wand can do
Artacadabra skibbidy boo

I dip it in red, I dab it in blue
Do you see purple? I do too
There's so much my magic wand can do
Artacadabra skibbidy boo

I dip it in yellow, I dab it in blue
And grassy green is showing through
There's so much my magic wand can do
Artacadabra skibbidy boo

Adapting Traditional Songs

At Young at Art we all got to be very good at converting traditional songs
and games to include art themes.

To the tune of "Brush Your Teeth" we chant:

You wake up in the morning
And it's a quarter to one
And you just can't think about having fun and
You brush your teeth.
Ch ch ch ch chchchchchch.

You wake up in the morning
It's a quarter to two

You get out all your papers and glue and
You brush your teeth
Ch ch ch ch chchchchch.

. . . It's a quarter to three, and you do a drawing about you and me and . . .
. . . It's a quarter to four, and you spill paint all over the floor and . . .
. . . It's a quarter to five, and all of your drawings come alive and . . .
. . . It's a quarter to six, and you and your mom play pickup sticks and . . .
. . . It's a quarter to seven, and you draw a picture about life in Heaven and . . .
. . . It's a quarter to eight, and you draw a picture of your favorite date and . . .
. . . It's a quarter to nine, and you really are thinking about drawing a line . . .
. . . It's a quarter to ten, and you draw and draw with a magic pen and . . .

To the tune of "Bingo" we sang:

There were some kids who loved to paint
And painting was their game. Oh!
P-A-I-N-T, P-A-I-N-T, P-A-I-N-T
And painting was their game. Oh!

There were some kids who loved to paste
And pasting was their game. Oh!
P-A-S-T-E, P-A-S-T-E, P-A-S-T-E
And pasting was their game. Oh!

My version of Pin the Tail on the Donkey transformed the donkey into Mona Lisa. Each child receives a card with instructions, either written or drawn, depending on their ages. I hang a large print of Mona Lisa up for the children to "improve." Instructions include:

• Make a hat for Mona.
• Design a necklace for Mona.
• Make a ring for Mona's hand.

Scarves, pins, favorite pets, flowers to hold, etc., can all be created out of craft materials and pasted directly on the print.

Art Activities

Below is a description of the activities that work best in each of the two age groups.

Ages 1–3:	Drawing:	with crayons on party bags
		with water-soluble markers on large paper
		with colored chalk on sidewalk or chalkboard
		with permanent markers on pennants or posters
		with makeup on faces
	Painting:	with tempera on large paper
		with watercolor blocks on plate or cup inserts
	Pasting:	with self-adhesive stickers
	Sculpture:	play dough—with hands and tools
	Printing:	handprints
		with alphabet stamps
Ages 4–6:	Drawing:	on balloon characters
		on cardboard puppets
		on blank white puzzles
		with chalk on the sidewalk
		on posters
		on large paper
	Painting:	with permanent paint on T-shirts
		with acrylics on umbrellas
		outdoors with squeeze bottles
		with watercolors
		on wooden plaques
		with sponges
		with markers on posters
	Collage:	with glue and assorted collage materials
		with Day-Glo or glow-in-the-dark stickers
		with glitter on party hats
	Sculpture:	with wood scraps and glue
		with assorted three-dimensional materials
		with self-hardening clay
	Printing:	with found objects
		with shape, alphabet, and number stamps

Painting an umbrella

Party Favors

Preparation for a party should mean getting things ready for children to make or decorate, not doing these things for them. The children can take home as party favors several art projects they make themselves. They will value these as highly as any candy or toys they receive at other parties.

Instead of spending time, energy, and money on finding just the "right" party bags, provide plain white ones for each child to decorate in his or her unique "right" way. A plain white paper tablecloth is the beginning of an ideal group art activity.

Set a cup or box of crayons at each child's place. They can be used for the art activities during the party, and become inexpensive and useful party favors as well. I always gave my son's guests and Young at Art clients who were over the age of six Anti-Coloring Books and markers. (When you purchase books by the dozen, most publishers will give you a 40–50 percent discount, so deal directly with the publisher to obtain maximum savings.)

Consider making the basics of one party activity the party favor as well.

This gives the favor some meaning, instead of being just "loot." At Young at Art, children decorated their own T-shirts or caps. Any plain white article of clothing would work as well, from socks to smocks. We decorated leotards for one group of young dancers. The girls added jewels and fabric paint to plain white ones, very effectively. Use permanent markers or fabric paint. (Close supervision is necessary whenever young children use permanent art materials.) Older children can decorate their creations with beads.

Umbrellas were another Young at Art favorite. Clear vinyl ones can be decorated with acrylic paints or permanent markers. Glitter can be used to add pizzazz. I'll never forget the bright and sunny day when twenty five-year-olds celebrated by painting and decorating clear vinyl umbrellas. When the party ended it was pouring outside. It was magical to watch the children open their umbrellas and leave, convinced that creating the umbrellas had somehow caused the change in the weather.

Even very young children can make their own party favors, although they should not require the use of permanent art materials. Lucite plates, cups, and mugs are perennial favorites with the under-four set. Parents love them, too! They contain simple drawings or paintings done freely by each child.

Painting a wooden letter

Pasting tissue on a bottle

You might give the children standard size paper, a package of crayons, and a picture frame. As each child completes his or her picture, slip it into the frame and let the child put it into the party bag. A Polaroid portrait of each child can identify the party bags and be delightful souvenirs as well.

Large wooden letters were provided to one group. We gave each child the first letter of his or her first name to decorate. They are great to hang on bedroom doors.

Pasting layers of colored tissue all over a clean, empty plastic bottle is a cost-efficient party project. All you need to buy is colored tissue paper and glue. When it is complete, cover the entire bottle with watered-down glue to seal and protect it. Plop in a tissue paper or live flower for a finishing touch.

The End

The ending of the party should occur before the children are tired and should very clearly be the last activity of the day. Short, simple endings that give children a clear understanding of their purpose are best. Consider singing a good-bye song such as "So Long, It's Been Good to Know You" while passing out party bags and coats.

CHAPTER 9

Books About Art for Children

The following list is not intended to be a list of books for you to go out and buy to read to your baby. They are intended to be a reference library for anyone who nurtures creativity in children or teaches art. They are all books that I own, having collected them over many years of teaching art. I have divided them by categories to help you locate a book about a certain art concept or idea that you may want to share with your child or a group of children. I can't imagine having a group paint with gold paint without having heard *The Midas Touch*. Some of the books are baby books, a few are intended for older children, and a very few are not even children's books at all, but I have found them to be a good substitute until I can find a children's book about the same subject. I never teach an art project without introducing it with a good story and lots of visual aids. Some of these books may be out of print, but available in a public library. Alibris.com is one of many companies that will locate out-of-print books for you. You will notice that my categories may not be anything at all similar to the publisher's description of them. *The Midas Touch*, for instance, would probably not be described as a color book, but that's what I use it for. I may focus attention on a portion of the story or its setting, quite apart from its central story line. Once, while preparing to teach quilt making to a group, I looked up the subject in *Children's Books in Print* to see if there was anything new. I was shocked to find no listing for quilt making, but I already owned twelve books that I would use when teaching quilt making! In most, the quilts themselves may have been incidental to the point of the story. I hope this list of categories of books will help you locate what you need.

Art Concepts

ACCIDENTAL ART

Aylesworth, Jim. *Old Black Fly*. New York: Henry Holt, 1992.

Bröger, Achim, and Michele Sambin. *Francie's Paper Puppy*. Natick, Mass.: Picture Book Studio, 1982.

Carrick, Malcolm. *Splodges*. New York: Viking, 1976.

Moss, Marissa. *Regina's Big Mistake*. Boston: Houghton Mifflin, 1990.

Pinkwater, Daniel Manus. *The Big Orange Splot*. New York: Scholastic, 1977.

Schaefer, Carole Lexa. *The Squiggle*. New York: Crown, 1996.

Shaw, Charles G. *It Looked Like Spilled Milk*. New York: Harper & Row, 1947.

Utton, Peter. *The Witch's Hand*. New York: Farrar, Straus and Giroux, 1989.

AESTHETICS

Crowley, Arthur, and Annie Gusman. *The Ugly Book*. Boston: Houghton Mifflin, 1982.

Gregorie, Caroline. *Uglypuss*. New York: Henry Holt, 1994.

Polacco, Patricia. *Just Plain Fancy*. New York: Dell, 1990.

BALANCE

Peek, Merle. *The Balancing Act*. New York: Clarion Books, 1987.

BIRD'S-EYE VIEW

Getz, David. *Floating Home*. New York: Henry Holt, 1997.

Graham, Judy, and Michael Ansell. *Bird's Eye*. La Jolla, Calif.: Green Tiger Press, 1981.

Jenkins, Steve. *Looking Down*. Boston: Houghton Mifflin, 1995.

Jonas, Ann. *Watch William Walk*. New York: Greenwillow Books, 1997.

BORDERS AND FRAMES

Hogrogian, Nonny. *The Contest*. New York: Greenwillow Books, 1976.

McVitty, Walter. *Ali Baba and the Forty Thieves*. New York: Harry N. Abrams, 1988.

CAMOUFLAGE

Hale, Irina. *Brown Bear in a Brown Chair*. New York: Atheneum, 1983.

Turk, Hanne. *Hieronymus*. Salzburg: Neugebauer, 1981.

CLOSE UP

Allingham, William. *The Fairies*. New York: Henry Holt, 1989.

Banyai, Istuan. *Zoom*. New York: Penguin, 1995.

Hoban, Tana. *Take Another Look*. New York: Greenwillow Books, 1981.

Loss, Joan. *What Is It? A Book of Photographic Puzzles*. Garden City, N.Y.: Doubleday, 1974.

Tildes, Phyllis Limbacher. *Animals in Black and White*. Watertown, Mass.: Charlesbridge, 1996.

COLORS

Lobel, Arnold. *The Great Blueness, and Other Predicaments*. New York: Harper & Row, 1968.

O'Neill, Mary. *Hailstones and Halibut Bones*. New York: Doubleday, 1961.

Scott, Rochelle. *Colors, Colors All Around*. New York: Grosset & Dunlap, 1965.

Sheehan, Cilla. *The Colors That I Am*. New York: Human Sciences Press, 1981.

BLACK/WHITE/GRAY

Coy, John. *Night Driving*. New York: Henry Holt, 1996.

Hasely, Dennis. *The Old Banjo*. New York: Macmillan, 1983.

Ipcar, Dahlov. *Black and White*. New York: Alfred A. Knopf, 1963.

Jonas, Ann. *Round Trip*. New York: Greenwillow Books, 1983.

Palazzo, Janet (retold by). *Why Opossum Is Gray*. Mahwah, N.J.: Troll, 1996.

Tildes, Phyllis Limbacher. *Animals Black and White*. Watertown, Mass.: Charlesbridge, 1996.

BLUE

Drummond, Allan. *The Willow Pattern Story*. New York: North-South Books, 1992.

Gates, Doris. *Blue Willow*. New York: Scholastic, 1940.

Grifalconi, Ann. *Kinda' Blue*. Boston: Little, Brown, 1993.

Inkpen, Mick. *The Blue Balloon*. Boston: Little, Brown, 1989.

Rice, Eve. *New Blue Shoes*. New York: Macmillan, 1975.

Whiteman, Candace. *Bring on the Blue*. New York: Abbeville, 1998.

BROWN

Bond, Jean Carey. *Brown Is a Beautiful Color*. New York: Franklin Watts, 1969.

BROWN AND BLACK

Berndt, Catherine Helen. *Pheasant and Kingfisher*. Greenvale, N.Y.: Mondo, 1987.

GREEN

Arnold, Tedd. *Green Wilma*. New York: Dial, 1993.

Lionni, Leo. *Little Blue and Little Yellow*. New York: McDowell, Obolensky, 1959.

Selkowe, Valerie M., and Jeni Crisler Bassett. *Spring Green*. New York: Lothrop, Lee & Shepard Books, 1985.

Stinson, Kathy, and Deirdre Betteridge. *Those Green Things*. Willowdale, Ontario, Canada: Firefly Books, 1995.

COLOR MIXING

Duvoisin, Roger. *The House of Four Seasons*. New York: Lothrop, Lee & Shepard Books, 1956.

Heller, Ruth. *Color*. New York: Putnam, 1995.

Jonas, Ann. *Color Dance*. New York: Greenwillow Books, 1989.

Lionni, Leo. *Little Blue and Little Yellow*. New York: McDowell, Obolensky, 1959.

Tison, Annette, and Talus Taylor. *Adventures of Three Colors*. Columbus, Ohio: Charles E. Merrill, 1980.

———. *Animals in Color Magic*. Columbus, Ohio: Charles E. Merrill, 1980.

Walsh, Ellen Stoll. *Mouse Paint*. Orlando, Fla.: Harcourt Brace Jovanovich, 1989:

COLOR'S MOOD

Grifalconi, Ann. *Kinda' Blue*. Boston: Little, Brown, 1993.

Seuss, Dr. *My Many Colored Days*. New York: Alfred A. Knopf, 1996.

COMPLEMENTARY COLORS

Andrew, Kulman. *Red Light STOP Green Light GO*. New York: Simon & Schuster, 1992.

Carle, Eric. *Hello, Red Fox*. New York: Simon & Schuster, 1998.

Kay, Helen. *One Mitten Lewis*. New York: Lothrop, Lee & Shepard Books, 1955.

McGuire, Richard. *The Orange Book*. New York: Children's Universe, 1992.

Walsh, Ellen Stoll. *Mouse Magic*. San Diego: Harcourt Brace Jovanovich, 2000.

COOL COLORS

Clement, Claude. *The Painter and the Wild Swans*. New York: Dial, 1981.

San Souci, Daniel. *North Country Night*. New York: Doubleday, 1990.

Shulevitz, Uri. *Dawn*. New York: Farrar, Straus and Giroux, 1974.

FLUORESCENT

Rockwell, Thomas, and Michael Horen. *The Neon Motorcycle*. New York: Franklin Watts, 1973.

GOLD

Craft, Carlotte (as told by). *King Midas and the Golden Touch*. New York: Morrow Junior Books, 1999.

MULTIPLE COLORS

Bryan, Ashley. *The Night Has Ears—African Proverbs*. New York: Atheneum, 1999.

DeRolf, Shane. *The Crayon Box That Talked*. New York: Random House, 1996.

Hubbard, Patricia. *My Crayons Talk*. New York: Henry Holt, 1996.

Littlefield, Holly. *Colors of Japan*. Minneapolis, Minn.: Carolrhoda Books, 1997.

Myers, Walter Dean. *Multicolors—The Story of Three Kingdoms*. New York: HarperCollins, 1995.

O'Neill, Mary. *Hailstones and Halibut Bones*. Garden City, N.Y.: Doubleday, 1961.

Shalom, Vivienne, and Dusan Petricic. *The Color of Things*. New York: Rizzoli, 1995.

ORANGE

McGuire, Richard. *The Orange Book*. New York: Rizzoli, 1992.

Pinkwater, Daniel Manus. *The Big Orange Splot*. New York: Scholastic, 1977.

PINK

Greenfield, Eloise. *First Pink Light*. New York: Scholastic, 1976.

POEMS ABOUT COLOR

O'Neill, Mary. *Hailstones and Halibut Bones*. New York: Doubleday, 1961.

Oram, Hiawyn, and David McKee. *Out of the Blue*. New York: Hyperion Books for Children, 1993.

PURPLE

Calleja, Gina. *Tobo Hates Purple*. Toronto: Annick Press, 1983.

Hest, Amy, and Amy Schwartz. *The Purple Coat*. New York: Macmillan, 1986.

Johnson, Crockett. *Harold and the Purple Crayon.* New York: Harper & Row, 1955.

————. *A Picture for Harold's Room.* New York: HarperCollins, 1985.

Joose, Barbara M. *I Love You the Purplest.* San Francisco: Chronicle Books, 1996.

Kessler, Leonard. *Mr. Pine's Purple House.* New York: Grosset & Dunlap, 1965.

Pearson, Tracey Campbell. *The Purple Hat.* New York: Farrar, Straus and Giroux, 1997.

RAINBOW

De Rico, Ul. *The Rainbow Goblins.* New York: Thames and Hudson, 1978.

Freeman, Don. *A Rainbow of My Own.* New York: Viking, 1966.

Nicklaus, Carol. *Mabel and the Rainbow.* New York: Platt and Munk, 1975.

Strom, Maria Diaz. *Rainbow Joe and Me.* New York: Lee & Low Books, 1999.

Thaler, Mike. *The Rainbow.* New York: Harlin Quist, 1967.

Whelan, Richard. *The Book of Rainbows.* Cobb, Calif.: O. G. Publishing, 1997.

RED

Bridwell, Norman. *Clifford the Small Red Puppy.* New York: Scholastic, 1972.

Bright, Robert. *I Like Red.* Garden City, N.Y.: Doubleday, 1955.

Cerf, Rosanne, and Jonathan Cerf. *Big Bird's Red Book.* Racine, Wis.: Western, 1978.

Irvine, Rex, and John Strejan. *Little Red Riding Hood.* Chatsworth, Calif.: Superscope Tape Products, 1973.

Lamorisse, A. *The Red Balloon.* Garden City, N.Y.: Doubleday, 1956.

Mari, Iela. *The Little Red Balloon.* New York: Barron's, 1979.

Parkin, Rex. *The Red Carpet.* New York: Macmillan, 1993.

Peek, Merle. *Mary Wore Her Red Dress and Henry Wore His Green Sneakers.* New York: Clarion Books, 1985.

Stinson, Kathy. *Red Is Best.* Toronto: Annick Press, 1982.

Whitman, Candace. *Ready for Red.* New York: Abbeville, 1998.

RED, WHITE, AND BLUE

Fisher, Leonard Everett. *Stars and Stripes: Our National Flag.* New York: Holiday House, 1993.

WARM COLORS

dePaola, Tomie (retold by). *The Legend of the Indian Paintbrush.* New York: G. P. Putnam's Sons, 1988.

McDermott, Gerald. *Musicians of the Sun*. New York: Simon & Schuster, 1997.

Peña, Amado, and Juanita Alba. *Calor: A Story of Warmth for All Ages*. Waco, Tex.: WRS Publishing, 1995.

WHITE

Shaw, Charles G. *It Looked Like Spilled Milk*. New York: Harper & Row 1947.

YELLOW

Asch, Frank. *Yellow*. New York: McGraw-Hill, 1971.

Bank, Molly. *Yellow Ball*. New York: Morrow Junior Books, 1991.

Ohlsson, Edward Fenton Ib. *The Big Yellow Balloon*. Garden City, N.Y.: Doubleday, 1967.

Rice, Eve. *Goodnight, Goodnight*. New York: Greenwillow Books, 1980.

Spinelli, Eileen. *In My New Yellow Shirt*. Illustrated by Hideko Takahashi. New York: Henry Holt, 2001.

Wheeler, Cindy. *Marmalade's Yellow Leaf*. New York: Alfred A. Knopf, 1982.

Whitman, Candace. *Yellow and You*. New York: Abbeville, 1998.

Wolff, Robert Jay. *Hello Yellow*. New York: Charles Scribner's Sons, n.d.

CREATIVE USES FOR THINGS

Crews, Donald. *Ten Black Dots*. New York: Greenwillow Books, 1968–1986.

Freeman, Don. *Add-a-Line Alphabet*. San Carlos, Calif.: Golden Gate Junior Books, 1968.

DARKNESS

Walter, Mildred Pitts. *Darkness*. New York: Simon & Schuster, 1995.

DIORAMAS

Keats, Ezra Jack. *The Trip*. New York: Scholastic, 1978.

DOORKIJKJE (VIEWING A SCENE THROUGH A DOOR OR WINDOW)

Hobar, Russell, and Quentin Blake. *Monsters*. New York: Scholastic, 1989.

Munro, Roxie. *The Inside-Outside Book of New York City*. New York: Dodd, 1985.

Wong, Olive. *From My Window*. Illustrated by Mark Bellerose. New York: Ginn, 1985.

LIGHT

Baumgart, Klaus. *Laura's Star*. Waukesha, Wis.: Little Tiger Press, 1997.

Bradbury, Ray. *Switch On the Night*. New York: Alfred A. Knopf, 1955.

Brinckloe, Julie. *Fireflies*. New York: Macmillan, 1985.

Brown, Marcia (trans.). *Shadow*. New York: Charles Scribner's Sons, 1982.

Conway, Diana Cohen. *Northern Lights*. Rockville, Md.: Kar-Ben, 1994.

Crews, Donald. *Light*. New York: Greenwillow Books, 1981.

dePaola, Tomie (retold by). *The Legend of the Indian Paintbrush*. New York: G. P. Putnam's Sons, 1988.

Dowling, Paul. *The Night Journey*. New York: Doubleday, 1996.

Dwyer, Mindy. *Aurora. A Tale of the Northern Lights*. Anchorage: Alaska Northwest, 1997.

Edwards, Pamela Duncan. *Barefoot Escape on the Underground Railroad*. New York: Scholastic, 1997.

Evans, Richard Paul. *The Christmas Candle*. New York: Simon & Schuster, 1998.

Flora, James. *The Fabulous Firework Family*. New York: Macmillan.

Graham, Joan Bransfield. *Flicker Flash*. New York: Houghton Mifflin, 1999.

James, Betsy. *Flashlight*. New York: Alfred A. Knopf, 1997.

Keller, Holly. *Henry's Fourth of July*. New York: Greenwillow Books, 1985.

Noyes, Alfred. *The Highwayman*. New York: Harcourt Brace, 1990.

Ray, David. *Pumpkin Light*. New York: Philomel Books, 1993.

Sabuda, Robert. *The Blizzard's Robe*. New York: Atheneum, 1999.

Simon, Seymour. *Lightning*. New York: Morrow, 1997.

Sturges, Philemon. *Ten Flashing Fireflies*. London: North-South Books, 1995.

Third Grade Art Students at Drexel Elementary School. *How the Sun Was Born—Como el Sol Nacio*. St. Petersburg, Fla.: Willowisp Press, 1993.

Walter, Mildred Pitts. *Darkness*. New York: Simon & Schuster, 1995.

LINE

Fox, Mem. *The Straight Line Wonder*. Greenvale, N.Y.: Mondo, 1997.

Green, Rhonda Gower. *When a Line Bends . . . a Shape Begins*. Boston: Houghton Mifflin, 1997.

Isadora, Rachel. *Ben's Trumpet*. New York: Mulberry Books, 1979.

Juster, Norton. *The Dot and the Line*. New York: Random House, 1963.

Lerner, Sharon. *Straight Is a Line*. New York: Lerner, 1970.

MacAgy, Douglas, and Elizabeth MacAgy. *Going for a Walk with a Line*. New York: Doubleday, 1959.

Newell, Peter. *The Stant Book*. Rutland, Vt.: Charles E. Tuttle, 1967.

Reeves, James. *Mr. Horrox and the Gratch*. Chicago: Wellington Publishing, 1969.

Roberts, Cliff. *The Dot*. New York: Franklin Watts, 1960.

Rockwell, Anne. *Sally's Caterpillar*. New York: Parent's Magazine Press, 1966.

Rouch, Hans-Georg. *The Lines Are Coming*. New York: Charles Scribner's Sons, 1939.

Selleck, Jack. *Elements of Design: Line*. Worcester, Mass.: Davis, 1974.

Tallon, Robert. *Worm Story*. New York: Holt, Rinehart and Winston, 1978.

Wood, Audrey. *Magic Shoelaces*. Singapore: Child's Play, 1980.

Yenawine, Phillip. *Lines*. New York: Delacorte Press, 1991.

LONG AND NARROW

Carle, Eric. *Do You Want to Be My Friend?* New York: Crowell, 1971.

Radunsky, Eugenia, and Vladimir Radunsky. *Skinny*. New York: Henry Holt, 1992.

Wood, Audrey. *Magic Shoelaces*. Singapore: Child's Play, 1980.

MURALS

Blake, Robert J. *A Tale from the Canyons*. New York: Philomel Books, 1999.

Knight, Margy Burns. *Talking Walls—The Stories Continue*. Gardiner, Me.: Tilbury House, 1996.

OPTICAL ILLUSIONS

Westray, Kathleen. *Picture Puzzler*. New York: Houghton Mifflin, 1994.

OVERLAPPING

Crews, Donald. *Parade*. New York: Mulberry Books, 1983.

PATTERNS

DOTS

Robertson, Janet. *Oscar's Spots*. Mahwah, N.J.: Troll, 1993.

PLAID

McElmurry, Jill. *Mad About Plaid*. New York: HarperCollins, 2000.

STRIPES

Baker, Keith. *Hide and Snake*. San Diego: Harcourt Brace Jovanovich, 1991.

Christelow, Eileen. *Henry and the Red Stripes*. New York: Clarion Books, 1982.

Shannon, David. *A Bad Case of Stripes*. New York: Blue Sky Press, 1998.

VARIOUS PATTERNS

Ata, Te (as told by). *Baby Rattlesnake*. San Francisco: Children's Book Press, 1989.

Chocolate, Debbi. *Kente Colors*. New York: Walker, 1996.

French, Fiona. *Anancy and Mr. Dry-Bone*. Boston: Little, Brown, 1991.

McDermott, Gerald. *Zomo the Rabbit*. San Diego: Harcourt Brace, 1992.

McKee, David. *Elmer and Wilbur*. New York: Lothrop, Lee & Shepard Books, 1994.

Pluckrose, Henry. *Patterns: Math Counts*. Chicago: Children's Press, 1995.

Sharratt, Nick. *My Mom and Dad Make Me Laugh*. Cambridge, Mass.: Candlewick Press, 1994.

Turpin, Lorna. *The Sultan's Snakes*. New York: Child's Play, 1990.

WILLOW PATTERNS

Drummond, Allan. *The Willow Pattern Story*. New York: North-South Books, 1992.

Gates, Doris. *Blue Willow*. New York: Scholastic, 1940.

ZIGZAG

Isadora, Rachel. *Ben's Trumpet*. New York: Mulberry Books, 1979.

Lacapa, Michael. *The Flute Player*. Flagstaff, Ariz.: Northland Publishing, 1990.

PERCEPTION

Gardner, Beau. *The Turn About, Think About, Look About Book*. New York: Lothrop, Lee & Shepard Books, 1980.

Yoshi. *The Butterfly Hunt*. New York: Simon & Schuster, 1993.

REFLECTIONS

Aylesworth, Jim. *Mary's Mirror*. New York: Holt, Rinehart and Winston, 1982.

Cowley, Joy. *In the Mirror*. Bothell, Wash.: Wright Group, 1983.

Day, Alexandra, and Christian Darling. *Mirror*. New York: Farrar, Straus and Giroux, 1997.

Ginsburg, Mirra, and Margot Zemach. *The Chinese Mirror*. Orlando, Fla.: Harcourt Brace Jovanovich, 1988.

Holl, Adelaide. *The Rain Puddle*. New York: Lothrop, Lee & Shepard Books, 1965.

Robinson, David. *Reflections*. New York: Henry Holt, 1978.

RHYTHM

Coleman, Evelyn. *To Be a Drum*. Morton Grove, Ill.: Albert Whitman, 1998.

SHADOWS

Canty, John. *Shadows*. New York: Harper & Row, 1987.

Cutting, Jillian. *My Shadow*. San Diego: Wright Group, 1988.

Freeman, Don. *Gregory's Shadow*. New York: Penguin Putnam, 2000.

Goor, Ron, and Nancy Goor. *Shadows Here, There, and Everywhere*. New York: Crowell, 1981.

Narahaski, Keiko. *I Have a Friend*. New York: Margaret K. McElderry Books, 1987.

Paul, Ann Whiteford. *Shadows Are About*. New York: Scholastic, 1992.

SHAPES

Palazzo, Tony. *The Magic Crayon*. New York: Lion Press, 1967.

AMORPHIC

Carrick, Malcom. *Splodges*. New York: Viking, 1976.

The Little Red Ant. New York: Grosset & Dunlap, 1978.

Moss, Miriam. *Jigsaw*. Brookfield, Conn.: Millbrook Press, 1997.

Pinkwater, Daniel Manus. *The Big Orange Splot*. New York: Scholastic, 1977.

Shaw, Charles G. *It Looked Like Spilled Milk*. New York: Harper & Row, 1947.

Silverstein, Shel. *The Missing Piece*. New York: Harper & Row, 1976.

———. *The Missing Piece Meets the Big O*. New York: Harper & Row, 1981.

Splish, Splash! New York: Grosset & Dunlap, 1981.

COMBINED

Baer, Gene, and Lois Ehlert. *Thump, Thump, Rat-a-Tat-Tat*. New York: HarperCollins, 1991.

Falwell, Cathryn. *Shape Space*. New York: Clarion Books, 1992.

Grifalconi, Ann. *The Village of Round and Square Houses*. Boston: Little, Brown, 1986.

Grover, Max. *Circles and Squares Everywhere!* San Diego: Harcourt Brace, 1996.

Hoban, Tana. *Circles, Triangles & Squares*. New York: Macmillan, 1974.

Hutchins, Pat. *Changes, Changes*. New York: Macmillan, 1971.

Potts, Jim. *The House That Makes Shapes*. Tucson, Ariz.: Harbinger House, 1992.

Stevenson, Robert Louis, and Ashley Wolff. *Block City*. New York: Dutton Children's Books, 1988.

Voss, Gisela. *Museum Shapes*. Boston: Museum of Fine Arts, 1993.

HEXAGON

Fulks, Gene, and Zena Bernstein. *Buzz, Buzz, Buzzing Bees*. New York: Holt, Rinehart and Winston, 1967.

HOLES

Carle, Eric. *Catch the Ball*. New York: Philomel Books, 1982.

———. *The Very Hungry Caterpillar*. New York: Philomel Books, 1994.

OVALS

Adams, Adrienne. *The Easter Egg Artists*. New York: Charles Scribner's Sons, 1976.

Hooper, Meredith, and Tenry McKenna. *Seven Eggs*. New York: Harper & Row, 1985.

Lionni, Leo. *An Extraordinary Egg*. New York: Scholastic, 1994.

Milhous, Katherine. *The Egg Tree*. New York: Aladdin, 1950, 1978.

Peet, Bill. *The Pinkish, Purplish, Bluish Egg*. Boston: Houghton Mifflin, 1963.

Polacco, Patricia. *Rechenka's Eggs*. New York: Philomel Books, 1988.

ROUND

Hoban, Tana. *Round and Round and Round*. New York: Greenwillow Books, 1983.

Inkpen, Mick. *The Blue Balloon*. Boston: Little, Brown, 1989.

Withers, Carl (retold by). *Painting the Moon*. New York: Dutton, 1970.

Zelinsky, Paul O. *The Wheels on the Bus*. New York: Dutton, 1990.

SPIRALS

Carle, Eric. *A House for Hermit Crab*. Natick, Mass.: Picture Book Studio, 1987.

Hoban, Tana. *Spirals, Curves, Fanshapes and Lines*. New York: Greenwillow Books, 1992.

SQUARE

Barrett, Peter, and Susan Barrett. *The Square Ben Drew*. New York: Scroll Press, 1972.

Hale, Irina. *Boxman*. New York: Viking, 1992.

Maloney, Cecilia. *The Box Book*. Racine, Wis.: Golden Press, 1978.

Salazar, Violet. *Squares Are Not Bad*. New York: Golden Press, 1967.

Siomades, Lorianne. *Look What You Can Make with Boxes*. Honesdale, Pa.: Boyds Mill Press, 1998.

Snape, Charles, and Juliet Snape. *The Boy with Square Eyes*. New York: Simon & Schuster, 1987.

Supraner, Robyn. *Draw Me a Square*. New York: Nutmeg Press, n.d.

STARS

Baumgart, Klaus. *Laura's Christmas Star*. Waukesha, Wis.: Little Tiger Press, 1999.

————. *Laura's Star*. Waukesha, Wis.: Little Tiger Press, 1997.

Davis, Karen. *Star Light, Star Bright*. New York: Green Tiger Press, 1992.

Field, Eugene. *Wynken, Blynken and Nod*. New York: Dutton, 1982.

Oughton, Jerrie. *How the Stars Fell into the Sky: A Navajo Legend*. Boston: Houghton Mifflin, 1992.

Trapani, Iza. *Twinkle, Twinkle, Little Star*. Danvers, Mass.: Whispering Coyote Press, 1994.

TRIANGLES

Burns, Marilyn. *The Greedy Triangle*. New York: Scholastic, 1994.

SIMPLICITY

Clement, Claude. *The Painter and the Wild Swans*. New York: Dial, 1986.

Polacco, Patricia. *Just Plain Fancy*. New York: Dell, 1990.

SIZE RELATIONSHIPS

Davis, Charles E. *Creatures at My Feet*. Flagstaff, Ariz.: Northland Publishing, 1993.

Fleming, Denise. *In the Tall, Tall Grass*. New York: Henry Holt, 1991.

Keats, Ezra Jack. *Peter's Chair*. New York: Puffin Books, 1967.

Kellogg, Steven. *Much Bigger than Martin*. New York: Puffin Pied Piper, 1976.

"The Teeny-Tiny Woman" in *Fairy Tales and Fables*. New York: Grosset & Dunlap, 1970.

SYMMETRY

Carle, Eric. *The Very Hungry Caterpillar*. New York: Philomel Books, 1994.

Conkling, Gladys. *I Like Butterflies*. New York: Holiday House, 1960.

Rockwell, Anne. *Sally's Caterpillar*. New York: Parent's Magazine Press, 1966.

Yoshi. *The Butterfly Hunt*. New York: Simon & Schuster, 1993.

TEXTURE

Hoban, Tana. *Is It Rough? Is It Smooth? Is It Shiny?* New York: Greenwillow Books, 1984.

Kundhardt, Dorothy. *Pat the Bunny*. New York: Simon & Schuster, 1940.

Saxe, John Godfrey. *The Blind Men and the Elephant*. New York: McGraw-Hill, 1994.

Witte, Pat, and Eve Witte. *The Touch Me Book*. Racine, Wis.: Golden Press, 1976.

Art History and Cultural Arts

Butler, Philippa. *Pawprints in Time*. New York: Penguin, 1998.

ACTION PAINTING

Glenn, Andrew. *Jackson Makes His Move*. New York: Frederick Warne, 1982.

Rosenberg, Liz, and Stephen Gammel. *Monster Mama*. New York: Philomel Books, 1993.

Spier, Peter. *Oh, Were They Ever Happy!* Garden City, N.Y.: Doubleday, 1978.

CAVE PAINTING

Baynes, Pauline. *How Dog Began*. New York: Henry Holt, 1985.

Bush, Timothy. *Grunt! A Primitive Cave Boy*. New York: Crown, 1995.

MANUSCRIPT ILLUMINATION

Robertson, Bruce, and Kathryn Hewitt. *Marguerite Makes a Book*. Los Angeles: J. Paul Getty Museum, 1999.

MEDIEVAL FRANCE

Price, Kathleen McCormick. *The Lady and the Unicorn*. Bridgeport, Conn.: Green Bark Press, 1994.

RENAISSANCE ITALY

Mayhew, James. *Katie and the Mona Lisa*. New York: Orchard Books, 1998.

Wooding, Sharon. *The Painter's Cat*. New York: G. P. Putnam's Sons, 1994.

CULTURE

ABORIGINAL

Berndt, Catherine. *Pheasant and Kingfisher*. Greenvale, N.Y.: Mondo, 1987.

Trezise, Percy. *The Cave Painters*. New York: HarperCollins, 1988.

AFRICAN

Bryan, Ashley. *The Night Has Ears—African Proverbs*. New York: Atheneum, 1999.

Coleman, Evelyn. *To Be a Drum*. Morton Grove, Ill.: Albert Whitman, 1998.

Musgrove, Margaret. *Ashanti to Zulu*. New York: Dial, 1976.

AFRICAN-AMERICAN

Herron, Carolivia. *Nappy Hair*. New York: Alfred A. Knopf, 1997.

Ringgold, Faith. *If a Bus Could Talk: The Story of Rosa Parks*. New York: Simon & Schuster, 1999.

AMERICAN FOLK ART

Nicholson, Nicholas B. A. *Little Girl in a Red Dress with Cat and Dog*. New York: Viking, 1998.

COLONIAL AMERICAN

Lewin, Betsy. *Araminta's Paint Box*. New York: Aladdin, 1990.

EGYPTIAN

dePaola, Tomie. *Bill and Pete Go Down the Nile*. New York: G. P. Putnam's Sons, 1987.

Langley, Andrew. *Cleopatra and the Egyptians*. Hove, England: Wayland, 1985.

Lattimore, Deborah Nourse. *The Winged Cat*. New York: HarperCollins, 1992.

Walsh, Jill. *Pepi and the Secret Names*. New York: Lothrop, Lee & Shepard Books, 1994.

GUATEMALAN

Rowan, Paula S. *Remember This*. Savannah, Ga.: Savannah College of Art and Design, 1997.

HAITIAN

Williams, Karen Lynn. *Painted Dreams*. New York: Lothrop, Lee & Shepard Books, 1998.

JAPANESE

Littlefield, Holly. *Colors of Japan*. Minneapolis, Minn.: Carolrhoda Books, 1997.

MEXICAN

Ancona, George. *Pablo Remembers the Fiesta of the Day of the Dead*. New York: Lothrop, Lee & Shepard Books, 1993.

Bunting, Eve. *Going Home*. New York: HarperCollins, 1997.

Czernecki, Stefan, and Timothy Rhodes. *Pancho's Piñata*. New York: Hyperion Paperbacks for Children, 1992.

Delacre, Lulu. *Golden Tales Myths, Legends and Folktales from Latin America*. New York: Scholastic, 1996.

Geeslin, Campbell. *In Rosa's Mexico*. New York: Alfred A. Knopf, 1996.

Gollub, Matthew. *The Moon Was at a Fiesta*. Santa Rosa, Calif.: Tutuga Press, 1994, 1997.

———. *The Twenty-Five Mixtex Cats*. New York: Tambourine Books, 1993.

———. *Uncle Snake*. New York: Tambourine Books, 1996.

Hoyt-Goldsmith, Diane. *Clay Hernandez—A Mexican American*. New York: Newbridge Communications, 1996.

Johnson, Tony. *Day of the Dead*. San Diego: Harcourt Brace, 1997.

———. *The Magic Maguey*. San Diego: Harcourt Brace, 1997.

Kleven, Elisa. *Hooray, a Piñata!* New York: Dutton, 1996.

Kurtz, Jane. *Miro in the Kingdom of the Sun*. Woodcuts by David Frampton. Boston: Houghton Mifflin, 1996.

Mathews, Sally Schofer. *The Sad Night: The Story of an Aztec Victory and a Spanish Loss*. New York: Clarion Books, 1994.

Morrow, Elizabeth. *The Painted Pig*. New York: Alfred A. Knopf, 1930.

NATIVE AMERICAN

Beadwork

Hunt, W. Ben, and J. F. "Buck" Burshears. *American Indian Beadwork*. New York: Macmillan, 1951.

McDermott, Gerald. *Arrow to the Sun*. New York: Puffin, 1974.

Button Blankets

Lewis, Paul Owen. *Frog Girl*. Hillsboro, Ore.: Beyond Words Publishing, 1997.

———. *Storm Boy*. Hillsboro, Ore.: Beyond Words Publishing, 1995.

McNutt, Nan. *The Button Blanket—A Northwest Coast Indian Art Activity Book*. Seattle: Sasquatch Books, n.d.

Inuit

Cohlene, Terri. *Ka·ha·si and the Loon—An Eskimo Legend*. Vero Beach, Calif.: Watermill Press, 1990.

Murphy, Claire Rudolf. *Caribou Girl*. Boulder, Colo.: Roberts Rinehart, 1998.

Kokopelli

Walker, Dave. *Cuckoo for Kokopelli*. Flagstaff, Ariz.: Northland Publishing, 1998.

Navajo Weaving

Grossenar, Virginia, and Sylvia Long. *Ten Little Rabbits*. San Francisco: Chronicle Books, 1991.

How the World Was Saved & Other Native American Tales. New York: Piers Harper Golden Books, 1994.

Miles, Miska. *Annie and the Old One*. Boston: Little, Brown, 1971.

Peña, Amado, and Juanita Alba. *Calor: A Story of Warmth for All Ages*. Waco, Tex.: WRS Publishing, 1995.

Northwest Coast Designs

Lelooska, Chief. *Echo of the Elders*. New York: DK Publishing, 1997.

———. *Spirit of the Cedar People*. New York: DK Publishing, 1998.

McDermott, Gerald. *A Trickster Tale from the Pacific Northwest*. New York: Harcourt Brace Jovanovich, 1993.

Steward, Hilary. *Looking at Indian Art of the Northwest Coast*. Seattle, Wash.: University of Washington Press, 1979.

Petroglyphs

La Pierre, Yvette. *Native American Rock Art*. Charlottesville, Va.: Thomasson-Grant & Lickle, 1994.

Philosophy and Tradition

Crow, Joe Medicine. *Brave Wolf and the Thunderbird*. New York: Abbeville, 1998.

Goble, Paul. *The Gift of the Sacred Dog*. New York: Aladdin, 1980.

Longfellow, Henry Wadsworth. *Hiawatha*. New York: Dial, 1983.

Matthaei, Gay, and Adam Cvijanovic. *The Ledgerbook of Thomas Blue Eagle*. Charlottesville, Va.: Thomasson-Grant & Lickle, 1994.

Raczek, Linda Theresa. *Rainy's Powwow*. Flagstaff, Ariz.: Rising Moon, 1999.

Seattle, Chief. *Brother Eagle Sister Sky*. New York: Dial, 1991.

Pueblo Pottery

Baylor, Byrd. *When Clay Sings*. New York: Aladdin, 1972.

Clark, Ann Nolan. *The Little Indian Pottery Maker*. N.p., n.d.

Hyde, Hazel. *Maria Making Pottery*. Santa Fe, N.M.: Sunstone Press, 1973.

Skin Painting

Bealer, Alex W. *The Picture-Skin Story*. New York: Holiday House, 1957.

dePaola, Tomie (retold by). *The Legend of the Indian Paintbrush*. New York: G. P. Putnam's Sons, 1988.

Friskey, Margaret. *Indian Two Feet and His House*. Chicago: Children's Press, 1959.

Tom-Toms

Cohlene, Terri. *Dancing Drum—A Cherokee Legend*. Vero Beach, Calif.: Watermill Press, 1970.

Totem Poles

Hoyt-Goldsmith, Diane. *Totem Pole*. New York: Holiday House, 1990.

Jensen, Vickie. *Carving a Totem Pole*. New York: Henry Holt, 1994.

Siberell, Ann. *Whale in the Sky*. New York: Dutton, 1982.

Zantua, Kanoe. *Princess Island Legends*. Ketchikan, Alaska: Angelo's Printing & Graphics.

Russian

Maxym, Lucy. *Russian Lacquer—Legends and Fairy Tales*. Farmingdale, N.Y.: Corners of the World, 1981.

Shakers

Raschka, Chris. *Simple Gifts—A Shaker Hymn*. New York: Henry Holt, 1998.

Ray, MaryLyn. *Shaker Boy*. San Diego: Browndeer Press, 1994.

Artists

ARTISTS BY NAME

JOSEFINA AGUILAR

Winter, Jeanette. *Josefina*. New York: Harcourt Brace Jovanovich, 1996.

MILTON AVERY

Kuskin, Karla. *Paul*. New York: HarperCollins, 1994.

WILSON BENTLEY

Martin, Jacqueline Briggs. *Snowflake Bentley*. Boston: Houghton Mifflin, 1998.

ROMARE BEARDEN

Hughes, Langston. *The Block*. New York: Viking, 1995.

Shange, Ntozake. *I Live in Music*. New York: Welcome Enterprises, 1978.

HIERONYMOUS BOSCH

Williard, Nancy. *Pish, Posh said Hieronymous Bosch*. Orlando, Fla.: Harcourt Brace Jovanovich, 1991.

CONSTANTINE BRANCUSI

Curtile, Sophie. *Le Cog*. New York: Metropolitan Museum of Art, 1990.

FILLIPPO BRUNELLESCHI

Bender, Michael. *Waiting for Fillippo: The Life of Renaissance Architect Fillippo Brunelleschi*. San Francisco: Chronicle Books, 1995.

ALEXANDER CALDER

Kalman, Marcia. *Roarr: Calder's Circus*. New York: Delacorte Press, 1991.

MARY CASSATT

McKellar, Shona. *A Child's Book of Lullabies*. New York: DK Publishing, 1997.

MARC CHAGALL

Kidd, Richard. *Almost Famous Daisy*. New York: Simon & Schuster, 1996.

Loumaye, Jacqueline. *Chagall, Mad Sad and Joyous Village*. New York: Chelsea House, 1984.

Raboff, Ernest. *Marc Chagall*. New York: Doubleday, 1982.

LEONARDO DA VINCI

Galli, Letizia. *Mona Lisa: The Secret of the Smile*. Garden City, N.Y.: Doubleday, 1996.

Lepscky, Ibi. *Leonardo da Vinci*. Hauppage, N.Y.: Barron's, 1984.

Provensen, A., and M. Provensen. *Leonardo da Vinci*. New York: Viking, 1984.

EDGAR DEGAS

Anholt, Laurence. *Degas and the Little Dancer*. Hauppage, N.Y.: Barron's, 1996.

Littlesugar, Amy. *Marie in Fourth Position*. New York: Penguin Putnam, 1996.

Skira-Venturi, Rosabiana. *A Weekend with Degas*. New York: Rizzoli, 1991.

Sweeney, Joan. *Bijou, Bonbon & Beau*. San Francisco: Chronicle Books, 1998.

ROBERT DELAUNAY

The Children's Studio and the National Museum of Modern Art, Georges-Pompidou Center, Paris, based on an original concept by Sophie Curtil. *Robert Delaunay*. New York: Harry N. Abrams, 1987.

GAUGUIN

Kidd, Richard. *Almost Famous Daisy*. New York: Simon & Schuster, 1996.

FRANCISCO GOYA
Venezia, Mike. *Francisco Goya*. Chicago: Children's Press, 1991.
RED GROOMS
Grooms, Red. *Ruckus Rodeo*. New York: Harry N. Abrams, 1988.
Strand, Mark. *Rembrandt Takes a Walk*. New York: Clarkson N. Potter, 1986.
KEITH HARING
Haring, Keith. *Big*. New York: Hyperion Books for Children, 1998.
———. *The Keith Haring Coloring Book*. New York: Fotofolio, 1992.
———. *My First Coloring Book*. New York: Fotofolio, 1993.
———. *10*. New York: Hyperion Books for Children, 1998.
EDWARD HICKS
Zadrzynska, Ewa. *The Peaceable Kingdom*. New York: M. M. Art Books, 1993.
WINSLOW HOMER
Littlesugar, Amy. *Jonkonnu: A Story from the Sketchbook of Winslow Homer*. New York: Philomel Books, 1997.
JACOB LAWRENCE
Duggleby, John. *Story Painter: The Life of Jacob Lawrence*. San Francisco: Chronicle Books, 1998.
Lawrence, Jacob. *Harriet and the Promised Land*. New York: Simon & Schuster, 1968.
Lawrence, Jacob, with Walter Dean Myers. *The Great Migrations*. New York: HarperCollins and the Museum of Modern Art, 1993.
ROY LICHTENSTEIN
Adelman, Bob. *Roy Lichtenstein's ABC*. Boston: Bulfinch Press, 1999.
Walker, Lou Ann. *Roy Lichtenstein—The Artist at Work*. New York: Lodestar Books, 1994.
RENÉ MAGRITTE
Garland, Michael. *Dinner at Magritte's*. New York: Dutton, 1995.
HENRI MATISSE
Benjamin, Roger. *Henri Matisse*. New York: Rizzoli, 1992.
Cohen, Leonard. *Dance Me to the Ends of Love*. New York: Welcome Enterprises, 1995.
Matisse, Henri. *Jazz*. New York: George Braziller, 1985.
Munthe, Nelly. *Meet Matisse*. Boston: Little, Brown, 1983.
MICHELANGELO
Fichetto, Laura. *Michael the Angel*. Garden City, N.Y.: Doubleday, 1993.
Parillo, Tony. *Michelangelo's Surprise*. New York: Farrar, Straus and Giroux, 1998.

CLAUDE MONET

Björk, Christina, and Lena Anderson. *Linnea in Monet's Garden*. New York: R & S Books, 1985.

Carmack, Lisa Jobe. *Philippe in Monet's Garden*. Boston: Museum of Fine Arts, 1998.

Kidd, Richard. *Almost Famous Daisy*. New York: Simon & Schuster, 1996.

Klee, Paul. *Dreaming Pictures*. Munich: Prestel-Verlag, 1997.

LeTord, Bijou. *A Blue Butterfly: A Story About Claude Monet*. New York: Doubleday, 1995.

GEORGIA O'KEEFFE

Venezia, Mike. *Georgia O'Keeffe*. Chicago: Children's Press, 1993.

Winter, Jeanette. *My Name Is Georgia*. San Diego: Harcourt Brace, 1998.

GRANDMA MOSES

Nikola-Lisa, W. *The Year with Grandma Moses*. New York: Henry Holt, 2000.

MAXFIELD PARRISH

Anderson, Jill. *The Maxfield Parrish Pop-Up Book*. Rohnert Park, Calif.: Pomegranate Art Books, 1994.

PABLO PICASSO

Anholt, Laurence. *Girl with a Ponytail: A Story About Pablo Picasso*. Hauppauge, N.Y.: Barron's, 1998.

Antoine, Veronique. *Picasso: A Day in His Studio*. New York: Chelsea House, 1993.

Hary, Tony. *Famous Children: Picasso*. Hauppauge, N.Y.: Barron's, 1994.

Lepscky, Ibi. *Pablo Picasso*. Chicago: Children's Press, 1984.

Venezia, Mike. *Picasso*. Chicago: Children's Press, 1988.

HORACE PIPPIN

Lyons, Mary E. *Starting Home: The Story of Horace Pippin*. New York: Charles Scribner's Sons, 1993.

JACKSON POLLACK

Glass, Andrew. *Jackson Makes His Move*. New York: Frederick Warne, 1982.

Kidd, Richard. *Almost Famous Daisy*. New York: Simon & Schuster, 1996.

BEATRIX POTTER

Wallner, Alexandra. *Beatrix Potter*. New York: Holiday House, 1995.

PIERRE-JOSEPH REDOUTÉ

Croll, Carolyn. *The Man Who Painted Flowers*. New York: G. P. Putnam's Sons, 1996.

REMBRANDT

Bonafoux, Pascal. *A Weekend with Rembrandt*. New York: Rizzoli, 1991.

Strand, Mark. *Rembrandt Takes a Walk*. New York: Clarkson N. Potter, 1986.

PIERRE-AUGUSTE RENOIR

Zadrzynska, Ewa, and Arnold Skolnick. *The Girl with the Watering Can*. New York: Chameleon Books, 1990.

FAITH RINGGOLD

Freeman, Linda, and Nancy Roucher. *Talking to Faith*. New York: Crown, 1996.

Ringgold, Faith. *Bonjour Lonnie*. New York: Hyperion Books for Children, 1996.

———. *Dinner at Aunt Connie's House*. New York: Hyperion Books for Children, 1993.

———. *Tar Beach*. New York: Crown, 1991.

DIEGO RIVERA

Braun, Barbara. *A Weekend with Diego Rivera*. New York: Rizzoli, 1994.

Winter, Jeanette. *Diego*. New York: Alfred A. Knopf, 1996.

HENRI ROUSSEAU

Canning, Kate. *A Painted Tale*. Hauppauge, N.Y.: Barron's, 1979.

Raboff, Ernest. *Henri Rousseau*. Garden City, N.Y.: Doubleday, 1970.

TOULOUSE-LAUTREC

Hart, Tony. *Famous Children: Toulouse-Lautrec*. Hauppauge, N.Y.: Barron's, 1994.

VINCENT VAN GOGH

Anholt, Laurence. *Camille and the Sunflowers: A Story About Vincent van Gogh*. Woodbury, N.Y.: Barron's, 1994.

Ison, Jean Shaddox. *The First Starry Night*. Dallas, Tex.: Whispering Coyote Press, 1997.

Loumaye, Jacqueline. *Van Gogh: The Touch of Yellow*. New York: Chelsea House, 1993.

Waldman, Neil. *The Starry Night*. Honesdale, Pa.: Boyds Mills Press, 1999.

ANDY WARHOL

Warhol, Andy. *Yum, Yum, Yum*. Boston: Bulfinch Press, 1996.

JAMES McNEIL WHISTLER

Merrill, Linda, and Sarah Ridley. *The Princess and the Peacocks*. New York: Hyperion Books for Children, in association with the Freer Art Gallery, Smithsonian Institution, 1993.

GRANT WOOD

Duggleby, John. *Artist in Overalls: The Life of Grant Wood*. San Francisco: Chronicle Books, 1995.

JAMIE WYETH

Seabrook, Elizabeth. *Cabbages and Kings*. New York: Viking, 1997.

N. C. WYETH

San Souci, Robert. *N. C. Wyeth's Pilgrims*. San Francisco: Chronicle Books, 1991.

ADULTS MAKING ART

Agee, Jon. *The Incredible Painting of Felix Clouseau*. New York: Farrar, Straus and Giroux, 1988.

Barrows, Allison. *The Artist's Model*. Minneapolis, Minn.: Carolrhoda Books, 1996.

Catalanotto, Peter. *The Painter*. New York: Orchard Books, 1995.

Cooney, Barbara. *Hattie and the Wild Waves*. New York: Viking, 1990.

———. *Miss Rumphius*. New York: Viking, 1982.

dePaola, Tomie. *Bonjour, Mr. Satie*. New York: G. P. Putnam's Sons, 1991.

Dunrea, Olivier. *The Painter Who Loved Chickens*. New York: Farrar, Straus and Giroux, 1995.

Goffstein, M. B. *An Artist*. New York: Harper & Row, 1980.

Kesselman, Wendy. *Emma*. New York: Dell, 1980.

Littlesugar, Amy. *Josiah True and the Art Maker*. New York: Simon & Schuster, 1995.

Mallat, Kathy, and Bruce McMillan. *The Picture That Mom Drew*. New York: Walker, 1997.

Nicholson, Nicholas B. A. *Little Girl in a Red Dress with Cat and Dog*. New York: Viking, 1998.

Striker, Susan. *The Anti-Coloring Book® for Adults*. New York: Holt, Rinehart and Winston, 1983.

ANIMALS MAKING ART

Borovsky, Paul. *The Strange Blue Creature*. New York: Hyperion Books for Children, 1993.

Browne, Anthony. *Willy's Pictures*. Cambridge, Mass.: Candlewick Press, 2000.

Deeter, Catherine. *Seymour Bleu*. New York: Simon & Schuster, 1998.

Gage, Amy Glaser. *Pascual's Magic Pictures*. Minneapolis, Minn.: Carolrhoda Books, 1996.

Glass, Andrew. *Jackson Makes His Move*. New York: Frederick Warne, 1982.

Hurd, Thacher. *Art Dog*. New York: HarperCollins, 1996.

Laden, Nina. *When Pigasso Met Mootisse*. San Francisco: Chronicle Books, 1998.

Lionni, Leo. *Matthew's Dream*. New York: Alfred A. Knopf, 1991.

McPhail, David. *Drawing Lessons from a Bear*. Boston: Little, Brown, 2000.

Rex, Michael. *The Painting Gorilla*. New York: Henry Holt, 1997.

Wolkstein, Diane. *Little Mouse's Painting*. New York: Morrow Junior Books, 1992.

Ziefert, Harriet. *Elemenopeo*. New York: Houghton Mifflin, 1998.

ARTISTS AT WORK

Goffstein, M. B. *Lives of the Artists*. New York: Farrar, Straus and Giroux, 1981.

Krull, Kathleen. *Lives of the Artists*. Orlando, Fla.: Harcourt Brace Jovanovich, 1995.

Lionni, Leo. *Matthew's Dream*. New York: Alfred A. Knopf, 1991.

Striker, Susan. *Artists at Work: An Anti-Coloring Book*. New York: Henry Holt, 1996.

KIDS MAKING ART

Berman, Linda M. A. *The Goodbye Painting*. New York: Human Sciences Press, 1983.

Bornstein, Ruth Lercher. *That's How It Is When We Draw*. New York: Clarion Books, 1997.

Borovsky, Paul. *The Strange Blue Creature*. New York: Hyperion Books, 1993.

Bröger, Achim, and Michele Sambin. *Francie's Paper Puppy*. Natick, Mass.: Picture Book Studio, 1982.

Cheltenham Elementary School Kindergarten. *We Are All Alike, We Are All Different*. New York: Scholastic, 1990.

Cohen, Miriam, and Lillian Hoban. *No Good in Art*. New York: Dell, 1980.

Collins, Pat Lowery. *I Am an Artist*. Brookfield, Conn.: Millbrook Press, 1992.

Cooney, Barbara. *Hattie and the Wild Waves*. New York: Viking, 1990.

Deeter, Catherine. *Seymour Bleu*. New York: Simon & Schuster, 1998.

Demi. *Liang and the Magic Paintbrush*. New York: Henry Holt, 1980.

dePaola, Tomie. *The Art Lesson*. New York: G. P. Putnam's Sons, 1989.

———. *Bonjour Mr. Satie*. New York: G. P. Putnam's Sons, 1989.

——— (retold by). *The Legend of the Indian Paintbrush*. New York: G. P. Putnam's Sons, 1988.

Edwards, Dorothy, and Priscilla Lamon. *Emmie and the Purple Paint*. New York: Oxford University Press, 1987.

Elliott, Dan. *Ernie's Little Lie*. Illustrated by Joe Mathieu. Featuring Jim Henson's Sesame Street Muppets. New York: Random House, 1983.

Freeman, Michael. *Grandfather's Pencil*. New York: Harcourt Brace Jovanovich, 1994.

Gage, Amy Glaser. *Pascual's Magic Pictures*. Minneapolis, Minn.: Carolrhoda Books, 1996.

Green, Donna. *My Little Artist*. New York: Smithmark, 1999.

Hamsa, Bobby. *Fast Draw Freddie*. Chicago: Children's Press, 1984.

Hest, Amy. *Jamaica Louise James*. Cambridge, Mass.: Candlewick Press, 1984.

Hoban, Russell. *Monsters*. New York: Scholastic, 1989.

Hubbard, Patricia. *My Crayons Talk*. New York: Henry Holt, 1996.

Hurd, Thacher. *Art Dog*. San Francisco: HarperCollins, 1996.

Isadora, Rachel. *The Pirates of Bedford Street*. New York: Greenwillow Books, 1988.

———. *Willaby*. New York: Macmillan, 1977.

Johnson, Crockett. *A Picture for Harold's Room*. New York: Scholastic, 1960.

Kent, Jack. *The Scribble Monster*. New York: Harcourt Brace Jovanovich, 1981.

Kidd, Richard. *Almost Famous Daisy*. New York: Simon & Schuster, 1996.

Lionni, Leo. *Matthew's Dream*. New York: Alfred A. Knopf, 1991.

Littlesugar, Amy. *Josiah True and the Art Maker*. New York: Simon & Schuster, 1995.

MacDonald, Elizabeth. *John's Picture*. New York: Viking Penguin, 1990.

Maynard, Bill. *Incredible Ned*. New York: G. P. Putnam's Sons, 1997.

McClintock, Barbara. *The Fantastic Drawings of Danielle*. Boston: Houghton Mifflin, 1996.

McPhail, David. *The Magical Drawings of Moony B. Finch*. N.p., 1978.

———. *Moony B. Finch, Fastest Draw in the West*. New York: Golden Books, 1994.

———. *Something Special*. Boston: Little, Brown, 1988.

Molarsky, Osmond. *A Sky Full of Kites*. Berkeley, Calif.: Tricycle Press, 1996.

Moss, Marissa. *Regina's Big Mistake*. New York: Houghton Mifflin, 1990.

Moss, Sally. *Peter's Painting*. Greenvale, N.Y.: Mondo, 1995.

Munsch, R., and Helene Desputeaux. *Purple, Green and Yellow*. Buffalo, N.Y.: Annick Press, 1992.

Russo, Marisabina. *Under the Table*. New York: Greenwillow Books, 1997.

Rylant, Cynthia. *All I See*. New York: Orchard Books, 1988.

Say, Allan. *Emma's Rug*. Boston: Houghton Mifflin, 1996.

Schaefer, Carole Lexa. *The Squiggle*. New York: Crown, 1996.

Stanley, Diane. *The Gentleman and the Kitchen Maid*. New York: Dial, 1997.

Thomas, Abigail. *Pearl Paints*. New York: Henry Holt, 1994.

Tusa, Tricia. *Bunnies in My Head*. Houston, Tex.: University of Texas, M. D. Anderson Cancer Center, 1998.

United Nations. *My Wish for Tomorrow*. New York: Tambourine Books, 1995.

Waddell, Martin. *Alice the Artist*. New York: Dutton, 1988.

Wilhelm, Hans. *Oh, What a Mess*. New York: Crown, 1988.

Williams, Karen Lynn. *Painted Dreams*. New York: Lothrop, Lee & Shepard Books, 1998.

Williams, Vera B. *Cherries and Cherry Pits*. New York: Scholastic, 1986.

Wilson-Max, Ken. *Max Paints the House*. New York: Hyperion Books for Children, 2000.

Ziefert, Harriet. *Elemenopeo*. New York: Houghton Mifflin, 1998.

The Environment and Weather

CLOUDS

Carle, Eric. *Little Cloud*. New York: Philomel Books, 1993.

Cutting, Brian, and Jillian Cutting. *Clouds*. Bothell, Wash.: Wright Group, 1988.

dePaola, Tomie. *The Cloud Book*. New York: Scholastic, 1975.

Locker, Thomas. *Cloud Dance*. San Diego: Silver Whistle, 2000.

Lustig, Ester, and Michael Lustig. *Willy Whyner, Cloud Designer*. New York: Four Winds Press, 1994.

Turkle, Brinton. *The Sky Dog*. New York: Scholastic, 1969.

RAIN

Archambault, John, and Bill Martin Jr. *Listen to the Rain*. New York: Henry Holt, 1988.

Grove, Don S. *One Rainy Night*. New York: Atheneum, 1974.

Kulan, Robert. *Rain*. New York: Morrow, 1978.

Serfozo, Mary. *Rain Talk*. New York: Macmillan, 1993.

Shulevitz, Uri. *Rain, Rain Rivers*. New York: Farrar, Straus and Giroux, 1969.

Tresselt, Alvin. *Rain Drop Splash*. New York: Lothrop, Lee & Shepard, 1946.

SCAPES
ALIEN
Canaday, John and John Arthur, eds. *Richard Estes: The Urban Landscapes.* Boston: Museum of Fine Arts, 1978.

Cutting, Brian, and Jillian Cutting. *Space.* San Diego: Wright Group, 1988.

Getz, David. *Alien.* New York: Henry Holt, 1997.

CITY
Cornelius, Chase, and Sue Cornelius. *The City in Art.* Minneapolis, Minn.: Lerner, 1966.

Tice, George A. *Urban Landscapes.* New Brunswick, N.J.: Rutgers University, 1975.

Yolen, Jane (poems selected by). *Sky Scrape/City Scape.* Honesdale, Pa.: Boyds Mills Press, 1996.

RURAL LANDSCAPES
Bruchac, Joseph. *Between Earth and Sky.* San Diego: Harcourt Brace Jovanovich, 1996.

Locker, Thomas. *Home.* San Diego: Harcourt Brace Jovanovich, 1998.

SEASCAPES
Cooney, Barbara. *Hattie and the Wild Waves.* New York: Viking, 1990.

Lee, Huy Voun. *At the Beach.* New York: Henry Holt, 1994.

SEASONS
AUTUMN
Archambault, John, and Bill Martin Jr. *Barn Dance!* New York: Henry Holt, 1986.

Birdwell, Norman. *Clifford's First Autumn.* New York: Scholastic, 1997.

Buscaglia, Leo. *The Fall of Freddie the Leaf: A Story of Life for All Ages.* New York: Henry Holt, 1982.

Ehlert, Lois. *Red Leaf, Yellow Leaf.* New York: Harcourt Brace Jovanovich, 1991.

Krensky, Stephen. *Lionel in the Fall.* New York: Henry Holt, 1982.

Maas, Robert. *When Autumn Comes.* New York: Henry Holt, 1990.

Riley, James Whitcomb. *When the Frost Is on the Pumpkin.* Boston: David R. Godine, 1991.

Rockwell, Anne. *Apples and Pumpkins.* New York: Macmillan, 1989.

San Souci, Robert. *Feathertop.* New York: Doubleday, 1992.

CHANGING
Allen, Marjorie N. *Changes.* New York: Macmillan, 1991.

Gilchrist, Jan Spivey. *Indigo and Moonlight Gold*. New York: Black Butterfly Children's Books, 1993.

Hazeltine, Alice I., and Elva S. Smith. *The Year Around: Poems for Children*. Eau Claire, Wis.: E. M. Hale, 1961.

Lindbergh, Reeve. *The Circle of Days*. Cambridge, Mass.: Candlewick Press, 1998.

SPRING

Kinsey-Warnock, Natalie. *When Spring Comes*. New York: Dutton Children's Books, 1993.

SUMMER

Crews, Nina. *One Hot Summer Day*. New York: Greenwillow Books, 1995.

WINTER

Gammell, Stephen. *Is That You, Winter?* San Diego: Harcourt Brace Jovanovich, 1997.

Lee, Huy Voun. *In the Snow*. New York: Henry Holt, 1995.

Martin, Jacqueline Briggs. *Snowflake Bentley*. Boston: Houghton Mifflin, 1998.

SKY

Bradbury, Ray. *Switch on the Night*. New York: Alfred A. Knopf, 1993.

Branley, Franklyn M. *The Big Dipper*. New York: HarperCollins, 1962, 1991.

Edens, Cooper. *Caretakers of Wonder*. New York: Green Tiger Press, 1980.

Field, Enid. *I Wonder . . . About the Sky*. Chicago: Children's Press, 1973.

Gibbons, Gail. *Sun Up, Sun Down*. Orlando, Fla.: Harcourt Brace Jovanovich, 1983.

Ginsburg, Maria. *How the Sun Was Brought Back to the Sky*. New York: Macmillan, 1975.

Isom, Joan Shaddox. *The First Starry Night*. Dallas, Tex.: Whispering Coyote Press, 1997.

Lee, Jeanne M. *Legend of the Milky Way*. New York: Henry Holt, 1982.

Rockwell, Anne. *The Dancing Stars: An Iroquois Legend*. New York: Crowell, 1972.

Yolen, Jane. *Nocturne*. San Diego: Harcourt Brace Jovanovich, 1997.

SUN

Gibbons, Gail. *Sun Up, Sun Down*. Orlando: Harcourt Brace Jovanovich, 1983.

Ginsburg, Maria. *How the Sun Was Brought Back to the Sky*. New York: Macmillan, 1975.

Grunsell, Angela. *The Sun*. New York: Franklin Watts, 1985.

Kramsky, Jerry, and Lorenzo Mattotte. *The Cranky Sun*. Boston: Little, Brown, 1994.

WEATHER

Fromby, Caroline. *Wild Weather Soup*. Chicago: Child's Play, 1995.

Koscielniak, Bruce. *Geoffrey the Groundhog Predicts the Weather*. Boston: Houghton Mifflin, 1995.

Rockwell, Anne. *The Storm*. New York: Hyperion Books for Children, 1994.

WIND

Ets, Marie Hall. *Gilberto and the Wind*. New York: Viking, 1963.

Hutchins, Pat. *The Wind Blew*. New York: Viking Penguin, 1978.

Lipson, Michael. *How the Wind Plays*. New York: Hyperion Books for Children, 1994.

Pierce, Robert. *The Day of the Wind*. New York: Golden Press, 1969.

Thompson, Kathleen A. *Sometimes I Am Like a Kite*. New York: Green Tiger Press, 1991.

Yolen, Jane. *The Girl Who Loved the Wind*. New York: HarperCollins, 1972.

Imaginary Creatures

ALIENS—OUTER SPACE

Anderson, Joan. *Richie's Rocket*. New York: Morrow, 1993.

Borovsky, Paul. *The Strange Blue Creature*. New York: Hyperion Books for Children, 1993.

Cutting, Brian, and Jillian Cutting. *Space*. San Diego: Wright Group, 1988.

Cutting, Jillian. *The Space Ark*. San Diego: Wright Group, 1988.

Getz, David. *Floating Home*. New York: Henry Holt, 1997.

Keats, Ezra Jack. *Regards to the Man in the Moon*. New York: Four Winds Press, 1987.

Mayer, Mercer. *The Alien*. Racine, Wis.: Western, 1995.

McNaughton, Colin. *Here Come the Aliens*. Cambridge, Mass.: Candlewick Press, 1995.

Sadler, Marilyn. *Alistair and the Alien Invasion*. New York: Simon & Schuster, 1994.

Strand, Mark. *The Planet of Lost Things*. New York: Potter, 1936.

Weisner, David. *June 29, 1999*. New York: Clarion Books, 1992.

Wilson, Max, and Ken Wilson. *Big Silver Space Shuttle*. New York: Scholastic, 1996.

DRAGONS

Bateson-Hill, Margaret. *Lao Lao of Dragon Mountain*. New York: Zero to Ten, 1998.

Davol, Marguerite W. *The Paper Dragon*. Illustrated by Robert Sabuda. New York: Atheneum, 1997.

Nolen, Jerdine. *Raising Dragons*. San Diego: Harcourt Brace Jovanovich, 1998.

Prelutsky, Jack, and Peter Sis. *The Dragons Are Singing Tonight*. New York: Scholastic, 1993.

Repchuk, Caroline. *The Glitter Dragon*. Illustrated by Colin and Moira Maclean. New York: Marlowe and Company, 1995.

MONSTERS

Berlan, Kathryn Hook. *Andrew's Amazing Monsters*. New York: Atheneum, 1993.

Hoban, Russell. *Monsters*. New York: Scholastic, 1989.

Komish, Daniel, and David Komish. *The Night the Scary Beasties Popped Out of My Head*. New York: Random House, 1998.

Mayer, Mercer. *There's a Nightmare in My Closet*. New York: Dial, 1968.

Sendak, Maurice. *Where the Wild Things Are*. New York: Harper & Row, 1963.

Viorst, Judith. *My Mama Says There Aren't Any Zombies, Ghosts, Vampires, Creatures, Demons, Monsters, Fiends, Goblins or Things*. New York: Aladdin, 1973.

TOOTH FAIRY

Karlin, Nurit. *The Tooth Witch*. New York: Harper & Row, 1985.

Kaye, Marilyn. *The Real Tooth Fairy*. New York: Harcourt Brace, 1990.

TROLLS

Brett, Jan. *Trouble with Trolls*. New York: Scholastic, 1992.

Imaginative Thinking

ACCIDENTAL ART

Aylesworth, Jim. *Old Black Fly*. New York: Henry Holt, 1992.

Blair, Margot. *The Red String*. Venice, Calif.: Children's Library Press, 1996.

Bröger, Achim, and Michele Sambin. *Francie's Paper Puppy*. Natick, Mass.: Picture Book Studio, 1982.

Carrick, Malcolm. *Splodges*. New York: Viking, 1976.

Crews, Donald. *Ten Black Dots*. New York: Greenwillow Books, 1968, 1986.

Moss, Marissa. *Regina's Big Mistake*. Boston: Houghton Mifflin, 1990.

Pinkwater, Daniel Manus. *The Big Orange Splot*. New York: Scholastic, 1977.

Seuss, Dr. *Hooray for Diffendoofer Day!* New York: Alfred A. Knopf, 1998.

Shaw, Charles G. *It Looked Like Spilled Milk*. New York: Harper & Row, 1947.

Turkle, Brinton. *The Sky Dog*. New York: Scholastic, 1969.

Utton, Peter. *The Witch's Hand*. New York: Farrar, Straus and Giroux, 1989.

ART ON INAPPROPRIATE PLACES

Edwards, Dorothy. *Emmie and the Purple Paint*. New York: Oxford University Press, 1987.

Isadora, Rachel. *The Pirate of Bedford Street*. New York: Greenwillow Books, 1988.

Munsch, Robert. *Purple, Green and Yellow*. Toronto: Annick Press, 1992.

Russo, Marisabina. *Under the Table*. New York: Greenwillow Books, 1997.

IMAGINATION

Dorros, Arthur. *Abuela*. New York: Dutton Children's Books, 1991.

Greenfield, Eloise. *Africa Dream*. New York: HarperCollins, 1977.

Keats, Ezra Jack. *Regards to the Man in the Moon*. New York: Four Winds Press, 1981.

Oram, Hiawyn, and Satoshi Kitamura. *In the Attic*. New York: Henry Holt, 1984.

Perry, Sarah. *If . . .* Malibu, Calif.: J. Paul Getty Museum and Children's Library Press, 1995.

Striker, Susan. *Nature's Wonders for the Young at Art®*. New York: Henry Holt, 1998.

———. *The Anti-Coloring Book® of Celebrations*. New York: Henry Holt, 1995.

———. *The Circus Anti-Coloring Book®*. New York: Henry Holt, 1995.

———. *The Newspaper Anti-Coloring Book®*. New York: Henry Holt, 1992.

———. *The Mystery Anti-Coloring Book®*. New York: Henry Holt, 1991.

———. *The Superpowers Anti-Coloring Book®*. New York: Grosset & Dunlap, 1984.

————. *The Sixth Anti-Coloring Book®*. New York: Henry Holt, 1984.

————. *The Inventor's Anti-Coloring Book®*. New York: Henry Holt, 1983.

————. *The Fifth Anti-Coloring Book®*. New York: Henry Holt, 1982.

————. *The Anti-Coloring Book® of Masterpieces*. New York: Henry Holt, 1982.

————. *The Fourth Anti-Coloring Book®*. New York: Henry Holt, 1981.

————. *The Anti-Coloring Book® of Red Letter Days*. New York: Holt, Rinehart and Winston, 1981.

————. *The Third Anti-Coloring Book®*. New York: Henry Holt, 1980.

————. *The Anti-Coloring Book® of Exploring Space on Earth*. New York: Henry Holt, 1980.

————. *The Second Anti-Coloring Book®*. New York: Henry Holt, 2000.

————. *The Anti-Coloring Book®*. New York: Henry Holt, 2000.

Utton, Peter. *Jennifer's Room*. New York: Orchard Books, 1994.

PICTURES COME ALIVE

Agee, Jon. *The Incredible Painting of Felix Clousseau*. New York: Farrar, Straus and Giroux, 1988.

Bröger, Achim, and Michele Sambin. *Francie's Paper Puppy*. Natick, Mass.: Picture Book Studio, 1982.

Canning, Kate. *A Painted Tale*. Woodbury, N.Y.: Barron's, 1979.

Demi. *Liang and the Magic Paintbrush*. New York: Henry Holt, 1980.

Johnson, Crockett. *A Picture for Harold's Room*. New York: Scholastic, 1960.

Jur, Bill Martin. *The Ghost-Eye Tree*. New York: Henry Holt, 1985.

Lionni, Leo. *Let's Make Rabbits*. New York: Pantheon, 1982.

Maynard, Bill. *Incredible Ned*. New York: G. P. Putnam's Sons, 1997.

McPhail, David. *Moony B. Finch, Fastest Draw in the West*. Racine, Wis.: Golden Books, 1994.

Potter, Katherine. *Spike*. New York: Simon & Schuster, 1994.

Reiner, Annie. *A Visit to the Art Galaxy*. New York: Green Tiger Press, 1990.

Sortland, Bjorn, and Lars Elling. *Anna's Art Adventure*. Minneapolis: Carolrhoda Books, 1999.

Velthuijs, Max. *The Painter and the Bird*. Reading, Mass.: Addison-Wesley, 1975.

WISHES/DREAMS

Breathed, Berkely. *A Wish for Wings That Work*. New York: Little, Brown, 1991.

Brown, Mac. *Arthur's Tooth*. Boston: Atlantic Monthly, 1985.

Carle, Eric. *The Secret Birthday Message*. New York: Harper Trophy, 1971.

Cazet, Denys. *Daydreams: Stories and Pictures*. New York: Orchard Books, 1990.

Farmer, Patti. *Bartholomew's Dreams*. Hauppaugh, N.Y.: Barron's, 1994.

Greenfield, Eloise. *Daydreamers*. New York: Dial, 1981.

Hague, Kathleen. *Out of the Nursery, Into the Night*. New York: Henry Holt, 1986.

Horowitz, Jordan. *Aladdin and the Magic Lamp*. New York: Cartwheel Books, 1993.

Keats, Ezra Jack. *Dream*. New York: Macmillan, 1974.

Kite, L. Patricia. *Dandelion Adventures*. Brookfield, Conn.: Millbrook Press, 1988.

Lionni, Leo. *Matthew's Dream*. New York: Random House, 1991.

Nixon, Joan Lowery. *Will You Give Me a Dream?* New York: Four Winds Press, 1994.

Zemach, Margot. *The Three Wishes: An Old Story*. New York: HarperCollins, 1986.

Media

COLLAGE

Davol, Marguerite W. *The Paper Dragon*. New York: Atheneum, 1997.

Gibbons, Gail. *Paper, Paper Everywhere*. New York: Harcourt Brace Jovanovich, 1983.

Hol, Coby. *Nicki's Little Donkey*. New York: North-South Books, 1993.

Hooper, Patricia, and Susan L. Roth. *How the Sky's Housekeeper Wore Her Scarves*. Boston: Little, Brown, 1995.

Hopkins, Lee Bennett. *School Supplies—A Book of Poems*. New York: Simon & Schuster, 1996.

Legge, David. *Bamboozled*. New York: Scholastic, 1994.

Lionni, Leo. *Let's Make Rabbbits*. New York: Pantheon, 1982.

Meilach, Dona, and Elvie Ten Hoor. *Collage and Found Art*. New York: Rinehold, 1964.

Oughton, Jerrie. *How the Stars Fell into the Sky: A Navajo Legend*. Boston: Houghton Mifflin, 1992.

Ranson, Candice, and Felicia Bond. *The Big Green Pocketbook*. New York: HarperCollins, 1993.

Sykes, Julie, and Tanya Linch. *This and That*. New York: Farrar, Straus and Giroux, 1996.

Toale, Bernard. *The Art of Paper Making*. Worcester, Mass.: Davis, 1982.

Whitman, Candace. *Bring on the Blue*. New York: Abbeville, 1998.

CRAFTS

BEADS

Reid, Margaret S. *A String of Beads*. New York: Dutton Children's Books, 1997.

BUTTONS

Reid, Margaret S. *The Button Box*. New York: Dutton Children's Books, 1990.

LACQUER

Maxym, Lucy. *Russian Lacquer: Legends and Fairy Tales*. Farmingdale, N.Y.: Corners of the World, 1981.

MOSAICS

Currier, Richard L. *The Art of Mosaics*. Minneapolis: Lerner, 1974.

Lewis, Beatrice, and Leslie McGuire. *Making Mosaics*. New York: Drake, 1973.

Stanley, Diane, and Perer Vennema. *Cleopatra*. New York: Morrow, 1994.

PAPER

Gibbons, Gail. *Paper, Paper Everywhere*. New York: Harcourt Brace Jovanovich, 1983.

Wilkinson, Beth. *Papermaking for Kids*. Layton, Utah: Gibbs Smith, 1997.

PUPPETS

Finger

Wood, Audrey, and Don Wood. *Piggies*. San Diego: Harcourt Brace Jovanovich, 1991.

Shadow

Bartalos. *Shadowville*. New York: Viking, 1995.

Wooden

Collodi, Carlo. *The Adventures of Pinocchio*. New York: Henry Holt, 1986.

Gauch, Patricia Lee. *Poppy's Puppet*. New York: Henry Holt, 1999.

Lucado, Max. *You Are Special*. New York: Scholastic, 1997.

RIBBONS

Satomi, Ichikawa. *Isabela's Ribbons*. New York: Philomel Books, 1995.

DRAWING

CHALK

Freeman, Don. *The Chalk Box Story*. Philadelphia, Pa.: Lippincott, 1976.

Hawkinson, John. *Pastels Are Great!* Chicago: Albert Whitman, 1968.

CRAYON

Charles, Oz. *How Is a Crayon Made?* New York: Simon & Schuster, 1988.

DeRolf, Shane. *The Crayon Box That Talked.* New York: Random House, 1996.

Girdler, Reynolds. *Crayon Techniques.* New York: Pitman, 1969.

Goffstein, Brook. *Artist's Helpers Enjoy the Evening.* New York: Harper & Row, 1987.

Hubbard, Patricia. *My Crayons Talk.* New York: Henry Holt, 1996.

Ryan, Pam Muñoz, and Jerry Pallotta. *The Crayon Counting Book.* Watertown, Mass.: Charlesbridge, 1996.

IN SAND

Lee, Huy Voun. *At the Beach.* New York: Henry Holt, 1994.

PENCIL

Cox, John. *Night Drawing.* New York: Henry Holt, 1996.

Foreman, Michael. *Grandfather's Pencil and the Room of Stories.* New York: Harcourt Brace Jovanovich, 1994.

Jeschke, Susan. *Perfect the Pig.* New York: Henry Holt, 1980.

McPhail, David. *Mooney B. Finch, Fastest Draw in the West.* Racine, Wis.: Golden Books, 1994.

RUBBING

Bunting, Eve, and Ronald Himler. *The Wall.* New York: Clarion Books, 1990.

SCRATCHBOARD

Lincoln, Abraham. *The Gettysburg Address.* New York: Houghton Mifflin, 1995.

Van Allsburg, Chris. *Ben's Dream.* Boston: Houghton Mifflin, 1982.

FIBER ARTS

DREAMCATCHERS

Heyer, Marilee. *The Weaving of a Dream.* New York: Puffin Books, 1986.

Osofsky, Audrey. *Dreamcatcher.* New York: Orchard Books, 1992.

KNITTING

Blackwood, Mary. *Derek the Knitting Dinosaur.* Minneapolis: Carolrhoda Books, 1987.

MACRAMÉ

Archambault, John, and Bill Martin Jr. *Knots on a Counting Rope.* New York: Henry Holt, 1987.

QUILTS

Bateson-Hill, Margaret. *Shota and the Star Quilt.* New York: Zero to Ten Unlimited, 1998.

Brumbeau, Jeff. *The Quilt Maker's Gift.* Hamilton, Minn.: Pfeifer, 2000.

Hopkinson, Deborah. *Sweet Clara and the Freedom Quilt.* New York: Dragonfly Books, 1993.

Johnston, Tony, and Tomie dePaola. *The Quilt Story.* New York: G. P. Putnam's Sons, 1985.

Jonas, Ann. *The Quilt.* New York: Greenwillow Books, 1984.

Kuskin, Karla. *Patchwork Island.* New York: HarperCollins, 1994.

Min, Willemien. *Peter's Patchwork Dream.* Brooklyn, N.Y.: Barefoot Books, 1991.

Polacco, Patricia. *The Keeping Quilt.* New York: Simon & Schuster, 1988.

Ringgold, Faith. *Bonjour Lonnie.* New York: Hyperion Books for Children, 1996.

———. *Dinner at Aunt Connie's House.* New York: Hyperion Books for Children, 1993.

———. *Tar Beach.* New York: Crown, 1991.

Smucker, Barbara. *Selina and the Bear Paw Quilt.* New York: Crown, 1995.

STITCHERY

Armstrong, Jennifer. *Pockets.* New York: Crown, 1998.

Denny, Norman, and Josephine Filmer-Sankey. *The Bayeux Tapestry.* New York: Atheneum, 1966.

Fair, Sylvia. *The Bedspread.* New York: Morrow, 1982.

Presilla, Marciel E., and Gloria Soto. *Life Around the Lake.* New York: Henry Holt, 1996.

WEAVING

Bodkin, Odds. *The Crane Wife.* San Diego: Gulliver Books, 1998.

Castaneda, Omar S. *Abuela's Weave.* New York: Lee & Low Books, 1993.

Griman, Nikki. *Aneesa Lee and the Weaver's Gift.* New York: Lothrop, Lee & Shepard Books, 1999.

Heyer, Marilee. *The Weaving of a Dream.* New York: Puffin Books, 1986.

Lattimore, Deborah Nourse. *The Dragon's Robe.* New York: HarperCollins, 1990.

Miles, Miska. *Annie and the Old One.* New York: Little, Brown, 1971.

Price, Kathleen McCormick. *The Lady and the Unicorn: A Tale of the Tapestries.* Bridgeport, Conn.: Green Bark Press, 1994.

Radley, Gail. *The Spinner's Gift.* New York: North-South Books, 1994.

Sanderson, Ruth. *Tapestries—Stories of Women in the Bible.* Boston: Little, Brown, 1998.

San Souci, Robert D. *A Weave of Words*. New York: Orchard Books, 1998.

Yarrow, Peter, and Leonard Lipton. *Puff, the Magic Dragon*. New York: Avon Books, 1979.

FOOD

Arnold, Katya, and Sam Swope. *Katya's Book of Mushrooms*. New York: Henry Holt, 1997.

Bloom, Valerie. *Fruits—A Caribbean Counting Poem*. New York: Henry Holt, 1992.

Brown, Marcia. *Stone Soup*. New York: Charles Scribner's Sons, 1947.

Desauliniers, Marcel. *An Alphabet of Sweets*. New York: Rizzoli, 1996.

Egielski, Richard. *The Gingerbread Boy*. New York: HarperCollins, 1997.

Ehlert, Lois. *Growing Vegetable Soup*. Orlando, Fla.: Harcourt Brace Jovanovich, 1987.

Elffers, Joost. *Play with Your Food*. New York: Stewart, Tabori & Chang, 1997.

Elffers, Joost, and Saxton Freymann. *Play with Your Pumpkins*. New York: Stewart, Tabori & Chang, 1998.

Everitt, Betsy. *Mean Soup*. San Diego: Harcourt Brace, 1992.

Fleming, Denise. *Lunch*. New York: Henry Holt, 1992.

Formby, Caroline. *Wild Weather Soup*. Swindon, England: Child's Play, 1995.

Freymann, Saxton. *Dr. Pompo's Nose*. New York: Arthur A. Levine Books, 2000.

Goldstone, Bruce. *The Beastly Feast*. New York: Henry Holt, 1998.

Kimmelman, Leslie. *Frannie's Fruits*. New York: Harper & Row, 1989.

Lord, John Vernon, and Janet Burroway. *The Giant Jam Sandwich*. Boston: Houghton Mifflin, 1972.

Michael Friedman Publishing Group. *Pumpkins*. New York: Friedman/Fairfax, 1998.

Pienkowski, Jan. *Dinner Time*. Los Angeles: Price Stern Sloan, 1981.

Pittman, Helena Claire. *Still Life Stew*. New York: Hyperion Books for Children, 1998.

Redhead, Janet Slater. *The Big Block of Chocolate*. Auckland, N.Z.: Ashton Scholastic, 1988.

Seuss, Dr. *Green Eggs and Ham*. New York: Random House, 1960.

Smith, Alastair. *What Happens to Your Food?* New York: Scholastic, 1997.

Warhol, Andy. *Yum, Yum, Yum*. Boston: Bulfinch Press, 1996.

INTERIOR DESIGN
CARPETS
Brisson, Pat. *Magic Carpet*. New York: Bradbury Press, 1991.

dePaola, Tomie. *The Legend of the Persian Carpet*. New York: G. P. Putman's Sons, 1993.

Say, Allen. *Emma's Rug*. New York: Houghton Mifflin, 1996.
CHAIRS
Keats, Ezra Jack. *Peter's Chair*. New York: Puffin Books, 1967.

Williams, Vera. *A Chair for My Mother*. New York: Morrow, 1982.
WALLPAPER
Francis, Frank. *The Magic Wallpaper*. London: Abelard-Schuman, 1970.

MASKS
Baylor, Byrd. *They Put On Masks*. New York: Charles Scribner's Sons, 1974.

Keats, Ezra Jack. *Hi, Cat*. New York: Macmillan, 1970.

Mueller, Virginia. *A Halloween Mask for Monster*. New York: Puffin Books, 1988.

Wagner, Ken. *Jack in the Sack*. Racine, Wis.: Western, 1970.

PAINTING
Agee, Jon. *The Incredible Painting of Felix Clousseau*. New York: Farrar, Straus and Giroux, 1988.

Heller, Ruth. *Color*. New York: Putnam, 1995.

Lee, Huy Voun. *At the Beach*. New York: Henry Holt, 1998.

———. *In the Park*. New York: Henry Holt, 1998.

———. *In the Snow*. New York: Henry Holt, 1998.

Myers, Walter Dean. *The Story of Three Kingdoms*. New York: HarperCollins, 1995.

Striker, Susan. *The Anti-Coloring Book of Masterpieces*. New York: Henry Holt, 1982.

———. *Young at Art: The First Anti-Coloring Book for Preschoolers*. New York: Simon & Schuster, 1985.

Velthiys, Max. *The Painter and the Bird*. Reading, Pa.: Addison-Wesley, 1975.

Ventura, Piero, and Marisa Ventura. *The Painter's Trick*. New York: Random House, 1977.

Withers, Carl (retold by). *Painting the Moon*. New York: E. P. Dutton, 1970.
ABSTRACT
Carrick, Malcolm. *Splodges*. New York: Viking, 1976.

Dickinson, Mike. *Smudge*. New York: Abbeville, 1988.

ACTION PAINTING

Ayles, Jim. *Old Black Fly*. New York: Henry Holt, 1992.

Glass, Andrew. *Jackson Makes His Move*. New York: Frederick Warne, 1982.

Rosenberg, Liz, and Stephen Gammel. *Monster Mama*. New York: Philomel Books, 1993.

Spier, Peter. *Oh, Were They Ever Happy!* Garden City, N.Y.: Doubleday, 1978.

Tresselt, Alvin. *Rain Drop Splash*. New York: Lothrop, Lee & Shepard, 1946.

BLACK WASH

Hasely, Dennis. *The Old Banjo*. New York: Macmillan, 1983.

DYEING

Sabuda, Robert. *The Blizzard's Robe*. New York: Atheneum, 1999.

FINGER PAINTING

Wiseman, Ann Sayre. *Finger Paint and Pudding Prints*. Reading, Mass.: Addison-Wesley, 1980.

PAINTING AS A CAREER

Lionni, Leo. *Matthew's Dream*. New York: Alfred A. Knopf, 1991.

PAINTING TECHNIQUES

Spilka, Arnold. *Paint All Kinds of Pictures*. New York: Henry Z. Walck, 1963.

STAINED GLASS

Sabuda, Robert. *Arthur and the Sword*. New York: Simon & Schuster, 1995.

Strom, Maria Diaz. *Rainbow Joe and Me*. New York: Lee & Low Books, 1999.

WET ON WET—WATERCOLOR TECHNIQUE

Bröger, Achim, and Michele Sambin. *Francie's Paper Puppy*. Natick, Mass.: Picture Book Studio, 1982.

Locker, Thomas. *Water Dance*. San Diego, Calif.: Harcourt Brace Jovanovich, 1997.

PAPER ENGINEERING

Baker, Keith. *The Magic Fan*. San Diego, Calif.: Harcourt Brace Jovanovich, 1989.

Bang, Molly. *The Paper Crane*. New York: Mulberry Books, 1985.

Brust, Beth Wagner. *The Amazing Paper Cuttings of Hans Christian Andersen*. New York: Ticknor and Fields Books for Young Readers, 1994.

Lobato, Arcadio. *Paper Bird*. Minneapolis, Minn.: Carolrhoda Books, 1994.

Lohf, Sabine. *Things I Can Make with Boxes*. San Francisco: Chronicle Books, 1990.

Melmed, Laura Krauss. *Little Oh*. New York: Lothrop, Lee & Shepard Books, 1997.

Pienkowski, Jan. *Dinner Time*. Los Angeles: Price Stern Sloan, 1981.

Say, Allen. *Tree of Cranes*. Boston: Houghton Mifflin, 1991.

Small, David. *Paper John*. New York: Sunburst, 1987.

PRINTING

Benjamin, Cynthia. *Footprints in the Snow*. New York: Scholastic, 1994.

Cox, Molly. *Whose Footprints?* New York: Crowell, 1990.

Delancy, A. *Monster Tracks?* New York: Harper & Row, 1981.

Dodd, Anne Wescott. *Footprints and Shadows*. New York: Simon & Schuster, 1992.

Geisert, Arthur. *The Etcher's Studio*. New York: Houghton Mifflin, 1997.

George, Jean. *Snow Tracks*. New York: E. P. Dutton, 1958.

Karashan, Donald H. *Picasso Linocuts: 1958–1963*. New York: Tudor, 1968.

Kirn, Ann. *Full of Wonder*. New York: World, 1959.

Lehan, Daniel. *Wipe Your Feet!* New York: E. P. Dutton, 1992.

Niedigh, Sherry. *Creatures at My Feet*. Flagstaff, Ariz.: Northland Publishing, 1993.

Pomeroy, Diana. *One Potato: A Counting Book of Potato Prints*. New York: Harcourt Brace, 1996.

———. *Wildflower ABC—An Alphabet of Potato Prints*. New York: Harcourt Brace, 1997.

Wiseman, Ann Sayre. *Finger Paint and Pudding Prints*. Reading, Mass.: Addison-Wesley, 1980.

Solga, Kim. *Make Prints!* Cincinnati: North Light Books, 1991.

HANDPRINTS

Edwards, Dorothy. *Emmie and the Purple Paint*. New York: Oxford University Press, 1987.

WOODCUTS

Azarian, Mary. *A Gardener's Alphabet*. Boston: Houghton Mifflin, 2000.

Kurtz, Jane. *Miro in the Kingdom of the Sun*. Woodcuts by David Frampton. Boston: Houghton Mifflin, 1996.

SCULPTURE

BOX SCULPTURE

Siomades, Lorianne. *Boxes*. Honesdale, Pa.: Boyds Mill Press, 1998.

CLAY

Aarrestad, Thomas. *The Potter Giselle*. Nashville, Tenn.: Ideals Children's Books, 1999.

Baylor, Byrd, and Tom Bahti. *When Clay Sings*. New York: Charles Scribner's Sons, 1972.

Baylor, Byrd, and Peter Parnall. *If You Are a Hunter of Fossils*. New York: Charles Scribner's Sons, 1980.

Cohen, Caron Lee (retold by). *The Mud Pony*. New York: Scholastic, 1988.

Engel, Diana. *The Little Lump of Clay*. New York: Morrow, 1989.

French, Fiona. *The Magic Vase*. Oxford: Oxford University Press, 1990.

Ginsberg, Mirra, and Joseph A. Smith. *Clay Boy*. New York: Greenwillow Books, 1997.

Hughes, Langston. *The Sweet and Sour Animal Book*. New York: Oxford University Press, 1994.

James, Betsy. *The Mud Family*. New York: G. P. Putnam's Sons, 1994.

Podwal, Mark. *Golem—A Giant Made of Mud*. New York: Greenwillow Books, 1995.

Ray, Mary Lyn. *Mud*. New York: Harcourt Brace Jovanovich, 1996.

Russell, Solveig Paulson. *Wonderful Stuff, the Story of Clay*. Chicago: Rand McNally, 1963.

Trapani, Iza. *I'm a Little Teapot*. Danvers, Mass.: Whispering Coyote Press, 1996.

Winter, Jeanette. *Josefina*. San Diego: Harcourt Brace Jovanovich, 1996.

FOUND OBJECTS

Freeman, Don. *Norman the Doorman*. New York: Puffin, 1981.

Greenblat, Rodney A. *Aunt Ippy's Museum of Junk*. New York: Harper-Collins, 1991.

Schermbrucker, Reviva. *Charlie's House*. New York: Viking Penguin, 1989.

MARBLE

Morrison, Taylor. *The Neptune Fountain—The Apprenticeship of a Renaissance Sculptor*. New York: Holiday House, 1997.

MOBILES

Freeman, Don. *Norman the Doorman*. New York: Puffin, 1981.

Lipman, Jean, and Margaret Aspinwall. *Alexander Calder and His Magical Mobiles.* New York: Hudson Hills Press, 1981.

Young, Miriam. *The Witch Mobile.* New York: Lothrop, Lee & Shepard Books, 1969.

ROCKS

Baylor, Byrd. *Everybody Needs a Rock.* New York: Aladdin, 1974.

Loff, Sabine. *Things I Can Make with Stones.* San Francisco: Chronicle Books, 1989.

Pfister, Marcus. *Milo and the Magical Stones.* New York: North-South Books, 1997.

Steig, William. *Sylvester and the Magic Pebble.* New York: Aladdin, 1969.

Van Allsburg, Chris. *The Wretched Stone.* Boston: Houghton Mifflin, 1991.

SAND

Trumbull, Ann, and Michael Foreman. *The Sand Horse.* New York: Atheneum, 1989.

SHADOW BOXES

Seeley, Laura L. *The Book of Shadow Boxes.* Atlanta, Ga.: Peachtree Publishers, 1990.

Soto, Gary. *Snapshots from the Wedding.* New York: G. P. Putnam's Sons, 1997.

STONE

Curlee, Lynn. *Rushmore.* New York: Scholastic Press, 1999.

Fine, Joan. *I Carve Stone.* New York: Crowell, 1979.

Parillo, Tony. *Michelangelo's Surprise.* New York: Farrar, Straus and Giroux, 1998.

WOOD

Coxe, Molly. *6 Sticks.* New York: Random House, 1999.

Davol, Marguerite W., and Sheila Hainanaka. *The Heart of the Wood.* New York: Simon & Schuster, 1992.

Denslow, Sharon Phillips, and Nancy Carpenter. *At Taylor's Place.* New York: Bradbury Press, 1990.

STRING

Blair, Margot. *The Red String.* Malibu and Venice, Calif.: J. Paul Getty Museum and Children's Library Press, 1996.

Reeves, James, and Quentin Blake. *Mr. Horrox and the Gratch.* Chicago: Wellington Publishing, 1991.

MUSEUMS AND MASTERPIECES

MASTERPIECES

Brown, Laurene Krasny, and Marc Brown. *Visiting the Art*. New York: Dutton Children's Books, 1986.

Clayton, Elaine. *Ella's Trip to the Museum*. New York: Crown, 1996.

Drawn & Quartered—Reshuffle the History of Art 234,256 Ways. Boston: Bulfinch Press, 1997.

Goldin, Diana, and Inge Heckel. *A Tale of Two Williams*. New York: Metropolitan Museum of Art, 1977.

Knox, Bob. *The Great Art Adventure*. New York: Rizzoli, 1993.

Logan, Claudia, and Joseph Zaremba. *Scruffy's Museum Adventure*. Boston: Museum of Fine Arts, 1996.

Mayhew, James. *Katie Meets the Impressionists*. New York: Orchard Books, 1997.

Reiner, Annie. *A Visit to the Art Galaxy*. New York: Green Tiger Press, 1990.

Trenc, Milan. *The Night at the Museum*. Hauppauge, N.Y.: Barron's, 1993.

Zadrzynska, Ewa. *The Peaceable Kingdom*. New York: M. M. Art Books, 1993.

TO FINISH

Carrick, Malcolm. *Splodges*. New York: Viking, 1976.

Dickinson, Mike. *Smudge*. New York: Abbeville, 1988.

Striker, Susan. *The Anti-Coloring Book® of Masterpieces*. New York: Henry Holt, 1982.

MUSEUMS

Boehm, Arlene. *Jack in Search of Art*. Boulder, Colo.: Roberts Rinehart, 1998.

Mayhew, James. Katie and the Mona Lisa. New York: Orchard Books, 1998.

Minnerly, Denise Bennett, and Gladys Walker. Molly Meets Mona and Friends. Bridgeport, Conn.: Green Bark Press, 1997.

Price, Kathleen McCormick. The Lady and the Unicorn: A Tale of the Tapestries. Bridgeport, Conn.: Green Bark Press, 1994.

Sortland, Bjorn. Anna's Art Adventure. Minneapolis, Minn.: Carolrhoda Books, 1999.

Music Inspires Art

Carle, Eric. *I See a Song*. New York: Crowell, 1973.

Gray, Libba Moore. *Little Lil and the Swing Singing Sax*. New York: Simon & Schuster, 1996.

Grifalconi, Ann. *Kinda' Blue*. Boston: Little, Brown, 1993.

Hasely, Dennis. *The Old Banjo*. New York: Macmillan, 1983.

Igus, Toyomi. *I See the Rhythm*. San Francisco, Calif.: Children's Book Press, 1998.

Isadora, Rachel. *Young Mozart*. New York: Jack Illustration, 1997.

Kailins, Mark. *Music over Manhattan*. New York: Doubleday, 1998.

Martin, Bill Jr. *The Maestro Plays*. New York: Henry Holt, 1970.

Matisse, Henri. *Jazz*. New York: George Braziller, 1985.

Pinkney, Andrea Davis. *Duke Ellington*. New York: Hyperion Books for Children, 1998.

Raschka, Chris. *Charlie Parker Played Be Bop*. New York: Orchard Books, 1992.

————. *Mysterious Thelonious*. New York: Orchard Books, 1997.

Schroeder, Alan. *Ragtime Tumpie*. Boston: Little, Brown, 1989.

Shange, Ntozake. *I Live in Music*. New York: Welcome Enterprises, 1978.

Strom, Maria Diaz. *Rainbow Joe and Me*. New York: Lee & Low Books, 1999.

Weatherford, Carole Boston, and Eric Velasquez. *The Sound That Jazz Makes*. New York: Walker, 2000.

Winch, John. *The Old Man Who Loved to Sing*. New York: Scholastic, 1993.

Winter, Jonah, and Jeanette Winter. *Once Upon a Time in Chicago*. New York: Hyperion Books for Children, 2000.

Ziefert, Harriet. *Animal Music*. Boston: Houghton Mifflin, 1999.

People

BODY DECORATING

English, Karen. *Nadia's Hands*. Honesdale, Pa.: Boyds Mills Press, 1999.

Munsch, Robert. *Purple, Green and Yellow*. Toronto: Annick Press, 1992.

BODY PARTS

Arnold, Ted. *Parts*. New York: Dial, 1997.

BOTTOMS

Singer, Marilyn. *Bottoms Up!* New York: Henry Holt, 1997.

FACES

Bennett, Jill (collected by). *People Poems.* Oxford: Oxford University Press, 1990.

Brenner, Barbara. *Faces.* New York: E. P. Dutton, 1970.

Cheltenham Elementary School Kindergarten. *We Are All Alike, We Are All Different.* New York: Scholastic, 2000.

Feelings, Tom, and Eloise Greenfield. *Daydreamers.* New York: Dial, 1981.

Galli, Letizia. *Mona Lisa—The Secret of the Smile.* New York: Delacorte, 1996.

Locker, Thomas. *Miranda's Smile.* New York: Dial 1994.

Messenger, Norman. *Making Faces.* London: Dorling Kindersley, 1992.

Rohmer, Harriet (collected by). *Just Like Me.* San Francisco: Children's Book Press, 1997.

Ventura, Piero, and Marisa Ventura. *The Painter's Trick.* New York: Random House, 1977.

Waterfield, Giles. *Looking at Art Faces.* Hove, England: Wayland, 1982.

Yudell, Lynn Deena. *Make a Face.* Boston: Little, Brown, 1970.

FEET

Benjamin, Cynthia. *Footprints in the Snow.* New York: Scholastic, 1994.

Lehan, Daniel. *Wipe Your Feet.* New York: Dutton Children's Books, 1992.

Morgenstern, Constance. *Good Night, Feet.* New York: Henry Holt, 1991.

FIGURES IN ACTION

Campbell, Katie. *The Steadfast Tin Soldier.* New York: Barnes & Noble Books, 1990.

Galdone, Paul. *The Gingerbread Boy.* New York: Clarion Books, 1975.

Robinson, Nancy. *Ten Tall Soldiers.* New York: Henry Holt, 1991.

Wilburn, Kathy. *The Gingerbread Boy.* New York: Grosset & Dunlap, 1984.

HANDS

Baer, Edith. *The Wonder of Hands.* New York: Macmillan, 1992.

English, Karen. *Nadia's Hands.* Honesdale, Pa.: Boyds Mills Press, 1999.

Holzenthaler, Jean. *My Hands Can.* New York: E. P. Dutton, 1978.

NOSES

Cowan, Catherine (retold by). *The Nose*, by Nicolai Gogol. New York: Lothrop, Lee & Shepard Books, 1994.

Freymann, Saxton. *Dr. Pompo's Nose.* New York: Arthur A. Levine Books, 2000.

PORTRAITS IN ART

Edwards, Michelle. *A Baker's Portrait.* New York: Lothrop, Lee & Shepard Books, 1991.

Lerner, Sharon. *Self-Portraits in Art.* Minneapolis, Minn.: Lerner, 1965.

Littlesugar, Amy. *Josiah True and the Art Maker.* New York: Simon & Schuster, 1995.

Nicholson, Nicholas B. A. *Little Girl in a Red Dress with Cat and Dog.* New York: Viking, 1998.

Stanley, Diane. *The Gentleman and the Kitchen Maid.* New York: Dial, 1997.

ROYALTY

Coen, Rena Neumann. *Kings and Queens in Art.* Minneapolis, Minn.: Lerner, 1965.

SCARECROWS

Brown, Margaret Wise, and David Diaz. *The Little Scarecrow Boy.* New York: HarperCollins, 1998.

Martin, Bill, Jr., and John Archambault. *Barn Dance.* New York: Henry Holt, 1986.

McGeorge, Constance, and Mary Whyte. *Waltz of the Scarecrows.* San Francisco: Chronicle Books, 1998.

Rupert, Rona. *Straw Sense.* New York: Simon & Schuster, 1993.

San Souci, Robert. *Feathertop: Based on the Tale by Nathaniel Hawthorne.* New York: Doubleday, 1992.

SKELETONS

Ahlberg, Janet, and Allan Ahlberg. *Funnybones.* New York: Mulberry Books, 1980.

Amadon, Alfred Mason, M.D. *The Fold-Out Atlas of the Human Body.* New York: Bonanza Books, 1984.

DeFelice, Cynthia C. *The Dancing Skeleton*. New York: Aladdin, 1989.

Moss, Jeff. *Bone Poems*. New York: Scholastic, 1997.

TEETH

Bate, Lucy. *Little Rabbit's Loose Tooth*. New York: Scholastic, 1975.

Kroll, Steven. *Loose Tooth*. New York: Holiday House, 1984.

Mackay, David, Brian Thompson, and Pamela Schaub. *The Loose Tooth*. Glendale, Calif.: Bowman, 1973.

Signs and Symbols

ALPHABET BOOKS

Grover, Max. *The Accidental Zucchini*. San Diego: Voyager Books, 1993.

Harris, John. *A Is for Artist*. Los Angeles: J. Paul Getty Museum, 1997.

Micklethwait, Lucy (devised and selected by). *I Spy: An Alphabet in Art*. New York: Greenwillow Books, 1992.

Pelletier, David. *The Graphic Alphabet*. New York: Orchard Books, 1996.

Roberts, Michael. *The Jungle ABC*. New York: Hyperion Books for Children, 1998.

LETTERING

Arnold, Tedd. *The Signmaker's Assistant*. New York: Dial, 1992.

Baer, Edith. *Words Are Like Faces!* New York: Pantheon, 1980.

Carle, Eric. *The Secret Birthday Message*. New York: HarperCollins, 1986.

Cathy, Marly, and Wendy Cathy. *A Is for Alphabet*. Glenview, Ill.: Scott, Foresman, 1967.

Diaz, Jorge. *The Rebellious Alphabet*. New York: Henry Holt, 1993.

Falls, C. B. *A B C Book*. New York: Doubleday, 1923.

Giles, John. *Oh, How I Wished I Could Read!* Rockford, Ill.: John Giles Communications, 1995.

Gourdi, Tom. *The Puffin Book of Lettering*. Baltimore, Md.: Penguin, 1961.

Korab, Balthazar. *Archabet: An Architectural Alphabet*. Washington, D.C.: Preservation Press, 1986.

Lancaster, John. *Decorated Lettering*. New York: Franklin Watts, 1990.

Lee, Huy Voun. *At the Beach*. New York: Henry Holt, 1994.

———. *In the Park*. New York: Henry Holt, 1998.

———. *In the Snow*. New York: Henry Holt, 1995.

Massin. *Letter and Image*. New York: Van Nostrand Rinehold, 1970.

Micklethwait, Lucy (devised and selected by). *I Spy: An Alphabet in Art*. New York: Greenwillow Books, 1992.

Morris, Ann. *The Little Red Riding Hood Rebus Book*. New York: Orchard Books, 1987.

Munro, Roxie. *Architects Make Zigzags: Looking at Architecture from A to Z*. Washington, D.C.: Preservation Press, 1986.

Ogg, Oscar. *The 26 Letters*. New York: Crowell, 1971.

Pelletier, David. *The Graphic Alphabet*. New York: Orchard Books, 1996.

Roth, Roger. *The Sign Painter's Dream*. New York: Crown, 1993.

Samoyault, Tiphaine. *Give Me a Sign! What Pictograms Tell Us Without Words*. New York: Viking, 1997.

Seuss, Dr. *On Beyond Zebra*. New York: Random House, 1955.

Wildsmith, Brian. *Brian Wildsmith's A B C*. New York: Franklin Watts, 1962.

HIEROGLYPHICS

De Manuelian, Peter. *Hieroglyphics from A to Z*. New York: Scholastic, 1991.

Walsh, Jill Paton. *Pepi and the Secret Names*. New York: Lothrop, Lee & Shepard Books, 1994.

NEWSPAPER

Pilkey, Dav. *The Paperboy*. New York: Scholastic, 1996.

Striker, Susan. *The Newspaper Anti-Coloring Book®*. New York: Henry Holt, 1992.

NUMBERS

Sullivan, Charles. *Numbers at Play*. New York: Rizzoli, 1992.

READING

Arnold, Tedd. *The Signmaker's Assistant*. New York: Dial, 1992.

Baer, Edith. *Words Are Like Faces!* New York: Pantheon, 1980.

Bradby, Marie. *More Than Anything Else*. New York: Orchard Books, 1995.

Giles, John. *Oh, How I Wished I Could Read!* Rockford, Ill.: John Giles Communications, 1995.

SIGNS AND SYMBOLS

Samoyault, Tiphaine. *Give Me a Sign! What Pictograms Tell Us Without Words*. New York: Viking, 1997.

CHAPTER 10

Songs About Art

There is nothing like a rhyme or a tune to help us remember facts and ideas. Help your child reach a deeper understanding of art concepts by adding the sing-along factor to each new art experience. In the "good old days" all early childhood teachers were required to play a musical instrument and a piano sat in the corner of every classroom. Music should be part of every child's day, but too often it isn't. As you might imagine, I had a hard time finding songs about things like tearing paper. I commissioned some and collected others.

The following is a list of songs included in this chapter, divided by subject.

Theme Song:
"Young at Art"

Color Songs:
"Crayon Neighbors" (Complementary Colors)
"Sing a Rainbow" (Multicolors)
"There's Music in the Colors"
"Purple Urple Goo"
"Green"
"Orange Is an Orange"
"Y-E-L-L-O-W"
"Look Blue"
"Today My Color Is Red"

"I Spy White"
"Black"
"Rainbow Song"
"Just Three Colors"
"Red, Yellow, Green Light"

Songs About Shapes:
"A Circle"
"That's a Square"
"Triangle"
"Stretch Out a Circle" (Ovals)
"Bob the Blob"

Lines:
"Long and Narrow"
"I Make Slanting Lines"

Songs About Paper Art:
"Paper Fun"
"Tear Paper"
"Cut Paper"
"Punch Paper"
"Stick to My Glue"
"Sticky Ickums"
"Peek-a-Boo Holes"

Art Concepts:
"Transparent"
"I Like to Make Faces" (Reflections)

Songs About Painting:
"Finger Paint—Brushy Paint"
"Splish Splash"
"Good Things to Remember"
"Finger Painting Goo"

Drawing:
"Scribbles"

Clay:
"Play with Clay"

Shadows:
"Can You Fool Your Shadow?"

Body Decorating:
"Color Me Clever"

Printing:
"Dip and Print"

Clean Up:
"Clean Up"

Young at Art

Music by John Weed
Lyrics by James Earle and Susan Striker

See the shape in the sand that I made with my hand I'm so young at art See the

thing that I do with my scissors and glue I'm so young at art. Do you

like my de - sign with the wiggly line? My cray-ons and paints have their ve-ry own shine. I

love to fill the hours of a rainy day, pound-ing my whatev-er from a lump of clay I'm a

flow - er in bud with my fingers in mud. I'm so young at art. From my

Crayon Neighbors

Lyrics by James Earle and Susan Striker
Music by Irv Dwier

Purple and yel-low live op-po-site so do orange and blue

Red and green live op-po-site on cray-on street, it's true. They're complementary

col-ors al-though some times they fight But when they shake

hands, they turn brown with de-light cray-on

neigh-bors Pur-ple and yel-low cray-on

neigh-bors Red and green cray-on

neigh-bors Blue and or-ange the friend-li-est

col-ors You've ev'-er seen

Sing a Rainbow

By Arthur Hamilton

There's Music in the Colors

Music by Willy Strickland and James Earle,
Kimbo Educational, Long Branch, N.J.
©1976 and 1983

There's mu - sic in the col - ors of yellow, red and blue.

So we put them in - to songs. They're painted just for you. There's

mu - sic in the col - ors of orange, purple, green

Look a - round you as you sing, I'm sure they will be seen. There's

mu - sic in the col - or of brown, black and white.

All told we've nine to col - or be - fore we say, "Good - night."

Red, yellow, blue, orange, pur - ple, green

brown, black and white. Col - or songs to sing to you be-

fore we say, "Good - night."

Purple Urple Goo

Music by Willy Strickland
Lyrics by James Earle

Soft Shoe Style

1. 2. 3. You take a gob of red paint. (Take a gob of red) and a gob of blue (and a gob of blue)

mix 'em both to-ge - ther. (mix 'em both together) that's pur-ple-ur- ple goo! (pur-ple-ur-ple goo)

(3rd time to Coda)

1.Pur - ple like jel-ly from a grape the skin of a fruit we call a plum. I
2.Pur - ple like pur-ple ur-ple ink the flow-er called a violet you can smell. There's a

love to mix this pur - ple goo and pur-ple up my fingers and my thumbs. You
pur - ple bruise here on my knee that shows you where I landed when I fell. You

Coda

3. Pur - ple ur - ple goo! (Pur - ple ur - ple goo!) Pur - ple

ur - ple goo! (Spoken) Goo!

Green
"Then You've Seen Green"

Music by Willy Strickland
Lyrics by James Earle

Orange Is an Orange

Music by Willy Strickland
Lyrics by James Earle

1. D.C. + 2nd verse
2. D.C.
   (Sing intro 4 times for endings)

Y-E-L-L-O-W

Music by John Weed
Lyrics by James Earle and Susan Striker

1. Y - E - L - L - O - dou - ble you col - or me chicken legs
2. Y - E - L - L - O - dou - ble you col - or me cuckoo bills

Y - E - L - L - O - dou - ble you col - or me scram - bled eggs.
Y - E - L - L - O - dou - ble you col - or me daf - fo - dils.

But - ter me muffins of corn Paint me ba - na - nas and sun in the

1. morn - ing.
2. morn - ing

Y - E - L - L - O - dou - ble you yel-low-y yel - low-y yel - low.

Look Blue

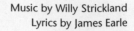

Music by Willy Strickland
Lyrics by James Earle

Today My Color Is Red

Music by Michael Barber
Lyrics by James Earle

I Spy White

Music by Willy Strickland
Lyrics by James Earle

Black

Music by Willy Strickland
Lyrics by James Earle

Rainbow Song

Just Three Colors

J. Raposo

Red, Yellow, Green Light

John S. Murray

Red light, red light what do you say? I say stop and stop right a-way.

Yellow light, yellow light what do you mean? I mean wait till the light turns green.

Green light, green light what do you say? I say GO! First look each way.

Thank you, thank you red, yellow, green. Now I know what the traffic lights mean.

A Circle

Music by John Weed
Lyrics by James Earle and Susan Striker

That's a Square

Music by John Weed
Lyrics by James Earle and Susan Striker

Triangle

Music by John Weed
Lyrics by James Earle and Susan Striker

Stretch Out a Circle

Lyrics by James Earle and Susan Striker
Music by Irv Dwier

Bob the Blob

Music by Irv Dwier
Lyrics by James Earle

Long and Narrow

Lyrics by James Earle and Susan Striker
Music by Irv Dwier

I Make Slanting Lines

Lyrics by James Earle and Susan Striker
Music by Irv Dwier

Paper Fun

Music by John Weed
Lyrics by James Earle and Susan Striker

Pa - per fun, pa - per fun We're all hav - ing pa - per fun

Pa - per fun, pa - per fun C'mon join our pa - per fun!

Tear Paper

Music by John Weed
Lyrics by James Earle and Susan Striker

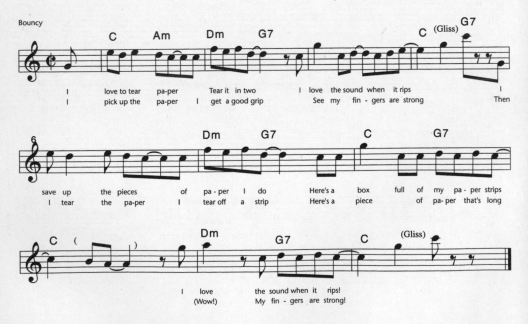

Bouncy

I love to tear pa-per Tear it in two I love the sound when it rips I
I pick up the pa-per I get a good grip See my fin - gers are strong Then

save up the pieces of pa-per I do Here's a box full of my pa-per strips
I tear the pa-per I tear off a strip Here's a piece of pa-per that's long

I love the sound when it rips!
(Wow!) My fin - gers are strong!

Cut Paper
(I Tried to Cut Paper with Scissors)

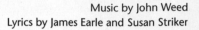

Music by John Weed
Lyrics by James Earle and Susan Striker

I tried to cut pa - per with scis - sors e - ven though I'm kind of small. I tried and I tried to cut pa - per but I could - n't cut pa - per at all. Then one day I picked up the scis - sors. I held them a spe - cial way. I cut with a scis - sors the first time I tried! Hey, I cut pa - per to - day!

Punch Paper

Music John Weed
Lyrics by James Earle and Susan Striker

Stick to My Glue

Lyrics by Jason Striker, age 3

Folk Song — "Skip to My Lou"

Stick, stick, stick to my glue! Stick, stick, stick to my glue!

Stick, stick, stick to my glue! Stick to my glue my pa - per.

Sticky Ickums

Music by John Weed
Lyrics by James Earle and Susan Striker

Jaunty

Stick-y ickums game I'm playing stick my paper with glue

Stick - y ickums I keep say-ing As I do what I do

Stick - y ick - ums past - ing glue - y - o - ey I drip

When the glue is used up I stick'em with a pa - per clip!

Stick - y ickums game I'm playing with my paper and paste.

Stick - y ick-ums I keep saying don't let the paste go to waste

Past - ing things to - geth - er   made me think of a song
All you sticky ickums let's sing a - long!

Peek-a-Boo Holes

Lyrics by James Earle and Susan Striker
Music by Irv Dwier

Let's punch a bunch of peek - a - boo holes,

peek - a - boo holes peek - a - boo holes

Let's punch a bunch of peek - a - boo holes Get

rea - dy, Let's be - gin

Peek - a- boo a bag - el (May I have some cream cheese).

Peek - a-boo a dough - nut (Cin - na - mon, please).

Peek - a-boo a key - hole (Where are my keys?)

Peek - a-boo a but - ton - hole (But - ton it, please).

Transparent

Lyrics by James Earle and Susan Striker
Music by Irv Dwier

wide?   Trans - pa - rent   You can   do   it.

See right through it   and   out   the oth - er   side.   Trans - pa - rent!

I Like to Make Faces

Lyrics by James Earle and Susan Striker
Music by Irv Dwier

I like to make   fa - ces   at shin - y   pla - ces

and   see   the shin - y   pla - ces look - ing   back.

I look   at the el - ec - tric toast - er.   I look at   the cof - fee - pot.

I make   a   face   and   see myself looking   back.

I stick out my tongue   at the tab - le   with   its   shin - y   glass

top.   The kitch - en floor winks   back   at me   af - ter it's waxed with a

mop.   I see   my - self   in   the win - dows   of   the   stores   that   I

pass. Be - fore I turn on the T - V set I see me in the

glass. I like to make fac - es at shin - y

plac - es and see the shin - y

plac - es look - ing back so look for those shin - y plac - es

then start mak - ing fac - es and watch those shin - y plac - es

look - ing back.

Finger Paint—Brushy Paint

Music by John Weed
Lyrics by James Earle and Susan Striker

Splish Splash

Lyrics by James Earle and Susan Striker
Music by Irv Dwier

Eb   Fm7/Bb Eb   Fm7/Bb   Bb7   Eb

Splish, splash, splatter, throw it. I'm hav-ing fun play-ing with paint.

Eb   Fm7/Bb Eb   Fm7/Bb   Bb7   Eb

Splish, splash, splatter, I know it. If Grand-ma saw me she'd faint. I

Fm7   Bb7   Eb   Bb7   Eb

drib-ble, drip, I driz-zle it. I doo-dle, dab, I droo-dle it. I

Ab   Eb   F7   Bb7

noo-dle, boo-dle oo-dle it. I pour it out. I make it spout.

Eb   Fm7/Bb Eb   Fm7   Bb7   Eb

Splish, splash, splatter, throw it. Green, blue, yellow and red

Eb   Fm7/Bb Eb   Bb7   Eb

Splish, splash, splatter, throw it. I'll keep it up 'til it's time for bed.

Good Things to Remember

from the book by Betty M. Barlowe
Shawnee Press, Inc.
Delaware Water Gap, PA

Put on a paint shirt, put on a paint shirt, put on a paint shirt, button it up.

Dip in your brush just a ti-ny lit-tle bit, If you want to paint to-day.

Finger Painting Goo

Music by John Weed
Lyrics by James Earle and Susan Striker

Scribbles

Music by John Weed
Lyrics by James Earle and Susan Striker

Bouncy Cmaj7 — Dm7 — G7 — Cmaj7 — Am7 — Dm7 — G7

Love my scribbles Yes I do Love my ups and downs. My
Love my scribbles Yes I do they go from side to side. I

Dm7 — G7 — Cmaj7 — Am7 — D7 — G7

wav - y lines that look so fine, will nev - er make me frown. I
zig, I zag, I cur - li - cue, I make 'em high and wide. I

Fmaj7 — Cmaj7 — C — Bb7 — A7

know some - day my scribbles will lead to let - ter "A." I
love to scrib - ble by myself or have my friend with me. We

Dm — G7 — Em7 — A7 — 1. D7 — G7 — 2. Dm7 G Dm7 G7 C G C

hold my crayons in my fist, my scrib - bles make my day.
scrib - ble as we sing this song. Here's what we scrib - ble, see?

Play with Clay

Music by John Weed
Lyrics by James Earle and Susan Striker

Can You Fool Your Shadow?

by Andrew Gunsberg

Verse 1

Can you fool your shadow? Shake your head Can you fool your shadow? Shake your head Can you fool your shadow? Shake your head But no matter what you do, you know your shadow does it too

Refrain

Oh, danc-ing, danc-ing, danc-ing, dancing all around No matter what you do your got it down No sha-dow's mat-ter what you try - you can-not get it by Your shadow fol-lows you just like you've got an-o-ther eye.

Verse 2: Can you fool your shadow? Lift your leg
Can you fool your shadow? Lift your leg
Can you fool your shadow? Lift your leg

But no matter what you do, you know,
your shadow does it too.

Coda

repeat and fade

Can you fool your shad - ow?

Color Me Clever

J. Caspell

Dip and Print

Music by John Weed
Lyrics by James Earle and Susan Striker

Dip it in the paint dish, dip and print, dip and print, dip and print.

Dab it in the paint dish, dip and print. Be a dip and prin - ter

dip and print a po - ta - to, your nose, your toes, or a toma - to.

Paint a tooth-brush, paint a sponge. Dip and print a car-rot you save from lunch.

Dip it in the paint dish, dip and print, dip and print, dip and print.

Dab it in the paint dish, dip and print. Be a dip and prin - ter!

Clean Up

Clean up, clean up, ever - y-bod - y ever - y-where

Clean up, clean up, every - y-bod - y do your share.

Art Concepts

Throughout chapters six and seven you will find a list of art concepts preceding every project. Over many years of teaching I have developed this list of all of the art concepts to which children should be introduced as they explore art materials. A child's understanding of simple art concepts will be built upon and expanded as the child gets older. I feel that it is important for anyone supervising a child doing an art project to be in touch with what the child is learning, while making allowances for creative diversion. Here is my completed list. Several art concepts are not appropriate for preschoolers and will not be introduced until later.

  I. Animals and Nature
    Increase perception of the world around us
 II. Art History
    Abstract Art
    Architecture
    Art by Accident
    Art History
    Crafts
    Landscape
    Montage
    Realism
    Still Life
    Surrealism

III. **Color**
   Analogous Colors
   Color Mixing
   Complementary Colors
   Cool Colors
   Monochromatic Color Schemes
   Recognition and Naming of Colors
   Tints and Shades
   Warm Colors
IV. **Design Principles**
   Aesthetics
   Balance
   Center of Interest
   Composition
   Formal Balance
   Harmony
   Informal Balance
   Light and Dark
   Pattern
   Unity
V. **Feelings and Personal Growth**
   Art Career Awareness
   Art Program Publicity
   Expressing Emotions
   Group Work
   Increasing Perception of the World Around Us
   Increasing Self-Awareness
   Using Your Imagination
   Utilizing Art to Convey a Message
VI. **Human Proportions**
VII. **Letters and Symbols**
   Lettering
   Symbolism
VIII. **Light and Shade**
   Contrast
   Highlight and Shading
   Silhouette

IX. Line Exploration

Parallel Lines

Scribbling

Understanding Line

Utilizing Line

Utilizing Lines to Create Shapes

X. Shape Exploration

Concentric Shapes

Creating Geometric Shapes

Recognizing Amorphic Shapes

Recognizing and Naming Geometric Shapes

Utilizing Amorphic Shapes

Utilizing Geometric Shapes

Utilizing Lines to Create Shapes

XI. Shapes in Space

Armature

Assemblage

Clay Coil

Mobiles

Modeling with Clay

Optical Illusions

Overlapping

Perspective

Relief Sculpture

Sculpture—Adding On

Sculpture—Removing

Sculpture—Wire

Size Relationships

XII. Technical Skills

Coloring In

Cooking and Baking

Curling Paper

Cutting on a Fold

Cutting Paper

Developing Photographs

Drawing and Painting on a Fold

Dyeing

Etching
Filmmaking
Incised Process Printing
Introduction to Photography
Lithography
Making and Using Patterns
Making and Using Stencils
Monoprinting
Mounting
Painting with a Brush
Painting with a Sponge
Painting with One's Fingers
Paper-Folding Techniques
Pasting
Precision and Measurement
Printing
Relief Printing
Sewing
Tearing Paper
Tracing
Understanding and Making Charts, Maps, and Diagrams
Using Hard Drawing Materials
Using Soft Drawing Materials
Weaving

Art Supplies

Throughout this book I have referred to and recommended art supplies to you. Some of the more unusual supplies are listed here for your convenience. Please turn to Appendix 3, Art Suppliers, on page 268 for the address, phone number, and e-mail address of each art supplier.

Archival-quality albums, folders, boxes, mats, etc.
    Light Impressions

Nontoxic Body Decorating Paint
Palmer Face Paint
PPP-189934 set
    United Art and Education

Beeswax
CKC-4112 50-piece pkg.
    United Art and Education

Blank Puzzles
    Compoz-A-Puzzle

Knobby Brushes
Knobby-R (round bristle)
Knobby-F (flat bristle)
    Henry S. Wolkins Co.

Paint Cup/Brushes Set
PCB10
    Henry S. Wolkins Co.

Marvy Brush Markers
A21330-1209 set of 12
A21330-2409 set of 24
    Dick Blick

Multicolor Crayon
Chunk-O-Crayon
Sac-Ch-O
    United Art and Education

Chunkie Markers
    Schoolmate Incorporated

Easy Grip Crayons
70-36484 set of 6
70-36483 set of 12

Chubbi Stump Crayons
30215 box of 40
  Hammett
  Kaplan

Childcraft Easels
g420073 three-way easel
g4144592 four-way easel
g4198572 wall-hung easel
g416667 two-sided easel
  Childcraft

Fadeless Double-sided Paper
Fadeless Duet Sheet
BJ-56554 pkg.

Wonder Foam Shapes and Sheets
A60947-1720
  Dick Blick

Fluorescent Construction Paper
#R04300
  Henry S. Wolkins Co.

Foam Brayers #BRF-DLX, BRF
  Henry S. Wolkins Co.

Fadeless Metallic Paper
BJ-57900 pkg.

Blank Flags and Dowels
EMB-C0168
  S&S

Gyotaku Rubber Fish
#339-2453 (set)
  Sax Arts & Crafts

Hexagon Papier-Mâché Box
CKC-6452
  United Art and Education

Fisher Jumbo Brush
70-40140
  Kaplan

Crayola Model Magic
  Binney & Smith
  Dick Blick

Melmac Plates
  Small Fry Originals

Tempera Markers
378-05 set of 6
  Kaplan

Multicolored Finger Paint Paper
SAC-FP-30
  United Art and Education

Multicolor Scratch Paper
658-SA2
  Henry S. Wolkins Co.

Notary Labels
Metallic Gold
05868
  Avery

Paint Marker
A21309-2005 Black
A21309-5005 Blue
A21309-8005 Brown
A21309-7005 Green
A21309-4505 Orange
A21309-3005 Red
A21309-3055 Pink
  Dick Blick

Easy-to-Grasp, Hexagonal Colored
Pencils
64355206
  Childcraft

Pencil Grips
A22927-0000
   Dick Blick

Photographic Sun Sensitive Paper
Nature Print
NPP-40
   Henry S. Wolkins Co.

Patterned Rollers
set 280-0399
set 280-2106

Play dough
Mary's soft dough
#7015
   Magic Cabin

Portfolios
Red Rope Fiber Envelopes
26" × 20" × 2"
A15105-1011
   Dick Blick

Scratchboard
657-5B1
   Henry S. Wolkins Co.

Stancup
Disposable Containers 300-1203
carton of 1,000
   Sax Arts & Crafts

Stubby Brushes
Stubby-30
   Henry S. Wolkins Co.

Geometric Stamps Pad Art Kit
64120709
   Childcraft

Washable Stamp Pads
Set g4288324 or g4288688
   Childcraft

Superman Pen
   Yaffa Pen Company

Stencil Paper
337-1556
   Sax Arts & Crafts

Scissors
Fiskars for Kids
FMC-9416 Blunt
FMC-9430 Pointed
   United Art and Education

Silver Scratchboard
SBS-8-50, 50 sheets
   Henry S. Wolkins Co.

Sterling Silver Jewelry Made from
Children's Drawing
   Totally Out of Hand
   Signature

White Sun Visor
EMA-GP457
   S&S Worldwide

Twisteez Craft Wire
RDW-TW120 120 feet
RDW-TW500 500 feet
   United Art and Education

Wire, Gold-Color Jewelry Wire
CKC-355
   United Art and Education

Wonder Foam
Shapes and Sheets
A60947-1720
approx. 720 pieces
   United Art and Education

Art Suppliers

Art to Remember
10625 Deme Drive, Unit "E"
Indianapolis, IN 46236
Phone 800-895-8777
Indianapolis area 317-826-0870
Fax 317-823-2822

Becker's School Supplies
12300 McNulty Road
Philadelphia, PA 19154
Phone 800-523-1490
Fax 215-464-8991

Bender-Burkot East Coast
School Supply
Highway 17 North, Serman Lane
Pollocksville, NC 28573
Phone 800-682-2638
Fax 800-717-2277
www.bender-burkot.com

Binney & Smith
Easton, PA 18044-0431

Caxton's Office and School Supply
312 Main Street
Caldwell, ID 83605

Phone 208-459-7421
Fax 208-459-7450
www.caxtonprinters.com

Childcraft Education Corp.
2920 Old Tree Drive
Lancaster, PA 17603
Phone 800-631-5652
Fax 888-532-4453
www.childcraft.com

Classroom Direct.com
2025 First Avenue North
P. O. Box 830677
Birmingham, AL 35283
Phone 800-248-9171
Fax 800-628-6250

Compoze-A-Puzzle
One Robert Lane
Glen Head, NY 11545
Phone 800-343-5887
Fax 516-759-1102
www.compozapuzzle.com

Constructive Playthings
13201 Arrington Road
Grandview, MO 64030

Phone 800-448-4115
Fax 816-761-5900

Dick Blick Art Materials
695 U.S. Highway 150 East
Galesburg, IL 61401
Phone 800-447-8192
Fax 800-621-8293
www.dickblick.com

Early Childhood.com
P. O. Box 7636
Spreckels, CA 93962
340 El Camino Real S.
Building 32
Salinas, CA 93901
Phone 800-627-2829
Fax 800-879-3753

Educational Products Inc.
1342 North I-35 East
Carrollton, TX 75006
Phone 800-365-5345
Fax 972-245-5632
www.educationalproducts.com

Holcomb's Educational Resource
3205 Harvard Avenue
Cleveland, OH 44105
Phone 800-362-9907
Fax 216-341-5151
www.holcombs.com

J. L. Hammett
1 Paliotti Parkway
Lyons, NY 14489
Phone 800-333-4600
Fax 800-873-5700
www.hammett.com

Kaplan
P.O. Box 609
1310 Lewis-Cemmon Road
Lewisville, NC 27023-0609
Phone 800-334-2014

Fax 800-452-7526
www.kaplanco.com

Kurtz Bros.
400 Reed Street
Clearfield, PA
Phone 814-765-6561
(order) 800-252-3811
Fax 606-431-0266

Light Impressions
P. O. Box 1011
Holyoke, MA 01041
Phone 800-628-1912

Magic Cabin
www.magicabin.com
Phone 877-876-1111

Nasco
901 Janesville Avenue
Fort Atkinson, WI 53538
Phone 800-558-9595
Fax 920-563-8296
www.nascofa.com

Office Depot—Business Services
Division
5280 Joliet Street
Denver, CO
Phone 800-800-2980 ext. 1037
Fax 303-373-7064

Office Depot—Business Services
Division
1105 Xenium Lane
Suite 100
Plymouth, MN 55441
Phone 800-392-4777
Fax 800-373-0005

Porch School Supply
4526 North Sewell
Oklahoma City, OK 73118
Phone 800-762-5774
Fax 405-525-5611

Quality Art
200 East 52 Street
Boise, ID 83714
Phone 208-672-0530
Phone 888-311-7707
Fax 208-672-5611

S & S Worldwide
P. O. Box 513
75 Mill Street
Colchester, CT 06415-0513
Phone 800-937-3482
Fax 800-566-6678

Sax Arts & Crafts
P. O. Box 510710
New Berlin, WI 53151
Phone 800-558-6696
Fax 800-328-4729
www.junebox.com

Schoolmate Incorporated
P. O. Box 225
Jackson, TN 38302
Phone 901-935-2000
Fax 901-935-2009
school@schoolmateinc.com

School Specialty
P. O. Box 1579
Appleton, WI 54912-1579
Phone 888-388-3224
Fax 888-388-6344

Signature
Box 2307
10 Steeple Street
Mashpee, MA 02649
Phone 508-539-0045
Fax 508-539-0509
signature@capecod.net

Small Fry Originals
2700 South Westmoreland
Dallas, TX 75224

972-248-9443
Fax 860-537-3451
www.snswide.com

Totally Out of Hand
48 Reilly Road
Easton, CT 06612
Phone 888-415-8772
www.totallyoutofhand.com

Toys to Grow On
2695 East Domingues Street
P. O. Box 17
Long Beach, CA 90801
Phone 800-542-8338
Fax 310-537-5403

Triarco Arts & Crafts
14650 28 Avenue N
Plymouth, MN 55447
Phone 800-328-3360
Fax 612-559-2215

Twisteez
Rabinowitz Design Workshop
8 Carmel Rd.
Bethany, CT 06524
Phone 203-393-2397

United Art and Education
P. O. Box 9219
Fort Wayne, IN 46899-9219
Phone 800-322-3247
Fax 800-858-3247

University Products
517 Main Street
P. O. Box 1011
Holyoke, MA 01041
Phone 800-628-1912

Yaffa Pen Company
21306 Sault Street
Canoga Park, CA 91303

Bibliography

Arnheim, Rudolf. *Art and Visual Perception: A Psychology of the Creative Eye.* Riverside, Calif.: University of California Press, 1974.

———. *Visual Thinking.* Riverside, Calif.: University of California Press, 1969.

Art: A Creative Curriculum for Early Childhood. Washington, D.C.: Creative Associates, 1979.

Bettelheim, Bruno. "A Personal Vision: Art, Art, Art." New York: New York Graphic Society, Museum of Modern Art, 1964.

Blocks: A Creative Curriculum for Early Childhood. Washington, D.C.: Creative Associates, 1979.

Boegehold, Betty D., Harriet K. Cuffro, William H. Hooks, and Gordon J. Kloof, eds. *Education Before Five.* New York: Bank Street College of Education, 1977.

Bos, Bev. *Don't Move the Muffin Tins: A Hands-off Guide to Art for the Young Child.* Roseville, Calif.: Turn the Page Press, 1978.

Brittain, W. Lambert. *Creativity, Art and the Young Child.* New York: Macmillan, 1979.

Burton, Leon, and Kathy Kuroda. *ArtsPlay: Creative Activities in Art, Dance and Drama for Young Children.* Old Tappan, N.J.: Addison-Wesley, 1981.

Cherry, Clare. *Creative Art for the Developing Child: A Teachers' Handbook for Early Childhood Education.* Rulander, N.C.: Pitman Publishing, 1972.

D'Amico, Victor. *Art for the Family.* New York: Museum of Modern Art, 1954.

Dean, Joan. *Room to Learn*. New York: Citation Press, 1972.

Dobbs, Stephen M., ed. *Art Education and Back to Basics*. Reston, Va.: National Art Education Association, 1979.

Dodge, Diane Trister. *Art: Trainer's Guide to a Creative Curriculum for Early Childhood*. Washington, D.C.: Creative Associates, 1979.

Gardner, Howard. *Art, Mind & Brain: A Cognitive Approach to Creativity*. New York: Basic Books, 1982.

———. *Artful Scribbles: The Significance of Children's Drawings*. New York: Basic Books, 1980.

Girdler Jr., Reynolds. *Crayon Techniques*. New York: Pitman, 1969.

Goodnow, Jacqueline. *Children Drawing: The Developing Child*. Cambridge, Mass.: Harvard University Press, 1977.

Hill, Dorothy M. *Mud, Sand and Water*. Washington, D.C.: National Association for the Education of Young Children, 1977.

Hirsch, Elisabeth S., ed. *The Block Book*. Washington, D.C.: National Association for the Education of Young Children, 1974.

Hood, M. V., Glenn Gildersleeve, Helen S. Leavitt, and Valentine Kirby. *Singing Days, the World of Music*: "Old Jack Frost" and "The Bonfire." Boston: Ginn, 1936.

Isaacs, Nathan. *A Brief Introduction to Piaget*. New York: Schocken Books, 1961.

Jenkins, Peggy Davison. *Art for the Fun of It: A Guide for Teaching Young Children*. Englewood Cliffs., N.J.: Prentice-Hall, 1980.

Kampmann, Lothan. *Creating with Clay*. New York: Litton Educational Publishing, 1971.

Karnes, Merle B. *Creative Art for Learning*. Arlington, Va.: Council for Exceptional Children, 1979.

Kellogg, Rhoda, with Scott O'Dell. *The Psychology of Children's Art*. New York: Random House, 1967.

Kellogg, Rhoda. *What Children Scribble and Why*. Palo Alto, Calif.: National Press, 1959.

Lewis, Hilda Present, ed. *Art for the Preprimary Child*. Reston, Va.: National Art Education Association, 1981.

Lowenfeld, Viktor. *The Lowenfeld Lectures, on Art Education and Therapy*. John A. Michael, ed. Philadelphia, Pa.: Pennsylvania State University Press, 1982.

———. *Your Child and His Art: A Guide for Parents*. New York: Macmillan, 1954.

Lowenfeld, Viktor, and W. Lambert Brittain. *Creative and Mental Growth*. New York: Macmillan, 1982.

Mendelowitz, Daniel M. *Children Are Artists*. Berkeley, Calif.: Stanford University Press, 1963.

Pile, Naomi F. *Art Experiences for Young Children*. New York: Macmillan, 1973.

Report of the NAEA Commission on Art Education. Reston, Va.: National Art Education Association, 1977.

Smith, Nancy R. *Experience and Art, Teaching Children to Paint*. New York: Teachers College Press, 1993.

Strickland, William, and James Earle. *There's Music in the Colors*. Long Branch, N.J.: Kimbo Educational, 1976 and 1983.

Striker, Susan. *Please Touch: How to Stimulate Your Child's Creative Development*. New York: Simon & Schuster, 1986.

Vanderbilt, Gloria, with Alfred Allen Lewis. *Gloria Vanderbilt Book of Collage*. New York: Van Nostrand, 1970.

Williams, Roger M., "Why Children Should Draw, The Surprising Link Between Art and Learning," *Saturday Review*, 3 Sept. 1977.

Acknowledgments

I would like to thank Charles Rue Woods for encouraging me to write this book, and for helping me finish it. Many thanks also to my wonderful new agent, Jennifer Unter, who jumped in late and is always in my corner. Fond farewell to Jonathan Diamond. I thank Deborah Brody for expert editorial assistance. Hats off to Heidi Fong and Kiyomi Todokoro for their elegant Chinese and Japanese calligraphy for the title Young at Art illustration that appears on page 27. Thanks to Jason and the many other children who contributed their enthusiasm and their artwork. Many were in classes at Young at Art or in Greenwich; many others were friends of my son. They include Jesse Conan, Ann Marie Craven, Victoria Hirshfeld, Trevor Hoey, Raine Kennedy, Jeffrey Lane, Jeffrey Moss, Elizabeth Newman, Katherine Severs, Jesse Sneddon, Gregory Wyles, and Evan Zeisel. Their parents were very generous to share their stories, photographs, and art with me. Laura and Raine Kennedy and Robin Miles kindly contributed many of their family's art stories. I would also like to thank my friend Zenda Dumas, who keeps things going in my home to free me to write and always knows where to find whatever I am looking for. I am grateful to Betty M. Barlowe, Melody House Publishing Company, Joe Raposo, James Earle, and Willy Strickland, who all contributed or permitted me to use their music, and Emma Rodriguez Oberheuser, who copied it. Special thanks to Frank Post, who always managed to do beautiful and painstaking drawings, often from sloppy photographs I provided him, and Maggie MacGowan and Judy Francis for their lovely black-and-white line illustrations. Dr. Fitzhugh Dodson was very generous to contribute his delightful poem about play dough. Thanks especially to Firoz Pathan of Mount Kisco's Mail Boxes Etc. for continuing to do a meticulous job of typing, despite a bout with the flu, to help me meet my deadline. My appreciation to Debbie Mathur for keeping track of all my art books and to Tim Marino and Dianne Besse for helping me with research. Profound thanks and admiration to early childhood educator Rhoda Kellogg, who did all of the fascinating and thorough research about the meaning, value, and significance of scribbling.

Index

adult expectations, 28, 31, 36, 43–44,
  63, 90
adult supervision, 2, 3–4, 12, 56, 115,
  118, 153
adult-made projects, 4, 5, 13, 95, 98,
  100, 112, 117
adults, 3
  at parties, 153, 154
  see also parents/parenting
age
  art projects, 15–16, 164
  crayons, 25
  finger painting, 60
  mandala, 29
  painting, 68
  painting with brush, 66
  scribbling, 39, 42, 45
alphabet, 2, 40
anal period, 60
analogous colors, 121, 122
Anti-Coloring Books, 6, 44, 165
art, importance of, 6, 8
art activities
  age groups, 164

  to avoid, 2
  for birthday parties, 158, 165
art activity development norms, 23t
art concepts, 2, 261–64
  books about (list), 169–81
  exploring, 138–49
  projects, 148–49t
art experiences, value of, 42, 121
Art Experiences for Young Children (Pile),
  111
art history, books about (list), 181–85
art materials, 3, 6, 7–8, 9, 11–12
  caring for, 69–70
  for collage, 105–7
  collecting, 105
  eating, 111
  list, 16–17
  for painting, 82
  stimulate creativity, 15
  storing, 17
art suppliers (list), 268–70
art supplies, 18
  list, 265–67
artists, books about (list), 185–93

Asch, Frank, 44
assemblage (relief sculpture), 100

background, self-stick, 104
Bemis-Jason Corp., 104
birthday cake, 150–51
    decorating, 151, 154, 156
birthday parties, 150–67, 151f
black, 67
    books about, 170, 171
    painting with, 72–73, 73f
    scribbling with, 40–41
    in shades, 85
black and white
    books about, 170
    projects, 123–24t
black crayon, 15–16
Bland, Jane Cooper, 6
blue
    books about, 170
    finger painting with, 62–63
    painting with, 74
    primary color, 81
blue and orange, 79, 81
blue collage experience, 101
blue scribble, 43–44
blueness, 74
body painting, 56, 60
body parts, printing, 88–89
books
    about art for children (lists), 168–215
    about circles, 139
    integrating into projects, 123–37t,
        142–49t
box sculpture, 118, 119f
Brittain, W. Lambert, 34
building, instinct for, 116, 118

Caroto, Giovanni Francesco
    portrait by, 4f, 5
Chagall, Marc, 2

chalk, drawing with, on blackboard, 50
Changes (Hutchins), 118
Childcraft, 83, 108
    Non-Spill Paint Pots, 70
Chunkie Markers, 45
Chunk-O-Crayon, 45, 50
circle experiences, 140f
circles, 29, 138–39, 142–44t
    stick-on, 103–5
clay, 16, 109, 111, 112–14
    with decorations stuck in it, 114f
    reconditioning, 113
    squish, poke, and pound on, 115
clay coils, 115, 116f
clay shapes, printing with, 91
clothing, 72, 166
Colbert, Colleen, 109
collage, 11, 52, 95, 97–108, 98f
    bumpy-texture, 107f
    of transparent materials, 107–8
collage box, 105–7
collagraphs, 91, 102
color(s), 67, 69
    drawing with four shades of one, 52–53
    exploring, 120–37
    finger paint, 61–62
    naming, 62–63, 72
    sequence of projects, 122–23
    transparent material, 107–8
color mixing, 67, 68, 80, 81, 82, 83, 84,
        85, 107, 111, 120, 121, 122, 123
    books about, 171
    projects, 136–37t
"Color Mixing Adventure" (Striker),
        136
color presentation, sequential, 66,
        67–68
color skills/concepts, 120–21
    list, 121
coloring, 13
coloring books, 5, 11, 43–44, 93

combine print, 102

comments, helpful, 37–38, 102, 113

complementary colors, 121, 122

   painting with, 79–81

   projects, 131t

computer art, 93

conceptual art, 10, 11f

constructions, 5, 109, 117, 118

contrast, 41, 44, 72, 121

coordination, 25, 58, 67, 112

Crayola Art and Craft, 99

Crayola Brush Tips, 50

Crayola Crayon Web site, 29

Crayola Model Magic, 16

crayons, 25, 40–41, 45, 48

Creative and Mental Growth (Lowenfeld
   and Brittain), 34

creative art, ten cardinal rules for
   teaching, 21–22

creativity, 7, 29, 67

   encouraging, 20–21, 120

   IQ and, 7

   nature of, 4

   parents observing, 13

   stifling, 2, 3, 12–13

   toys and, 9–10

Creativity, Education's Stepchild
   (Lowenfeld), 15

critical thinking, 1, 9, 120

criticizing, correcting, directing, 5, 26,
   40–41

crumbling, 94

cultural arts, books about (list), 181–85

cutting, 13, 94

   with scissors, 95–97

day care centers, 5, 12

decollage, 103

development, 2, 6, 8, 15

   arrested, 12

   emotional, 115

   milestones in, 1

   scribbling in, 33, 34, 36, 54

diamonds, 29

Dodson, Fitzhugh, 110–11

drawing, 2, 11, 24–55, 58, 108, 120

   with chalk on blackboard, 50

   creative development in, 54f

   with four shades of one color, 52–53

   with markers, 48–49, 48f

   with pencil, 51

   scribbling and, 2

   in three dimensions, 119

drawing activities, sequence of, 40–55

drawing materials, 55

Earle, James, 162

easels, 70–71, 71f, 74

Easter eggs, 10

Edwards, Dorothy, 88

Einstein, Albert, 57

Elmer's Wilhold, 99

Emmie and the Purple Paint (Edwards and
   Lamond), 88

emotionally disturbed children, 7

entertainment for parties, 157–58

environment and weather, books about
   (list), 193–96

eraser drawing, 51

experimentation, learning through, 75,
   77

eye-hand coordination, 42

fabrics, 106

finger paint, 18

   edible, 61

finger painting, 59–60, 65f, 75, 88

   with blue, 74

   with blue, yellow, 62–63

   with food, 58–62, 59f

   with red, 62

fingerprinting, 88–89

Fiskars, 97
fluorescent colors
  books about, 172
  projects, 130t
folding, 94
food
  finger painting with, 58–62, 59f
  for parties, 157
food painting, 15
food printing, 90
footprints, 88
Footprints in the Snow, 88
found objects, 106
found-objects printing, 89–90
Freud, Sigmund, 60

games, 2
  about circles, 139
  integrating into projects, 123–37t,
    142–49t
  for parties, 153, 158–60
Gardener's Alphabet, A, 87
Gardner, Howard, 139
geometric shapes, 103
  projects, 142–48t
Gesell, Arnold, 25
glue, 18, 99, 116, 118
glue prints, 91
goals set by child, 79, 80, 95
green, 83
  books about, 171
  secondary color, 81
group activities, 12, 118, 150–67
Gyotaku, 90

hammer, 116
handprints, 88, 89
Hello Yellow (Wolff), 44, 74
Hoban, Tina, 139
hole punching, 95
holiday art, 12, 72

human being, drawing, 30–33, 32f–33f,
  40
Hutchins, Pat, 118

I Wish I Had a Computer That Makes
    Waffles, 110–11
imaginary creatures, books about (list),
  196–200
incised process, 87
independence, ingredients for, 10
intellectual development, 15, 35–36, 42

Jung, Carl, 29

Kellogg, Rhoda, 1–2, 26
Kinda' Blue, 74
kinesthetic activity, 25, 42, 50, 67
Klee, Paul, 2
Knudsen, Kathy, 110

Lamond, Priscilla, 88
language development, 25, 36, 37
large-motor skills, 78
learning, 6, 66
  color in, 42, 43
  through experimentation, 77, 79
  through kinesthetic activity, 67
  through play and art, 13
learning styles, 119, 123, 139
learning-disabled children, 6–7
Lent, Blair, 81
Lewis, Robin Baird, 42
lines, 28, 29, 34
linoleum printing, 87
Lionni, Leo, 83, 120, 122
lip prints, 88
lithography, 87
Little Blue and Little Yellow (Lionni), 83,
  120, 122
Look at the Moon, 91
Lowenfeld, Viktor, 14–15, 34, 115

McGuire, Richard, 81
magic, at parties, 161–62, 161*f*
mandala form, 29–34, 29*f*, 30*f*, 31*f*, 32*f*, 33*f*
manipulative materials, 7–8, 15, 107–17
    modeling with, 117, 118–19
markers
    brush-tipped, scribbling with, 49–50, 49*f*
    drawing with, 48–49, 48*f*
    easy-grip, scribbling with, 45–47, 45*f*
mathematics, 5
May Horses (Wahl), 81
media, 11
    books about (list), 200–210
messes, 1, 8, 13, 56–57, 60
    finger paint, 64, 65
Midas Touch, The, 168
Miro in the Kingdom of the Sun, 87
Model Magic, 111
monochrome, 121
monoprint, 88
motor activity, 69
    in scribbling, 24–25, 34, 41
multimedia art projects
    integrating, 123–37*t*, 142–49*t*
multiple colors
    projects, 133–34*t*
multiple copies, 92, 93
multiple intelligences, 139
music, 2
    books about (list), 211
    see also songs/singing
musical chairs, 158
Musical Paints (game), 158–60
"My Paint Brush" (Earle and Striker), 162

nails, 116
naming, 28, 138
    colors, 121

negative space, 95
neutral colors
    projects, 129–30*t*
nursery schools, 5, 12

objects, drawing, 46–47, 46*f*, 47*f*
O'Dell, Scott, 26
One Mitten Lewis, 80
orange, 83
    books about, 172
    secondary color, 81
Orange Book, The (McGuire), 81

paint, 56
    blowing through straw, 77–78, 78*f*
    smearing, tasting, 60
paint containers, 70, 79, 80, 81, 82–83
"paint scrapers," 65
paintbrushes, 49, 64, 69*f*
    in color mixing, 84
    painting with, 66–67
painting, 2, 11, 41, 56–86, 102, 108, 120
    age and, 16
    with a brush, 66–67
    with complementary colors, 79–81
    creative development in, 57*f*
    with multiple colors, 85–86
    with roller, 78–79
    with sponge, 77
    with squeeze-bottle, 99, 100
    with a straw, 77–78, 78*f*
    three-dimensional objects, 117
    transition to, 49
    with two primary colors to create
        secondary color, 81–84
painting techniques (list), 75
palettes, 84, 86, 122
paper, 2, 17–18, 94–108
    altered, 77
    for finger painting, 61
    for painting, 69, 72

paper (cont'd)
  for rubbing, 52
  for scribbling, 40, 41
  sun-sensitive, 93
parents/parenting, 10, 11, 12, 34, 39, 59
  disapproval by, 14
  and scribbling, 3–4
parties
  format, 153
  preparation for, 154–57, 165
party activities, 158–60
party box, 154, 155–56
party favors, 165–67
pasting, 13, 94, 99, 102, 103, 120
pencil, drawing with, 50
people, books about (list), 211–14
perceptual concepts, 103
personality, 34–35, 37
photo montage, 102–3
photocopy machines, 92
photography, 93
Picasso, Pablo, 2, 3, 43, 62
Pile, Naomi, 111
Pin the Tail on the Donkey (game),
    163
pipe cleaners, 118–19
plasticine, 111
Play-Doh, 109
play dough, 16, 109, 111–12
Please Touch (Striker), 14
praise and encouragement, 7, 15, 26,
    37–38, 58, 112
preschools, 40
primary colors, 52, 67, 121
  painting with, to create secondary
    color, 81–84
  projects, 124–26t
printing, 2, 16, 87–93
printmaking, 11, 52
problem solving, 1, 3, 15, 104, 120
process over product, 14, 19, 51, 72

Psychology of Children's Art, The
    (Kellogg and O'Dell), 26
pumpkin, painting, 117f
purple, 84
  books about, 172–73
  secondary color, 81
Purwin, Sig, 79

Quick-Stick, 104

reading, 1, 28
  scribbling and, 1, 2, 5, 6, 13, 36
realistic drawing, 33, 35, 63
realistic objects, 13, 25, 28, 31, 98,
    100–101, 105
  molds of, 112
  shapes, 138
rectangles, 104
red
  books about, 173
  finger painting with, 62
  painting with, 73–74
  primary color, 81
red and blue, 84
red and green, 79, 80
Red Balloon, 62
red collage experience, 100–101
Red Is Best (Stinson and Lewis), 42,
    62
red scribble, 42–43
redness, 42, 73
reflective colors
  projects, 128–29t
relief process, 87
removing/subtracting, 5, 94, 109
repetition, 15, 62, 70, 81, 101
  learning through, 42
  printing as, 88
representational art, 40, 105
resist effect, 79
Richardson, Susan, 19

right-/left-handed, 72
    scissors, 96, 96f
"Ring Around the Rosie," 139
roller (brayer)
    painting with, 78–79, 91, 92
Roughneck Carry Caddy, 17
Round and Round and Round (Hoban), 139
roundness, 139
rubber stamps, 90–91, 91f
rubbing, 51–52

Sanford Craypas, 52–53
Sargeant pastels, 53
saving artwork, 10, 15, 18–20, 38–39, 72,
    104
scavenger hunt, 160
schools
    eliminating art programs, 36, 58
science, 5
scissors, 16
    cutting with, 95–97
    right- and left-handed, 96, 96f
Scola chalks, 50
Scratch-Art, 73
scratchboard, 55
scribbles, 26f
    basic, 26–27, 27f, 37
scribbling, 1–2, 24–28, 31, 34–36,
    38–40, 41, 55, 58, 69, 102, 112
    with black, 40–41
    blue, 43–44, 74
    with brush-tipped marker, 49–50, 49f
    creative development in, 53f
    with easy-grip marker, 45–47, 45f
    goal of, 50
    importance of, 3–4, 5, 7, 54
    with pencil, 51
    red, 42–43
    regression to, 13
    yellow, 44–45
scribbling development, 39f, 40

sculpture, 2, 11, 41, 102, 108, 109–19, 120
    categories of, 116–19
secondary colors, 52, 67, 121
    painting with two primary colors to
        create, 81–84
    projects, 122–28t
Seitz, William, 97
self-confidence, 12
    ingredients of, 10
self-discovery, 75–76
self-motivation, 15, 42, 95
self-stick labels, 16
    design with, 103–5
shades, 84–85, 121
    projects, 134–35t
    red, 100
shape facts (list), 140–41
shapes, 28, 29–30, 42
    exploring, 138–49
signs and symbols, books about (list),
    214–15
Simple Simon (game), 160
sing-alongs, 158
Small World Toys, 108
Smith, David, 119
smooth-/soft-textured objects, 100
snacks
    integrating into projects, 120,
        123–37t, 142–49t
Sobo, 99
songs/singing, 41, 216–59
    adapting traditional, 162–63
    birthday party, 167
    about circles, 139
    integrating into projects, 120,
        123–37t, 142–49t
sponge, painting with, 77
spray painting, 75
squares, 29, 103, 104, 138, 142–44t
Stancups, 70
Statue (game), 160–61

stenciling/stencils, 87, 92

stereotypes, 34, 63

Stinson, Kathy, 42

stories, 120

storing art, 18–19

story time
  at birthday parties, 158

Striker, Susan, 136, 162

Stubby Brushes, 69, 80

Styrofoam, 100

Styrofoam tray prints, 92

subject matter, 5, 31, 63, 69

surface(s)
  getting children to use acceptable, 14,
    42–43
  for rubbing, 51–52
  textured/relief, 45, 51

symbol recognition, 5, 6, 28

tadpoles, 31

tape, 16, 103

tasting, 40, 60, 109

teachers, 5–6, 12, 37, 38–39
  lack of knowledge about preschool
    art, 63–64

tearing paper, 94–95

technology, 92

tempera paint, 64, 66, 79, 89, 92, 99, 118
  altering, 76–77

tension, relief of, 113, 115

textures, 51–52, 77, 106

three-dimensionality, 100, 108, 109, 116

tints, 84–85, 100, 121
  projects, 134–35t

tissue, pasting on bottle, 167, 167f

tools, sculpture, 112, 114

touching, 14, 106

toys, 9–10

Toys to Grow On, 90–91

transparent materials, collage of, 107–8

treasure hunt, 100, 101

triangle experiences, 141f

triangles, 29, 103, 104, 138, 141, 142–44t

Twisteez, 119

two-dimensionality, 108

umbrella, painting, 165f, 166

verbalizing, 52, 76

vocabulary, 52, 63, 76, 102

Wahl, Jan, 81

warm and cool colors, 121
  projects, 132t

watercolors, 86, 86f

white
  books about, 170, 174
  in tints, 84–85

Williams, Roger M., 6

wire sculpture, 116, 117, 119

Wolff, Robert Jay, 44

woodcut printing, 87

wooden letters, painting, 166f, 167

workspace, 8–9

writing, 28, 58
  scribbling and, 1, 2, 5, 6

yellow
  books about, 174
  finger painting with, 62–63
  painting with, 74–75
  primary color, 81

yellow and blue, 83

yellow and purple, 79, 80

yellow and red, 83–84

yellow collage experience, 101–3

yelow scribble, 44–45

Yellow Yellow (Asch), 44, 74

Young at Art, 104
  adapting traditional songs, 162–63
  birthday parties, 150–51, 153,
    154–55, 157, 158, 165, 166

About the Author

SUSAN STRIKER has been an art educator for more than twenty-five years and currently teaches elementary school art in Greenwich, Connecticut. She is the recipient of Connecticut's Celebration of Excellence Award for Creativity in the Classroom and has been named a Distinguished Teacher by the Greenwich public schools. In addition to the Anti-Coloring Book series, she is the author of *Please Touch*. She lives in Easton, Connecticut. You can visit her at www.susanstriker.com.